Training Young Distance Runners

Third Edition

Training Young Distance Runners
Third Edition

Larry Greene

Russ Pate

Human Kinetics

Library of Congress Cataloging-in-Publication Data

Greene, Larry,
    Training young distance runners / Larry Greene, Russ Pate. -- Third edition.
        pages cm.
    Includes bibliographical references and index.
    1. Running for children. 2. Marathon running--Training. I. Pate, Russ R. II. Title.
    GV1061.18.C45G74 2015
    796.42'52--dc23
                                            2014024311

ISBN: 978-1-4504-6884-8 (print)

The web addresses cited in this text were current as of June 2014, unless otherwise noted.

Acquisitions Editor: Tom Heine; **Senior Managing Editor:** Amy Stahl; **Copyeditor:** Patsy Fortney; **Indexer:** Dan Connolly; **Permissions Manager:** Martha Gullo; **Graphic Designer:** Kathleen Boudreau-Fuoss; **Cover Designer:** Keith Blomberg; **Photograph (cover):** © Human Kinetics; **Photographs (interior):** Neil Bernstein, unless otherwise noted; **Photo Asset Manager:** Laura Fitch; **Visual Production Assistant:** Joyce Brumfield; **Photo Production Manager:** Jason Allen; **Art Manager:** Kelly Hendren; **Associate Art Manager:** Alan L. Wilborn; **Illustrations:** © Human Kinetics; **Printer:** Sheridan Books

We thank Pine Crest School in Ft. Lauderdale, Florida, for assistance in providing the location for the photo shoot for this book.

Human Kinetics books are available at special discounts for bulk purchase. Special editions or book excerpts can also be created to specification. For details, contact the Special Sales Manager at Human Kinetics.

Printed in the United States of America   10   9   8   7   6   5   4   3   2   1

The paper in this book is certified under a sustainable forestry program.

Human Kinetics
Website: www.HumanKinetics.com

United States: Human Kinetics
P.O. Box 5076
Champaign, IL 61825-5076
800-747-4457
e-mail: humank@hkusa.com

Canada: Human Kinetics
475 Devonshire Road Unit 100
Windsor, ON N8Y 2L5
800-465-7301 (in Canada only)
e-mail: info@hkcanada.com

Europe: Human Kinetics
107 Bradford Road
Stanningley
Leeds LS28 6AT, United Kingdom
+44 (0) 113 255 5665
e-mail: hk@hkeurope.com

Australia: Human Kinetics
57A Price Avenue
Lower Mitcham, South Australia 5062
08 8372 0999
e-mail: info@hkaustralia.com

New Zealand: Human Kinetics
P.O. Box 80
Torrens Park, South Australia 5062
0800 222 062
e-mail: info@hknewzealand.com

                                                                        E6148

Contents

Acknowledgments

We are grateful to the outstanding staff at Human Kinetics for their continued support of *Training Young Distance Runners, Third Edition*. Special thanks to Human Kinetics' Tom Heine and Amy Stahl for your encouragement and helpful advice to improve this new edition. Thanks also to Coach Paul Baur and the runners at Pine Crest School in Fort Lauderdale, who did such a great job of demonstrating the technique drills and the stretching and strength training exercises in chapters 5 and 6.

Larry Greene and Russ Pate

In so many ways, this book is inspired by the valuable lessons I learned from my former coaches: John Mixon, the late John Brogle, Malcolm Coomber, and Al Schmidt. I am forever grateful to you all.

Larry Greene

I would like to express my sincerest appreciation to two groups. First, I am privileged to work with a remarkably talented and committed group of colleagues in the University of South Carolina's Children's Physical Activity Research Group (CPARG). The faculty, staff, postdocs, and graduate students who comprise CPARG are collectively responsible for any and all of my research accomplishments. Second, it has been an enormous pleasure for me to work with a tremendous group of people for over three decades in conducting running events under the auspices of the Carolina Marathon Association in Columbia, South Carolina. Thanks to both wonderful groups!

Russ Pate

Introduction

- At what age should kids start training for competitive distance running?

- What limits, if any, should coaches set on the distances young runners cover in workouts and races?

- Which training methods are best for helping young runners develop endurance, speed, strength, and good form?

- What sorts of foods are ideal for ensuring optimal growth, health, and performance in young runners?

- Do girls and boys have different training and nutritional needs?

- How can coaches and parents help young runners boost their motivation, willpower, self-confidence, and other aspects of mental fitness for distance running?

These are just a few of the questions that motivated us to write the first edition of *Training Young Distance Runners*, which was published in 1996. Our goal was to provide coaches, parents, and young runners with the best information and training guidelines, because we knew that a well-researched resource would lead to many positive outcomes. For example, as young runners ourselves, we experienced the unparalleled feelings of satisfaction and confidence that come from working hard to accomplish performance goals in cross country, track, and road racing. That hard work and dedication in our youth served us well in our personal, family, and professional adult lives. We also knew that the spirited teamwork and camaraderie that made running so much fun in our youth are the foundation of true friendships, some of which last forever. And from our work as exercise scientists, we knew that sound training and nutrition in the teenage years set the stage for a lifetime of physical fitness and good health. We were motivated to write the first edition, as well as this new edition, by the desire to share these great gifts of running.

When we wrote the first edition of *Training Young Distance Runners*, few books on the subject were available, and the Internet was in its infancy. In doing research for this third edition of the book, we were awestruck by the vast amount of information now available for young runners and their coaches and parents. As we reviewed new books, websites, blogs, and videos, we were impressed by the open exchange of ideas and discussion about training methods, racing strategies, nutrition, running gear, and more. We couldn't help but notice that elite high school runners and coaches now have something like celebrity status, sharing their training secrets in interviews featured on popular running websites and in magazines. All of these developments are very positive for our sport.

In researching Internet resources and talking with coaches, we also noticed many striking differences in views on the best approaches to training young runners. For example, a debate surrounds the question of whether coaches should limit the number of miles or kilometers in young runners' training programs. Coaches also have different opinions about how much to emphasize the development of endurance—through long and relatively low-intensity workouts—versus speed, using high-intensity interval training. Regarding diet, recommendations vary on the optimal amount of carbohydrate, fat, and protein for young runners. Another interesting debate involves footwear and, with the barefoot running revolution, whether young runners should wear shoes at all.

In *Training Young Distance Runners, Third Edition,* we tackle key debates and offer guidance for building successful programs based on important findings from well-designed research and the insights and experiences of top coaches and runners. We provide sound scientific principles to help coaches determine the best types and amounts of training for individual athletes. And we rely on established knowledge about growth and maturation to help parents in their role of ensuring their children's optimal health and performance. As former elite distance runners with long-standing careers in exercise science and health promotion, we are thrilled and honored to share our approaches to training young distance runners with you.

Part I
Running Fundamentals

We know that you have questions about training for young distance runners, and we're eager to answer them. We'd like to begin by asking you a few questions.

If you're a coach, how do you usually go about planning training programs? What factors influence your decisions about the types and amounts of training for your runners? Are you confident that your program will help them reach their highest potential?

If you're a parent, how do you know whether you're providing optimal nutrition for your child's health and running performance? How can you be certain that you're offering your child sound advice about running and positive emotional support?

If you're a runner, how can you be most confident that your training is on the right track for accomplishing your goals from season to season and year to year?

Over many years we've heard different answers to these important questions. Some of the answers come from intuition, or a "gut sense" of the best ways to train. Other answers are based on copying the methods used by elite coaches and runners. These approaches certainly have some benefits. For example, we know excellent coaches who, simply as a result of their intuition, believe that training should be fun and interesting. Their programs include games, contests, and variety in training methods and settings. We definitely applaud this strategy for planning training. However, on its own, intuition is limited. For example, it can lead to the flawed reasoning that more is better when it comes to training—that is, if 40 miles (about 64 km) per week helps runners improve, 80 miles (about 129 km) will help them improve twice as much. In addition, intuition fuels the common misconception that young athletes are simply small versions of adult athletes. Many coaches of young runners accept this idea and, to the detriment of their athletes, assign the same methods that adult runners use, just scaled down a bit.

What about designing training based on the methods of elite runners? To an extent, this strategy can be effective. For example, if a runner learns that a world-class runner does weight training, he might add the method to his program. But basing most or all of one's training on someone else's is usually a recipe for poor performance and injuries. Closely following an elite runner's training program works only for athletes who are already elite runners, with similar levels of ability, fitness, and motivation.

To complement these two approaches (intuition and adopting the methods of elite runners), our approach to training young runners is based on *running fundamentals*. This method is a useful guide for developing training programs based on established knowledge about the physical and psychological capacities of young athletes. It also takes into consideration the way young runners' bodies and minds adapt to training for distance running. Our approach is based on scientific research and the insights of highly experienced and successful coaches and runners. We also relay our own experiences as lifelong runners and exercise scientists.

We've devoted part I of this book to running fundamentals, focusing on established developmental principles for training and racing (chapter 1); the science of running physiology (chapter 2); proper nutrition for young endurance athletes (chapter 3); mental fitness for peak performance (chapter 4); and running technique, or form (chapter 5). These chapters provide the background knowledge for part II, in which we guide you through a step-by-step process for building complete training programs over a young runner's career.

Peak Development

One of the main challenges in developing effective training programs for young distance runners is accounting for growth and maturation during adolescence. These developmental changes greatly influence the young runner's physical and psychological capacities, nutritional needs, and responses to training. In this chapter we discuss 10 developmental principles that guide decisions about the best approaches to training and racing.

Developmental Principle 1: Limit Training Before Puberty

We're often asked about the best age for kids to begin training for cross country, road racing, and the distance events in track and field. That's a tough question because scientific research on the subject is lacking and anecdotes simply aren't reliable. Even so, the question is too important to overlook. The reason is that coaches, parents, and health professionals have raised many concerns about potential negative effects of competitive running at a young age. We've formed our view on when training should begin by considering these questions: At what age are children physically capable of running long distances? Do their bodies' physiological systems—for example, their hearts and muscles—adapt positively to training? What are the long-term psychological effects of training and racing at a young age? Have any serious health risks been documented for young children who participate in distance running?

You might be surprised to know that, at least physiologically, children as young as 6 years old are fairly well suited for aerobic activities such as distance running. We know this from research on children's $\dot{V}O_2$max values. $\dot{V}O_2max$ is a measure of how much oxygen the body can use to supply energy for maximal exercise. People with high $\dot{V}O_2$max values have superior aerobic fitness. This means that the heart can supply the muscles with a sufficient amount of oxygen-rich blood, and the muscles can quickly process the oxygen to generate energy for contractions. $\dot{V}O_2$max is vital to success in distance running because muscles fatigue quickly when their demand for oxygen is not fully met. (We examine the relationship between $\dot{V}O_2$max and running performance more closely in chapter 2.)

Research shows that, pound for pound, normally active 6- to 8-year-olds have $\dot{V}O_2$max values as high as, or sometimes even higher than, recreational adult runners who train 30 to 40 miles (about 48 to 64 km) a week. The view that young children are physiologically capable of running long distances is backed by world age-group records for races as long as the marathon (26.2 miles, or 41.2 km). The records for 8-year-olds are 3:34:30 for boys and 3:13:24 for girls; for 11-year-olds the records are 2:47:17 for boys and 2:49:21 for girls. Many adult marathoners have trained at high levels for years without reaching these marks. Research also shows that young children adapt physiologically to endurance training in ways that improve running performance. Before puberty, for example, children who perform moderate levels of endurance training experience about a 10 percent increase in $\dot{V}O_2$max, slightly less than the 15 percent increase observed, on average, in adults.

From this information, you might conclude that young children are indeed capable of training for and competing in long-distance races. Before you start planning programs for 8-year-olds, however, consider the following other important points:

- Neither scientific nor anecdotal evidence suggests that distance runners must start training at a young age to reach their greatest potential. Most world-class runners did not begin training until they were in their mid to late teens. And, with very few exceptions, the children who held age-group records for the 5K through the marathon did not develop into elite adult runners.

- Research consistently shows that, before puberty, physiological adaptations to training aren't always correlated with performance in long-distance events. For prepubescent children, the factors that best predict distance running performance are simply related to physical maturity: taller, stronger, and faster children lead the pack in distance races, just as they excel in other sports such as basketball, baseball, and soccer.

- Although many children have naturally high levels of aerobic fitness, making them physiologically capable of performing low-intensity endurance activities, they are limited in their capacity to generate energy for high-intensity activities. The body has two primary systems for producing energy during exercise: the aerobic system, which operates when a sufficient amount of oxygen is available to the muscles, and the anaerobic system, which operates when the oxygen supply cannot keep up with the muscles' demand during high-intensity activity. One of the most consistent findings in pediatric exercise science is that the anaerobic system is not fully developed until children have passed through puberty.

- Physically immature youth who undertake high volumes of intense training are at relatively high risk for injuries, abnormal growth and maturation, and psychological burnout.

Considering these points, we recommend that children not begin regular and specialized training for distance running at least until the early stages of puberty, around ages 11 to 13 (see table 1.1). By no means are we saying that kids under 11 shouldn't participate in running events such as 1- or 2-mile fun runs at school or in community races. We encourage children of all ages to run for fun and health. Instead, we advise holding off on regular training, which we define as more than three days a week over periods of several months, and specialized training, which means focusing only on running as opposed to other sports and physical activities.

While children are experiencing major physical changes during puberty, we recommend limiting the volume and intensity of training. One reason is that normal pubertal development can improve running performance on its own. For example, the growth spurt of the lungs and heart, which occurs at an average age of 11.5 years in girls and 13.5 years in boys, boosts the delivery of oxygen-rich blood to the muscles, which naturally increases $\dot{V}O_2$max. Another example is the elevated level of growth hormone, which enables stronger muscle contractions, increasing running speed and efficiency.

Not all developmental changes automatically improve running performance, a point that also supports curbing early training. Consider rapid growth in height. At the average age of 10.5 for girls and 12.5 for boys, the growth rate increases dramatically from approximately 2.2 inches (5.5 cm) per year to approximately 4.1 to 4.7 inches (10.5 to 12 cm) per year. The highest rate of growth, which is called *peak height velocity*, occurs at around age 11.5 for girls and 13.5 for boys. Now consider the 13-year-old boy who grows 2 inches (5 cm) over a single summer—suddenly he's all legs. The growth spurt should improve his running by increasing leg length and thus stride length. However, he now has trouble coordinating his

Table 1.1 Hallmarks of Puberty

Hallmark	Characteristics	AVERAGE AGE	
		Girls	Boys
Beginning of pubertal growth spurt	Accelerated skeletal growth of the arms, legs, feet, and trunk	10.5	12.5
Peak height velocity	Sharpest increase in the rate of height gain	11.5	13.5
Growth spurt of the heart and lungs	Accelerated growth of the heart and lungs in diameter and volume	11.5	13.5
Beginning development of secondary sex characteristics	Growth of reproductive organs; breast development and widening of the hips in females; appearance of facial hair, widening of the shoulders, and lowering of the voice in males	10.5	11.5
Menarche	Onset of menstruation	12.5-13.0	—
End of pubertal growth	Skeletal growth diminishes or ceases	15.5	17.5

Coaches Kathy and Rob Hipwood

Los Alamos High School
Los Alamos, New Mexico

Blake Wood

In 2014, Kathy and Rob Hipwood entered their 21st season as co-head coaches of girls' and boys' cross country at Los Alamos High School. The husband-and-wife team met at Adams State University in Colorado, where they both competed in cross country and track. Over the years, the Los Alamos girls' teams have won 14 New Mexico state championships and earned numerous national rankings. The boys' teams have also dominated, winning four state championships, finishing second 12 times, and finishing four seasons with national rankings.

How do you adapt your training program to account for individual differences in maturation and experience?—Our coaching philosophy has always been based on the principle of gradual progression, taking into account an athlete's age and experience. To accommodate the backgrounds and ages of our runners, we place them in one of five groups, ordered by highest to lowest training volumes: I, II, IIg (g = girls), III, and IV. The volume is based on minutes of running per week. Most of our athletes train six days per week, with Sunday reserved for active or complete rest. A full week of training for the groups adds up to 400 (group I), 360 (group II), 320 (group IIg), 280 (group III), and 240 (group IV) minutes. The volume naturally progresses with longer running times and faster paces for older and more experienced athletes. For example, a boy who ran cross country in middle school and has shown early interest and dedication might work his way from group III as a freshman, to group II as a sophomore, and group I as a senior. Freshman newcomers and those from the middle school program who don't have much experience start in group IV their freshman year, and their progression depends on their off-season motivation and training throughout high school.

Most freshman girls start in group IV and then spend two years in group III. Very motivated and healthy girls run in group IIg late in their high school careers, and occasionally a girl with an extensive training background runs in group I. As with the boys, progression from one level to the next is based on individual adaptation, motivation, and current health status. Athletes who remain on the same level for more than a one year increase training paces and can add some volume on Sundays.

What limits do you set on training and racing for your youngest runners?—All of our runners participate in most races during a season. However, runners with little or no athletic background take an additional day off from training each week, and they finish their season earlier than the varsity runners do. So, they ultimately run fewer races. We also try to schedule some lower-key meets in which we encourage athletes to avoid "taking it to the bottom of the well." At times, a talented youngster who usually runs varsity may compete at the subvarsity level to lessen the physical and mental intensity of competition.

How do you design training for consistent improvement over a high school runner's career and beyond?—We believe that our progressive plan with multiple groups and modest mileage allows for gradual adaptation over time. While many of our runners will never progress to group I, athletes with aspirations to compete at the collegiate level naturally gravitate toward the higher running volumes and faster paces. One goal has always been for our athletes to view cross country and track as the foundation for an active lifestyle well beyond high school.

We have come to believe that the biggest challenge to consistent improvement and the ability to compete beyond high school is getting athletes to embrace the recovery elements of proper nutrition, hydration, and sleep. So, we constantly educate them about the importance of recovery after demanding training sessions.

In what ways does your training program differ for boys and girls?—Outside of total volume, the training differences between the boys and girls are subtle. Whereas the boys' volume progresses throughout high school, at some point we often limit the mileage increases for the girls and try to focus more on improving strength, general training paces, and intensity. Our boys and girls perform strength training. But for the girls, as their bodies change, functional strength work is especially critical for handling increased training demands and avoiding injury and staleness. We also may incorporate cross-training more often for our girls to balance training loads and tissue regeneration.

How do you make training engaging and fun for young runners?—We believe that working hard and achieving challenging goals in running is naturally fun. But with over 80 kids of varying abilities in our program, we include social activities and training games in our program. We have team dinners and occasionally take postmeet trips to an amusement park. Fun training may include single-file rabbit runs, in which athletes who are surging to the front call out a favorite movie, song, or food. Our kids might do a Rambo run, in which they jump over obstacles, climb up bleachers, or do hopping or skipping exercises in follow-the-leader fashion. They also play speed games such as capture the flag and ultimate Frisbee, and we do team relays that include backward running, wheelbarrow races, hand–foot crawls, and sprinting.

---

longer legs because the nervous system, which controls movement, doesn't immediately adapt to changes in limb length. Also, during the growth spurt body parts grow at different rates. The feet and legs, for example, usually lengthen faster than the trunk, making many teenagers seem gangly or awkward in their movements. These developmental changes may actually cause the runner to temporarily perform worse because his uncoordinated stride wastes energy and leads to fatigue.

Rapid limb growth also means that children who train intensely for distance running are at risk for muscular and skeletal injury. Bones lengthen at each end in soft tissue called *epiphyseal growth plates*. During puberty, the growth plates are weaker than hardened bone and susceptible to fractures under the heavy, repetitive stresses experienced in long-distance running. The growing athlete's joints and muscles are also susceptible to injury because muscle mass and strength develop more slowly than bone. Eventually, the epiphyseal growth plates ossify, or harden, and muscle mass increases. Until these two critical growth processes are complete, however, children are at increased risk of injury from excessive training.

Excessive training before puberty can also affect hormones in ways that may interfere with normal maturation and optimal health. Estrogen, for example, is a hormone that ensures healthy growth and development in girls. This hormone plays a major role in menstruation, which is a normal process of maturation in girls and young women. Under certain conditions, including suboptimal nutrition, estrogen is not produced at regular levels during puberty in female runners. As a result, they may experience delayed menarche or irregular menstrual cycles. In chapter 3 we discuss a major health problem called the *female athlete triad*, which encompasses suboptimal nutrition, abnormal menstrual function, and weakened bones. Compared with normally active girls, those who train excessively for distance running are at risk for this condition.

Fortunately, most young runners avoid harmful levels of training. They naturally stop pushing themselves before reaching their limits. However, we've known at least a few young runners who were self-motivated to push to extremes, and we've known coaches and parents who pushed young runners too far. For these children, running injuries are fairly common.

Another concern for those who specialize in running at a young age is psychological burnout. Take the 10-year-old who's running 40 miles (64 km) a week and racing 10Ks on a regular basis. Eventually, she may grow tired of running, especially because improvement depends on increasing training loads over time. If a child is running 40 miles (64 km) a week at age 10, at age 16 she'll need to run 70 (113km), or maybe even 90 or 100 miles (145 or 161 km), to keep improving. That much running leaves little time for activities other than school, sleeping, and eating. When training becomes that consuming, it isn't fun anymore, and most young people drop out of running.

Most girls and boys, by the ages of 12 and 14, respectively, have experienced key developmental changes that enable them to safely begin a low-mileage, low-intensity training program, leaving lots of room for gradual improvement over time. Again, we're not saying that younger children should avoid participating in distance running altogether. Instead, our advice is to delay specialized training on a year-round basis. Beginning at age 7 or 8, children who enjoy running may participate in fun runs and organized track and field programs that last a few months each year. Future distance runners will benefit from participating not only in middle-distance races (up to 1 mile, or 1,600 meters), but also in sprinting, jumping, and throwing events. When track season is over, they should participate in soccer, basketball, and other youth sports they enjoy. We recommend multisport participation because it's important to develop all-around physical fitness before beginning specialized training for track and cross country (see developmental principle 3).

Developmental Principle 2: Consider Individual Differences

Table 1.1 shows the average ages at which key developmental changes occur. Striking differences characterize these hallmarks of puberty. For example, two 12-year-old boys on a cross country team might begin puberty five or six years apart. The early-maturing boy might show the first signs of puberty at age 10, whereas his late-maturing teammate might not get there until 15 or 16. The boys are the same chronological age, but they are very different in terms of *biological age*, or physical maturity.

To develop effective programs, coaches must have a good sense of each athlete's biological age and physical readiness for training. A herd approach, in which everyone on the team does the same workout, can be harmful. This is especially true when late-maturing youth try to keep up with early-maturing teammates who have gained advantages in size, muscle development, and physiological fitness. An awareness of individual differences in development is also critical for those who coach both girls and boys, because some pubertal changes influence running performance differently in girls and boys.

Coaches can gain a good sense of their athletes' biological ages by being aware of the hallmarks of puberty. The obvious changes in secondary sex characteristics, such as breast development in girls and the appearance of facial hair in boys, indicate that puberty is underway. Also, as discussed earlier, the pubertal growth spurt is a particularly important stage of development. Coaches should be aware of sharp increases in their athletes' height and limb length to avoid overtraining during periods of rapid growth.

Besides accounting for differences in biological age, coaches must consider *training age*, which refers to the number of years an athlete has been training regularly. A 16-year-old who has been training since age 13 has a training age of 3 years, whereas a 16-year-old who just came out for the team six months ago has a training age of 0.5 years. Even though these two runners are the same biological age, they should train differently. The newcomer's program should include fewer miles or kilometers and a greater emphasis on general training.

Developmental Principle 3: Emphasize General Fitness for Beginners

Some people think of running as a natural movement that requires little athletic skill, unlike hitting a home run or sinking a three-pointer. By this view, runners

Effects of Puberty on Performance in Boys and Girls

Boys and girls experience several common developmental changes that lead to improved running performance, including increases in limb length and height, muscle mass, and dimensions of the heart and lungs. However, because of the effects of sex-specific hormones that are released during puberty—estrogen in girls and testosterone in boys—some changes tend to favor boys. For example, testosterone stimulates a greater production of hemoglobin, an iron-containing protein in red blood cells. Hemoglobin is the vehicle for transporting oxygen in the blood. So, blood with a higher concentration of hemoglobin can carry more oxygen to the working muscles. As a result of increased testosterone levels during puberty, boys experience an automatic improvement in $\dot{V}O_2$max, whereas in girls hemoglobin levels remain the same or decline. Testosterone also stimulates muscle growth and the ability to produce anaerobic energy. At puberty, girls do get a little boost because their bodies produce a small amount of testosterone, but boys are at a greater advantage because they produce far more testosterone than girls do.

As a result of increased estrogen levels during puberty, girls tend to gain body fat. The average body fat composition of 6-year-old girls is 14 percent; it increases to 25 percent in 17-year-old girls. In contrast, body fat composition averages only 11 percent in 6-year-old boys and 15 percent in 17-year-old boys. Runners who have relatively high percentages of body fat are at a disadvantage because carrying extra fat increases the energy required for distance running. Estrogen also stimulates widening of the pelvic bones in young women. A wider pelvis can lead to misalignment of the legs, which worsens running technique and increases the risk of hip, knee, and ankle injuries.

These differences in the effects of puberty on boys and girls certainly don't mean that girls who run are doomed to poor performance and injuries. In most high school events, if the best female runners competed in male races, they would place fairly high. Also, girls who train for endurance sports have a significantly lower body fat percentage than their nonathletic peers. Girls who train well experience a marked increase in $\dot{V}O_2$max, which compensates for the slight decrease in hemoglobin that they experience. The same is true for the increased risk of injury girls face as a result of wider hips: smart training prevents injuries.

Even so, the differences between the sexes are important because they call for individualized training. Because puberty has a small influence on muscle mass and strength in girls, they benefit from extra strength training, including weight lifting and circuit training. And, although sound nutrition is a key to success for all runners, girls may have different nutritional needs than boys, which we discuss in chapter 3.

would just need a lot of endurance and willpower to succeed, so their primary training method should be piling on the miles or kilometers. The more you learn about the fundamentals of distance running, however, the more you'll appreciate that optimal performance is the product of developing many physical and psychological capacities. The physical capacities include cardiorespiratory fitness, a combination of muscular strength and endurance, proper technique (running form), and speed. The psychological capacities include motivation, self-confidence, concentration, and pacing and tactical skills.

To appreciate one example of the athletic skill required in distance running, consider the ability to control the elastic, springlike properties of muscles and tendons. The calf, thigh, and buttock muscles and their tendons stretch when the foot contacts the ground during the running stride. The stretched leg muscles generate force by contracting, or shortening, to propel the body upward and forward in the takeoff phase of the running stride. This active muscle contraction requires energy that is created through metabolic processes, or the breakdown of stored dietary nutrients, primarily carbohydrate and fat. In training and competition, distance runners can easily deplete a critical source of nutrient energy called *glycogen*, resulting in fatigue. Skilled runners, however, can generate propulsive force without completely relying on metabolic energy, sparing glycogen and thus delaying fatigue. Like stretching a rubber band, lengthening the calf, thigh, and gluteal muscles and their connected tendons creates elastic energy that can be used for powerful recoil, which helps propel the runner's body upward and forward. Runners who can take advantage of the elastic energy in their muscles and tendons get something like a free ride—their legs behave like bouncing balls or pogo sticks, generating force without using up precious metabolic energy sources.

The ability to use elastic energy isn't automatic. It requires great muscle strength and neuromuscular control, or the ability to precisely time muscle contractions. Just before the foot contacts the ground, a skilled runner generates neural commands to contract the muscles that will be stretched on impact. These contractions stiffen the springs, so to speak, of the muscles and tendons for a more powerful recoil. Runners won't develop this skill by piling on the training miles or kilometers. In fact, long, slow distance running can dampen the springiness of muscles and tendons, impairing their ability to generate elastic energy. Runners can develop this skill instead through methods such as circuit training and technique drills. Also, games such as basketball and ultimate Frisbee train the neuromuscular system to take advantage of elastic energy. (You'll learn how to incorporate these methods into training programs in part II.)

Figure 1.1 illustrates the fitness capacities that are essential for success in distance running. In the lower part of the figure are general fitness capacities, which can be developed through training that doesn't directly simulate the physical and mental demands of a distance race. Consider cardiorespiratory fitness, the capacity of the heart and the blood vessels to supply the muscles with sufficient oxygen-rich blood. To develop this general capacity, runners don't always need to run. Instead, they can try swimming, bike riding, or even in-line skating. Or consider strength endurance, the capacity to generate forceful muscle contractions over a long time. As you'll learn in chapter 6, strength endurance can be developed through circuit training, weight training, and hill running.

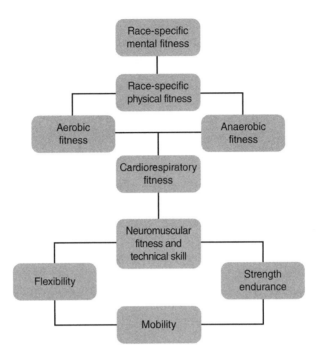

Figure 1.1 General and race-specific fitness capacities.

In the middle part of figure 1.1 are race-specific fitness capacities, which are developed through training that simulates the demands of competition. To develop race-specific fitness, runners must train by covering competitive distances at racing speeds, using high-intensity interval training, or participating in time trials or actual competitions. The top part of figure 1.1 mentions mental fitness, which we cover in chapter 4.

Programs for young runners should emphasize general capacities because they form a fitness base that helps them undertake more specialized, intense training. Consider the demands of a high-intensity interval training session for an 800-meter runner: 4 × 200 meters at her race pace, with a 20-second recovery period between the 200s. To perform this workout successfully and safely, the runner must have strong general fitness, including ample flexibility and sound technique to move her limbs through the extensive range of motion required for such fast running. If her hamstring muscles are tight and her range of motion at the hip joint is limited, she risks straining or tearing those muscles. If her technique is poor—let's say she's overstriding, which creates a braking action with every foot strike—she'll waste energy and fatigue quickly. Clearly, without basic strength endurance and neuromuscular fitness, her running technique will suffer. In addition, if she hasn't developed cardiorespiratory endurance, she won't recover adequately during the 20-second recovery intervals between the 200s.

In part II, on training design, you'll see that methods for developing general fitness capacities are especially important for beginners and for all runners in the initial stages of preparing for competitive seasons. However, this emphasis doesn't mean that a beginner's program should not include race-specific methods such as high-intensity interval training. We recommend mixing all the types of training throughout a season, starting with a relatively low percentage of specialized training and increasing it gradually.

Developmental Principle 4: Increase Training Loads Gradually

Designing quality training programs requires determining appropriate workloads, which are defined by volume, intensity, and frequency. *Volume* means the amount of training, which includes the number of miles or kilometers covered. *Intensity* refers to the effort exerted, which is reflected in the speed of a run. *Frequency* is defined by how often the athlete trains. There are two main reasons for starting with manageable training loads and increasing them gradually. First, athletes who do too much too soon limit their potential for building up to advanced training loads; and second, the three components must increase systematically for the athlete to improve.

Marsha is a 15-year-old whose training age is 1.5 years. Marsha currently averages 18 miles (29 km) over four days of training per week, including the moderate-intensity running she does to develop cardiorespiratory endurance as well as the high-intensity running she does to develop anaerobic fitness and race-specific fitness. To ensure progressive improvement, Marsha's coach will increase her weekly volume over time: 26 miles (42 km) at age 16, then 34 miles (55 km) at age 17, and 42 miles (68 km) at age 18. As the total volume increases, so should the intensity and frequency. At age 15, Marsha might do one fast interval session per week to develop anaerobic power and race-specific fitness. By 17 or 18, she might do two or three interval sessions per week. In addition, Marsha's overall frequency of training might increase from four to six or seven days per week between ages 15 and 18.

Because no simple formula exists for determining optimal increases in training loads, the best coaches weigh many factors, including the runner's developmental status, motivation, history of responding to certain types of training, and potential for handling training loads over a career. This sort of planning is guided by well-defined goals. The process of setting individualized goals and designing the optimal training loads for achieving them is called *periodization*. Part II guides you through periodization step by step.

Developmental Principle 5: Increase Competition Distances Gradually

To support young runners in achieving their ultimate potential, we adhere to the principle that beginners should compete in shorter races and then increase the distances from season to season and year to year. In track season, for example, beginners should focus on the shortest distance race—800 meters. With training and experience, runners can move up in distance if they show promise at the longer races. Why start out with short races? Successful racing means running as fast as you can over a given distance without slowing down and losing form. It's very difficult for beginners to accomplish this aim in a long race such as 5,000 meters. Most beginners simply lack the concentration and pacing skills to maintain a fast pace for that long.

Table 1.2 provides general guidelines for the distances over which young runners should compete during track season. Organized by chronological and training age, the guidelines reflect the principle and goal to race at the fastest pace possible—a pace that is neither too easy nor too hard to maintain. By starting out with shorter races, beginners achieve this goal more quickly than if they try to trudge through longer events. However, the guidelines are somewhat flexible. For example, a 12-year-old who has just begun competing doesn't always have to run 800 meters. To gain fitness and experience, he will benefit from occasionally racing in shorter and longer events, from 400 to 3,000 meters.

Table 1.2 Recommended Racing Distances for Track

Chronological age (years)	Training age (years)	Racing distance (meters)
12 to 14	Up to 2	800 to 1,500-1,600
14 to 16	2 to 4	800 to 3,000-3,200
16 to 18	4 to 6	800 to 5,000

Developmental Principle 6: Emphasize Training for Mental Fitness

A high level of physiological fitness for distance running must be matched by mental fitness, which is made of willpower and motivation, self-confidence, skill in controlling effort and pace, and intelligence in planning and carrying out racing tactics. We've talked about how training for physiological fitness has its limits in young runners. Consider, however, that training for mental fitness isn't as restricted by developmental factors. Remember that physiological adaptations to training, such as increases in $\dot{V}O_2max$, don't necessarily predict improved running performance, at least until young runners are physically mature. Also, recall that runners who do a lot of physical training during periods of rapid growth and maturation risk injuries.

Young runners have much to gain from developing qualities of mental fitness. One straightforward reason is that they lack the training and racing experiences that build these qualities. Take the example of pacing skill. The best adult distance runners are masters at controlling their pace. They are especially good at even-paced running and negative-split running, which means covering the last half of a race faster than the first. These pacing strategies are optimal for conserving energy and avoiding early fatigue. In track races, elite adult runners are also able to judge and adjust their effort and speed to hit target splits, such as 400-meter splits, along the way to achieving their final time goals. In contrast, most young runners start races too fast and don't have a sense of their split times.

The ability to precisely control effort and pace over a long distance requires extraordinary mental fitness. Just think about what's involved in pacing. The runner must continuously sense how fast his limbs are moving, how hard he's breathing, and how fatigued he feels. Then he must compare this sensory information with a memory of how the effort should feel for the target pace. Split times really help in determining and adjusting pace, but doing math on splits when fatigued is no simple mental task. Our point is that young runners have much to gain from training to improve these mental abilities. Chapter 4 and part II provide examples of training methods for developing pacing skills and other aspects of mental fitness.

Developmental Principle 7: Emphasize Proper Technique

We've talked about how children are well suited for distance running because they have naturally high levels of aerobic fitness, indicated by their high $\dot{V}O_2$max measures. However, this advantage can be easily offset by another physiological determinant of performance called *running economy*. An analogy for running economy is fuel efficiency for a car. If you compare two cars traveling at the same speed, the more efficient car uses less gasoline. Compared with adult runners, children and adolescents are very inefficient. We know this from many studies that have consistently shown that young runners use much more oxygen than adults when running at comparable speeds. When demands for oxygen reach high levels, fatigue follows.

A major cause of poor running economy in children and adolescents is flawed technique. As you'll learn in chapter 5, this includes overstriding, heel striking, turning the upper body, and flailing arms. These flaws can waste energy by slowing the runner's forward progression and by diverting muscle force to counterproductive movements. Many flaws in form are related to developmental factors. Earlier in this chapter, for example, we discussed how the adolescent growth spurt can temporarily worsen coordination and running technique. Rapid growth can also weaken postural muscles in the abdomen and back, which are essential for stabilizing the upper body and avoiding counterproductive movements. Technique training, especially for beginners, is essential for breaking bad habits and preventing new ones that will be difficult to correct later on.

In addition to improving performance by conserving energy, technique training can prevent injuries. Flaws such as overstriding place excessive stress on bones, joints, and muscles. Good form smooths out the distribution of forces loaded on the musculoskeletal system, reducing injury risk. Chapter 5 outlines the details of how technique influences performance and injury risks and offers tips for

Pointers for Parents

A developmental approach to distance running accounts for growth and maturation, emphasizes the gradual improvement of various capacities of fitness, and places a premium on optimal health. Because parents are intimately involved in these aspects of their children's lives, they can be supportive by doing the following:

- **Take a developmental view of your child's running.**

   An understanding of key developmental principles for young distance runners will best prepare you to offer your child helpful advice, positive emotional support, and responsible care. Suppose that your child is experiencing a pubertal change—say, a dramatic growth spurt—that is hurting his training and racing performance. He's frustrated and dejected because of the setbacks. Taking a developmental view, you recognize that this is a natural and temporary situation, one that will eventually enable him to train and race at higher levels. Along with training adjustments made by your child's coach, your advice and emotional support can make a tremendous difference in helping him get through the changes with a positive attitude.

- **Be prepared to talk with your child about matters of growth and maturation.**

   Let's face it—not all children feel comfortable talking with their parents about the changes their bodies are experiencing in puberty and adolescence. You might, however, be surprised by your child's questions and concerns. So, it's best to be prepared to talk. This means learning about the hallmarks of puberty, the effects of pubertal changes on running performance, and health risks associated with excessive training during periods of rapid growth and maturation. In cases of abnormal growth and maturation, or if your child's health is compromised by excessive training, we strongly recommend that you seek professional medical help, beginning with your family physician.

- **Focus on positive health outcomes.**

   Much of this book is about training to improve competitive performance, which naturally relates to the interests of coaches and young runners themselves. However, we also focus on many matters of health for young runners, including nutrition and injury prevention. Of course, these matters directly concern parents, whose roles involve promoting positive health outcomes. To achieve this aim, you'll need to learn as much as you can about running and health, pay close attention to signs that indicate your child's health status, ensure that your child receives appropriate health care when necessary, and serve as a role model through your own positive health behaviors.

developing good running form. Chapter 6 covers specific technique drills and other methods, such as weight, circuit, and flexibility and mobility training, that are critical to developing efficient running form.

Developmental Principle 8:
Set Your Sights on Self-Improvement

A good bit of energy for distance running is fueled by dreams. Some young runners dream of qualifying for or winning their state championship, earning a college scholarship, or even competing in the Olympic Games. Dreams serve as strong motivators for pushing through the long runs, the exhausting interval sessions, and the last stages of grueling races. The reality, of course, is that only a small percentage of today's young runners will develop into tomorrow's Olympic athletes, and those who do reach the world's elite ranks get considerable help from their genes. Even so, all young runners can be on par with elite runners in at least one way: focusing on self-improvement as the most important measure of success.

The next time you read an article about a world-class runner or see one being interviewed on television or the Internet, pay attention to what they talk about. Beyond the championships, the medals, and the money, you'll hear messages about taking on the challenges of self-improvement. "I need to work on my kick, because I know that I can run faster over the last 400," an elite athlete might say. "I'm losing form going uphill, so I need to include more hill training in my program," another might say; or another, "I'm letting my nerves get to me too much before races, so I'm planning to experiment with relaxation techniques."

The bottom line is that self-improvement from day to day, season to season, and year to year paves the road to achieving one's highest goals and results in unparalleled satisfaction, making the hard work worthwhile and, yes, even enjoyable.

Developmental Principle 9:
Never Compromise Health

Without question, training for young distance runners should be designed for peak performance. Given the physical demands of running, however, a fine line often separates peak performance from injury and illness. To keep their athletes on the right side of the line, coaches must adhere to the philosophy that training should never compromise health. In the long run, one of the most important objectives of youth sport is influencing values and behaviors in ways that ensure a healthy lifestyle in adulthood. Participating in cross country and track is especially valuable considering the high incidence of diseases that are linked to physical inactivity, including obesity, high blood pressure, coronary heart disease, diabetes, and even some forms of cancer. If you're a parent or a coach, you can pave the young runner's path to a physically active life by emphasizing healthy training practices such as increasing training loads gradually, using technique and strength training methods geared toward injury prevention, stressing optimal nutrition, watching for signs of overtraining, and advising athletes to rest if they are injured or ill.

Developmental Principle 10: Make It Fun

The adage "Last but not least" applies doubly here. Although the best outcomes for young runners depend on applying developmental principles 1 through 9, this last one can make all the difference in the end. That's because none of the principles we've presented so far has much practical value if young runners don't view their training and racing experiences as fun. Take the principle of aiming for self-improvement. The odds that young runners will improve are very low if they don't fully enjoy the sport. Obviously, if they grow to dislike it, they'll drop out along the way. For coaches, all the knowledge in the world about the science of distance running doesn't amount to much if their athletes find training a bore. It's true that well-designed training programs can naturally instill a sense of enjoyment. The reason is that sound programs enable runners to challenge themselves to work hard and to reach their goals, which can be inherently rewarding and, indeed, fun. However, there's a lot more to cultivating exciting and engaging experiences for young runners. The best coaches have the most creative imaginations; they use games, contests, and special events to spice up their training programs. Throughout this book, we share suggestions for adding variety and making training fun.

Striding Ahead

To design effective training programs for young distance runners, coaches need to be knowledgeable about human development, specifically about how children and adolescents grow and mature. We've stressed this point in this chapter's 10 developmental principles. You'll see all the principles in action in part II (chapters 6 through 10), in which we guide you through a process for planning training programs. First, however, we'll help you learn more about the fundamentals of distance running, starting with its physiological basis.

2

Teen Physiology

On May 27, 2001, Alan Webb, a high school boy from Reston, Virginia, shocked the running world. Racing against world-class professionals at the prestigious Prefontaine Classic in Oregon, Webb ran the mile in 3:53.4, breaking the U.S. high school record of 3:55.3 set 36 years earlier by the legendary Jim Ryun. When you consider that a 5:00 mile is an impressive feat for high school boys, Webb's 3:53.4 is truly astounding. One way to grasp this remarkable achievement is to break it into 100-meter segments. A 3:53 mile strings together 16 consecutive 100s, averaging about 14.5 seconds for each, plus another 9 meters to reach 1,609 meters, which equals 1 mile. At that pace you'd cover the mile at 3:53.3, breaking Alan Webb's record by 0.1 second.

Maybe that seems at least a little less daunting. After all, many high school boys can run 100 meters in 14.5 seconds with ease. But why, despite the highest levels of motivation, can't they keep up the pace for another 1,509 meters? In terms of the body's energy-making capacities, what would it take to match Webb's feat? For all the high school runners who might start out on pace for the record, what factors would ultimately cause them to feel fatigue and slow down? And what capacities must young runners develop through training to sustain such fast-paced running and defy fatigue? These questions are at the heart of running physiology, the topic of this chapter. As you'll see, knowledge about the physiological basis of running is essential for designing effective training programs for young endurance athletes. Before you read on, make sure that you're well rested, because our physiology lesson guides you through an attempt at breaking the U.S. high school record for the mile run.

Fantasy Run for the Record

"Last call for the mile run," announces the starter. Your competitors and you, a first-rate field, toe the line. The stadium is packed, the air is filled with expectation, the track is fast, and the weather couldn't be better. It's a perfect day for an attempt on the high school record in the mile run. Again, for boys, the challenge is to string together 16 nonstop 100-meter segments (plus another 9 meters) averaging about 14.5 seconds, or 58 seconds for each 400 meters. That's the pace for a 3:53.3 mile, dipping just under Alan Webb's record. For girls, we'll set our sights on a 4:24.0 mile, which would break the stunning U.S. high school record of 4:24.11, which was set in 2014 by Mary Cain, of Bronxville, New York. You'll need to average 16.4 seconds for each 100-meter run, or 65.6 seconds per 400.

The starting pistol fires, and before you know it, you're 20 meters down the track. As you settle into target pace, a wave of confidence sweeps over you. So far, this is easy. Your leg muscles are generating powerful forces against the track that propel you upward and forward. If you can sustain the same amount of force in each muscle contraction for every stride from here to the finish line, the record will be yours. Of course, you'll rely on the competition to bring out your best effort, you'll need the crowd to spur you on, and you'll have to draw on supreme determination and willpower to overcome the fatigue that will inevitably set in. Many factors must align perfectly for you to have a chance at the record. Ultimately, however, success depends on whether your body can produce a sufficient amount of energy, at a fast enough rate, to sustain those powerful muscle contractions. This energy, you might be surprised to know, ultimately comes from a single chemical compound in the body called *adenosine triphosphate*, or ATP.

Got ATP?

ATP is a molecule that stores the energy muscles need to contract and thereby generate force in running, as well as in all other physical activities. Muscles are composed of parallel bundles of fibers, each surrounded by nerve endings that transmit neural signals, and by capillaries that deliver nutrients and oxygen (see figure 2.1). Muscle fibers are made of protein filaments called *myosin* and *actin*. The physical interaction between myosin and actin filaments, fueled by energy from ATP, is the basic mechanism of muscle contraction.

A voluntary muscle contraction begins with neural signals that travel from the brain to the nerve endings in muscle fibers. The neural signals trigger an intricate series of biochemical events that enable myosin and actin to overlap and bind with each other. As shown in figure 2.2, the binding occurs when a myosin crossbridge connects with an actin filament. Although many preliminary chemical reactions are involved, a muscle contraction occurs when energy is released from the splitting of ATP molecules. This energy causes the myosin crossbridge to bend and generate tension against the actin filament. This action, called the *power stroke*, causes actin and myosin to slide past each other, shortening the muscle fiber. The process occurs in millions of muscle fibers within a single muscle, causing the entire muscle to contract. When muscles contract, they generate forces that pull on their tendons, which then pull on the bones to which

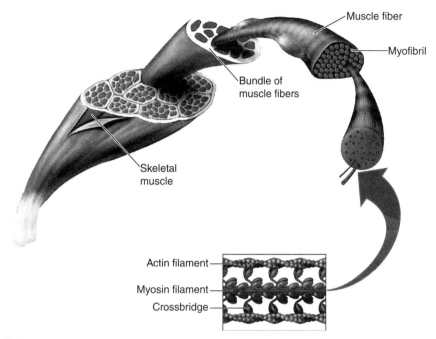

Figure 2.1 Structural elements of a muscle.

they are attached. This action results in limb movements such as the running stride.

Once again, your record run depends on having enough ATP to sustain muscle contractions that are forceful enough to move your body at a speed of 14.5 seconds (boys) or 16.4 seconds (girls) per 100 meters over the distance of 1 mile. But there's a catch: your muscles normally store only a small amount of this precious substance. Consider that at the start of a mile race, if you had to rely on your ATP stores as your only source of energy, you'd cover only about 10 to 20 meters, and then you'd experience complete and utter fatigue. You literally would be unable to take another step. But at least you'd reach the 20-meter mark side by side with Alan Webb or Mary Cain—that's because the muscles of elite runners don't contain much more ATP than anyone else's muscles.

Replenishing ATP With Creatine Phosphate

Fortunately, you don't have to worry about running out of fuel at the 20-meter mark of a distance race. The reason is that the body can replenish its ATP stores. This occurs through various energy pathways, which are complex biochemical processes that re-form ATP after it is broken down to fuel muscle contractions. Here's an all-important point about running physiology: the rate of ATP resynthesis ultimately determines whether runners will have sufficient energy to sustain fast-paced efforts. In other words, you'll be able to stay on pace for the high

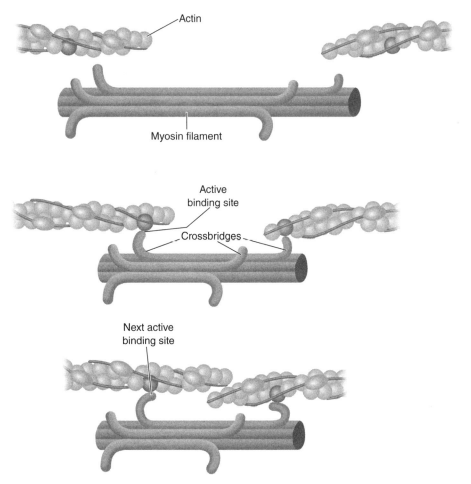

Figure 2.2 The power stroke of myosin crossbridges causes myosin and actin to slide past each other, shortening the muscle fiber and causing the whole muscle to contract.

school mile-run record only if your body can replenish ATP fast enough to meet its energy needs. If your body's energy pathways fall behind in ATP production, you'll experience fatigue and have no choice but to slow down.

At the 20-meter mark of a distance race, the body relies heavily on an energy pathway called the *ATP–creatine phosphate (ATP–CP) system*. When stored ATP is split to release the energy that fuels muscle contractions, two molecules are formed: adenosine diphosphate (ADP) and phosphate. (For science buffs, this pathway is diagrammed in figure 2.3.) To replenish ATP rapidly, the body must have a source of energy to bind the phosphate molecule back to ADP. One immediately available energy source is creatine phosphate (CP).

The phosphate molecule in CP binds with ADP to re-form ATP. The ATP-CP energy pathway will get you past the 20-meter mark in a distance race, but it won't get you much farther. Like ATP, creatine phosphate is stored in very small amounts in the body.

$$\text{ATP} + H_2O \longrightarrow \text{ADP} + \overset{\text{Phosphate}}{\overbrace{H_3PO_4}}$$

Figure 2.3 The ATP molecule is hydrolyzed, or split by water, yielding ADP and phosphate. To re-form ATP, energy is required to bind the phosphate to ADP.

Creatine phosphate is an immediate source of energy for binding phosphate to ADP. When creatine phosphate stores are exhausted, the energy for producing ATP must come from the body's stored carbohydrate and fat.

A little extra creatine phosphate can be produced in the body from dietary creatine, which is found in beef and other meats. If your diet includes at least a little meat, your muscles likely have enough creatine phosphate for you to reach about 50 meters on pace for the mile record. As you may know, many athletes in power sports such as football and competitive weightlifting take creatine as a dietary supplement to boost their creatine phosphate levels. Creatine supplements are known to increase muscle size and strength in power athletes. Distance runners, however, don't really benefit from supplementing their diets with creatine. The main reason is that this molecule contributes relatively little energy in events over 100 meters. In addition, creatine supplements can increase body weight through water accumulation and muscle gain. Carrying the extra weight can drain the distance runner's energy.

Considering the limited stores of creatine phosphate, our prospects for a new record are looking bleak at the 50-meter mark of our mile race. But don't despair—food and oxygen are coming to the rescue with the potential for yielding abundant energy.

Energy From Food and Oxygen

In a 100-meter race, sprinters use stored ATP and creatine phosphate to meet a large part of their energy needs. In contrast, middle-distance (800 to 1,500 meters) and long-distance (3,000 to 5,000 meters) runners rely most heavily on nutrient metabolism, or the breakdown of stored food energy, to replenish ATP. (This is why optimal nutrition, the topic of chapter 3, is so important for distance runners.) The primary nutrient sources of energy for distance runners are carbohydrate and fat. Carbohydrate makes up foods such as bread, pasta, rice, potatoes, fruits, and vegetables. Fat is mainly found in meats, butter, and vegetable oils.

The body has three energy pathways for replenishing ATP through carbohydrate and fat metabolism: anaerobic glycolysis, aerobic glycolysis, and aerobic lipolysis. These pathways are distinguished by two factors. The first is whether they use oxygen to re-form ATP. Energy pathways that use oxygen are called *aerobic*, and those that do not use oxygen are called *anaerobic*. The second factor that distinguishes the pathways is whether they use carbohydrate or fat as energy sources.

Pointers for Parents

You might think that knowledge about running physiology is important only for scientists and coaches. However, to carry out their many supportive roles, parents also need to know about the subject.

- **Be aware of the adage "Kids are not miniature adults."**

  As emphasized in chapter 1, children and adolescents have unique physiological characteristics that change on the path to adulthood. Some coaches and young runners overlook this fact in their enthusiasm for winning championships. They adopt training methods that are more appropriate for adults and, in doing so, risk physical injury and psychological burnout. We encourage you to have collegial conversations with your child's coaches to learn how the training program is designed and adapted specifically for youth.

- **Help your child understand that good running isn't just psychological.**

  Many young runners attribute competitive success and failure mainly to psychological factors such as motivation and willpower. Although the mental side of running is tremendously important, it's just one side. Kids need to understand that their potential in running greatly depends on their genetic makeup, metabolic capacities, and state of growth and maturation. They also need to appreciate how training can improve physiological capacities. You may need to reinforce these points, especially when your child is frustrated by falling short of performance goals and looking for answers on how to attain them.

- **Be prepared for dynamic changes during adolescence.**

  This advice was introduced in chapter 1, where we detailed key pubertal changes. Recall, for example, that during puberty boys tend to add muscle, whereas girls tend to add fat. The addition of normal amounts of muscle and fat during puberty should not negatively influence running performance. On the other hand, kids who add disproportionately large amounts of muscle or fat mass may experience temporary or long-term declines in performance. With awareness of these physiological facts, you can provide rational as well as emotional support when your child is going through changes that affect performance.

- **Encourage your child to keep learning about running physiology.**

  The value of studying this topic extends far beyond youth sport. Many kids who take an interest in running physiology naturally adopt a lifelong commitment to taking good care of their bodies. They're the kids who grow up purposefully choosing healthy foods, making sure they're getting enough sleep, and avoiding unhealthy behaviors such as alcohol and drug abuse. To encourage lifelong study about how the body works, learn alongside your child, and regularly discuss key lessons.

- *Anaerobic glycolysis* is the breakdown of carbohydrate to form ATP when oxygen is lacking in the muscles. Dietary carbohydrate is stored in the muscles and liver as glycogen, which is composed of smaller molecules called *glucose*. Anaerobic glycolysis supplies most of the energy for shorter, faster races up to 400 meters.

- *Aerobic glycolysis* is the breakdown of carbohydrate to form ATP when oxygen is present in the muscles. This is the predominant energy pathway for the youth running events from 800 to 5,000 meters.

- *Aerobic lipolysis* is the breakdown of fat to form ATP when oxygen is present in muscle cells. This pathway supplies most of the energy in longer, relatively slow-paced distance running, such as the marathon (26.2 miles, or 42.2 km).

Oxygen is truly the star player in the game of energy metabolism. It's like the 7-foot, 6-inch basketball center whose team scores big when he's in the offensive court, but who sometimes can't get down the court fast enough. When that happens, the team doesn't score as much. When oxygen is lacking in muscle cells, the anaerobic pathway yields only a small amount of ATP. Compared with anaerobic glycolysis, the aerobic pathway produces up to 18 times more ATP from the breakdown of the same amount of glucose. Aerobic lipolysis produces up to 65 times more ATP from a molecule of fat. These numbers partly explain why a high level of aerobic power—in other words, the body's capacity to use oxygen to replenish ATP—is so essential for success in distance running. Recall from chapter 1 that the highest level of aerobic power is measured as $\dot{V}O_2$max.

Breathe Naturally

Because more oxygen in the working muscles results in more ATP, you might wonder whether runners should adjust their breathing to maximize oxygen intake. The best advice is to let breathing occur naturally, preferably through both the mouth and the nose. Research shows that under normal circumstances, the runner's natural breathing pattern brings more than enough air into the lungs to fully load oxygen onto hemoglobin, which carries oxygen in red blood cells. Changing breathing patterns won't load any more oxygen onto hemoglobin and therefore won't result in more oxygen being delivered to the muscles.

Roles of the Energy Pathways

All three energy pathways are involved in replenishing ATP in distance running. However, they contribute in varying degrees depending on two main factors: the distance covered and the running intensity, which refers to speed and effort. As the distance gets shorter and running intensity increases, a greater proportion of energy is supplied through the anaerobic (versus aerobic) pathway. During extremely high-intensity efforts, the cardiovascular system—the heart and blood vessels—can't supply enough oxygen-rich blood to fully sustain aerobic metabolism. The flip side is that as distances get longer and intensity decreases, the aerobic pathways play bigger roles. This important point is illustrated in figure 2.4.

You might ask, How much energy comes from the anaerobic versus aerobic pathways in the competitive events in which young runners compete? That's an excellent question because the answer provides key information for designing training programs that target the specific physiological capacities that runners need to develop. Consider, for example, the roles of the energy pathways in a 1-mile or 1,500-meter race. Studies of competitive runners have revealed that, at these distances, 75 to 85 percent of energy needs are met aerobically, and 15 to 25 percent are met anaerobically (Gastin, 2001; Spencer and Gastin, 2001). In a 5,000-meter race, the contribution of the aerobic pathway can increase to around 95 percent. Table 2.1 shows estimated contributions of the aerobic and anaerobic pathways for racing 800 to 5,000 meters. Note that even in the longer events, runners rely on some anaerobic energy, especially for midrace surges, sprint finishes, and uphill running.

The percentages in table 2.1 come from studies on competitive *adult* runners. Because of a lack of research, we don't know exactly how much energy comes

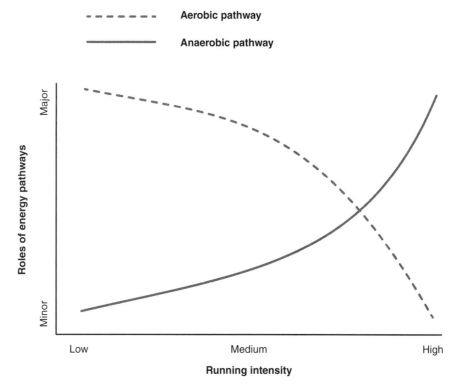

Figure 2.4   Relative roles of the energy pathways in low- to high-intensity running.

Table 2.1 Estimated Contribution of the Energy Pathways

Distance	PERCENTAGE OF CONTRIBUTION TO GENERATING ATP	
	Aerobic pathway	Anaerobic pathway
800 m	60-65	35-40
1,500 m to 1 mile (1,600 m)	75-85	15-25
3,000 m	85-90	10-15
5,000 m	90-95	5-10

These data come from studies of highly trained adult runners (Gastin, 2001; Spencer & Gastin, 2001). Research has not been conducted to determine the contribution of each energy pathway in elite young runners.

from the various energy pathways in young runners. But, as we discussed in chapter 1, studies have shown that children and adolescents are limited in their ability to produce ATP anaerobically. Compared with adult runners, young runners rely more heavily on aerobic metabolism.

Aerobic Fitness Makes the Difference

Early in an 800- to 5,000-meter race, if you lack aerobic fitness and you're running too fast, your muscles will be forced to rely heavily on anaerobic metabolism. This pathway rapidly generates energy for high-intensity activity when the cardiovascular system can't supply the muscles with oxygen quickly enough. However, the anaerobic pathway has some major drawbacks for distance runners. Recall that anaerobic glycolysis yields a relatively small amount of energy. In addition, this pathway relies on glycogen as a nutrient fuel source. The problem is that our bodies, specifically our muscles and liver, store only limited amounts of glycogen. A girl weighing 110 lb (50 kilograms), for example, might have stores of only 200 to 250 grams of glycogen in her whole body. Several days of intense training without sufficient carbohydrate replacement from the diet can lead to glycogen depletion, a major cause of fatigue in distance running.

Revving Up Your Metabolic Engine

In a physiological nutshell, the distance runner's basic challenge is to sustain the fastest pace that doesn't cause excessive fatigue and slowing. This challenge is met by relying as much as possible on the aerobic pathways. However, it takes a while for the oxygen-delivery system, the heart and blood vessels, to rev up. Therefore, a runner who starts a training session or a race without warming up properly must rely heavily on anaerobic metabolism to supply ATP until the heart begins pumping enough blood and the vasculature directs that blood to the working muscles. The main consequence of relying too heavily on anaerobic energy early in a race is lactic acid accumulation, which causes fatigue. Chapter 6 addresses how to warm up properly for training and racing.

Coach Jeff Messer, PhD

Desert Vista High School
Location: Phoenix, Arizona

Jeff Messer (second from right in bottom row in photo) is uniquely qualified to apply running physiology to the design of training programs for young endurance athletes. He has a PhD in exercise physiology and teaches the subject at Mesa Community College, where he serves as director of the Human Performance Laboratory. Before becoming head coach of the girls' cross country team at Desert Vista High School in 2013, Dr. Messer was co-head coach of the Xavier College Preparatory (Phoenix) cross country team, a perennial nationally ranked high school program. In this profile, Dr. Messer discusses the importance of training to develop aerobic power.

Margot Kelly Photography

How do you apply knowledge about the physiological energy pathways to designing training programs for young runners?—Research in exercise physiology has provided coaches with useful information about the contributions of the aerobic and anaerobic energy systems to race performance (Gastin, 2001; Spencer and Gastin, 2001). We have learned, for example, that in a 1,500-meter race, about 80 percent of the energy for ATP production comes from the aerobic pathway. In 3,000- and 5,000-meter races, aerobic metabolism supplies about 90 percent and 95 percent of energy needs, respectively. Based on this information, we know that youth training programs should primarily emphasize the development of aerobic power. An important principle is that distance runners can rely on aerobic metabolism to the extent that they develop it through training.

Which training methods are best for developing aerobic power?—Ideal methods include tempo runs, progression runs, and repetition sessions with very modest recovery intervals. An example is a 3-mile (4.8 km) tempo run designed for a 16-year-old girl whose goal is to run 18:36 for 5,000 meters in November, when we have our cross country state championship. In July, when we start training for cross country, her pace for the tempo run will be about 15 percent slower than her goal race pace. To run 18:36, she will need to average 6-minute miles. So, in July her pace for the tempo run will be around 6:54 per mile. By October, we lower the tempo run pace to about 5 to 7 percent slower than goal race pace, which is 6:18 to 6:25 per mile. Or, instead of an even-paced tempo run in October, I might plan a progression run, which involves decreasing the pace. For the runner aiming for an 18:36 5K, target mile splits for a late-season 3-mile (4.8 km) progression run would be 6:25, 6:20, and 6:15.

How do you teach your athletes to work at the right intensity for building aerobic power?—I cue my runners to pay attention to what's going on in their bodies, such as their breathing rate in relation to their foot strike. For example, in a tempo run, if they are breathing in every second foot strike, they are likely relying too much on anaerobic metabolism. I also teach my runners to self-assess their energy level and adjust their intensity accordingly. Before a one-hour aerobic foundation run, I give instructions that at the end they should feel as though they could keep running for another 10 minutes. Or, at the end of a 3- to 4-mile (4.8 to 6.4 km) tempo run, they should be able to run another half mile at the same pace. If they can't keep going for another half mile, their intensity was too high. On the other hand, if they easily can run another mile, they didn't work hard enough for building aerobic power.

How do you ensure that your athletes also develop anaerobic capacity and speed?—I design programs on the principle of conjugate periodization, which means that we train every relevant performance capacity for distance running on a year-round basis. At some point in a race, distance runners need to recruit fast-twitch muscle fibers and summon top-end speed. So, throughout the year, we include sprinting in our training sessions twice a week. At the end of a tempo run, for example, our girls do five or six 200-meter repetitions faster than race pace. Or they might do 100-meter repetitions with the middle 60 meters at a full sprint.

Another drawback to the anaerobic pathway involves one of its by-products, lactic acid. This substance is actually essential for generating energy during high-intensity work. However, the accumulation of lactic acid in the muscles is a major cause of fatigue in running. The acidic component of lactic acid physically interferes with the overlapping of the protein filaments that enable muscles to generate tension. Lactic acid can also limit the activity of enzymes that are involved in ATP production. For these reasons, a high level of aerobic fitness is the main physiological determinant of success in distance running.

Getting back to our fantasy attempt to break the high school record for the mile run, let's say that you've reached the 800-meter mark on target pace. If you have a very high level of aerobic fitness, at this point your muscles will minimize their reliance on the anaerobic pathway. As a result, you'll avoid lactic acid accumulation, which is a major cause of fatigue at this competitive distance. Still, because this pathway does provide a portion of ATP for a mile race, you'll also need a high level of anaerobic fitness to stay on pace and, especially, to pick up the pace if you fall behind. We discuss anaerobic fitness later in the chapter.

Improving Maximal Aerobic Power

Let's face the facts: unless you're a world-class distance runner, you simply don't currently have the aerobic power to keep up with Mary Cain or Alan Webb very far into a mile race. However, young runners have a remarkable capacity to improve

Principle of Training Specificity

Two key concepts introduced in this chapter underscore why successful coaches study exercise physiology. First, the body produces energy for distance running through three pathways, and, second, several metabolic factors cause fatigue in distance races. It follows that training must be comprehensive, stressing each energy pathway to the proper degree. This is determined by how much energy that pathway contributes to a given competitive event. A 5,000-meter runner, for example, needs to do more training to develop aerobic fitness than a 1,500-meter runner does. And because lactic acid accumulation is a primary cause of muscle fatigue in 1,500-meter races, coaches must design sessions to train the 1,500-meter runner's body to hold off lactic acid accumulation and, when it inevitably starts to accumulate, to tolerate its effects. These two concepts are related to an important principle of training, called *specificity*, which states that physiological adaptations are specific to the type, intensity, and duration of training. In part II, you'll learn how to apply this principle to designing training programs.

their aerobic power through training. We know this from many studies that have measured training-related changes in $\dot{V}O_2$max in adolescents (Bar-Or and Rowland, 2004). On average, $\dot{V}O_2$max in untrained girls is around 35 to 45 milliliters per kilogram of body weight per minute. The average range for untrained boys is 40 to 50. Following a moderate training program, approximately 15 miles (24 km) per week over two to three months, untrained adolescents experience about a 15 percent increase in $\dot{V}O_2$max. With additional months and years of more intense training, adolescent runners can boost their $\dot{V}O_2$max values to 50 to 60 (girls) and 60 to 70 (boys) milliliters per kilogram of body weight per minute. The highest $\dot{V}O_2$max values recorded for elite adult distance runners are around 75 for women and 85 for men.

Training-induced increases in $\dot{V}O_2$max are caused by adaptations in the runner's heart, blood vessels, and muscle cells (see table 2.2). Training increases the dimensions of the heart's chambers, the thickness of its muscle wall, and the strength of its contractions. These changes enable the heart to pump more blood to the working muscles. Although training usually doesn't influence maximal heart rate (the highest number of heartbeats per minute during the most intense exercise), it reduces heart rate during submaximal exercise and at rest. Well-trained distance runners have resting heart rates as low as 35 to 45 beats per minute (bpm), much lower than normal rates of around 70 bpm.

Other responses to endurance training occur in the skeletal muscles. To handle the increased blood supply during high-intensity running, the vasculature adapts by channeling more blood flow to the working muscles and away from tissues and organs that don't require a large amount of oxygen. New capillaries are formed, enabling more oxygen to reach muscle cells and more lactic acid to be cleared from the muscles. Within muscle cells, the most important adaptation to training is an increase in the number and size of mitochondria, the structures in which oxygen is used to generate ATP, and an increase in the mitochondrial enzymes

Table 2.2 Physiological Adaptations to Training

Energy pathways stressed by training	Physiological changes
Aerobic	↑ VO$_2$max ↑ Maximal cardiac output ↓ Resting and submaximal heart rate ↑ Blood flow and oxygen delivery to working muscles ↑ Capillary density ↑ Lactic acid clearance from muscles ↑ Size and number of mitochondria ↑ Aerobic enzyme concentration and activity ↑ Capacity to metabolize fat
Anaerobic	↑ Anaerobic enzyme concentration and activity ↑ Maximal lactic acid production ↑ Capacity to buffer lactic acid

that catalyze reactions in the aerobic energy pathways. These adaptations enable the runner to work at higher intensities without having to go farther down the anaerobic pathway, where the hazards of glycogen depletion and lactic acid accumulation lurk. As you'll see in chapters 6 and 7, the training methods for developing cardiorespiratory fitness and maximal aerobic power include continuous aerobic running, tempo running, and aerobic interval training.

Muscle Fibers for Endurance and Speed

Although a high level of aerobic fitness is essential for success in distance running, other factors are also involved, some of which are determined by genetics rather than training. One of the most important genetic factors is muscle fiber type. We all inherit two major types of muscle fibers, which are generally referred to as *type I* and *type II*. Type I fibers are also called *slow-twitch fibers* because they generate contractile force slowly, resulting in low power output. Slow-twitch fibers are built for endurance. They contain many mitochondria and a large amount of myoglobin, a molecule that transports oxygen into the mitochondria. Slow-twitch fibers operate with ATP formed through the aerobic pathway, and they are able to resist fatigue during low- to moderate-intensity exercise.

In contrast, type II fibers, also called *fast-twitch fibers*, contract rapidly and forcefully for speed and power, but they fatigue more quickly than slow-twitch fibers do. There are several subtypes of fast-twitch fibers, with names such as *fast-glycolytic (FG)* and *fast-oxidative-glycolytic (FOG)* fibers. Fast-glycolytic fibers rely exclusively on ATP generated through anaerobic metabolism, whereas fast-oxidative-glycolytic fibers can contract aerobically, which means that they combine the characteristics of slow-twitch and fast-twitch fibers.

Table 2.3 shows common ratios of slow-twitch to fast-twitch muscle fibers in elite athletes in various sports. People born with a high percentage of slow-twitch fibers tend to excel in endurance activities, whereas those born with a high

Table 2.3   Ratio of Slow-Twitch to Fast-Twitch Muscle Fibers in Elite Athletes in Various Sports

Athlete group	Slow-twitch fibers (%)	Fast-twitch fibers (%)
Cyclists	50	50
Swimmers	50	50
Cross-country skiers	75	25
Sprinters (track and field)	26	74
Middle-distance runners	50	50
Long-distance runners	80	20

Adapted from Noakes (2003).

percentage of fast-twitch fibers tend to excel in activities that demand short bursts of power and speed.

Notice in table 2.3 that the ratio of fiber types in elite middle-distance runners, who compete in 800- to 1,600-meter races, is 50:50. Let's say that you happen to have been born with a very high percentage, 75 percent, of fast-twitch fibers of the fast-glycolytic subtype, which are built for speed. If you're trying to break the U.S. high school record in the mile run, the first 300 to 400 meters will feel easy because you'll be running much slower than your maximal speed. However, your fast-glycolytic fibers aren't built for endurance. They have few mitochondria and

Using Heart Rate to Determine Optimal Training Intensity

To develop a specific energy pathway, training must stimulate physiological stress in a critical zone. Training below the zone's threshold won't result in desired adaptations, and neither will training too hard. How do you know whether you're training in the critical zones for developing the aerobic and anaerobic pathways? The most objective feedback comes from tests of oxygen consumption and blood lactic acid concentration in an exercise physiology lab. Such tests, however, are neither practical nor necessary for runners in their daily training. To obtain useful physiological data, all you need is a watch and some experience with taking your pulse, which reflects how fast your heart is beating. Heart rate is a useful measure of physiological processes because it increases in proportion to the muscles' oxygen demands.

Because certain ranges of heart rates are associated with specific adaptations of the energy pathways, you have a guide for determining target training intensities and paces. For example, research shows that $\dot{V}O_2$max increases in beginning runners who train at 65 to 75 percent of maximal heart rate. So, if a beginner named Jenna has a maximal heart rate of 204 beats per minute, she would need to run continuously at a pace that raises her heart rate to between 133 and 153 beats per minute (204 × 0.65 = 132.6 and 204 × 0.75 = 153) to increase her $\dot{V}O_2$max. In part II, we show you how to take your pulse, determine your maximal heart rate, and calculate training paces for developing the energy pathways.

a small amount of myoglobin, so they are not efficient in using oxygen to make ATP, relying instead on anaerobic glycolysis, which produces lactic acid.

On the other hand, let's say that you were born with a very high percentage of slow-twitch fibers. It's possible that you might be running at top speed to reach 200 meters on pace for the U.S. high school mile record. One of this book's authors, Russ Pate, didn't have great sprinting speed as a high school runner. Russ's best time for the mile in high school was 4:44, which is good but not quite record setting. By his late 20s, however, Russ was a world-class marathoner, with a PR (personal record) of 2:15. He also improved his mile PR to a respectable 4:17. In 1975, when he was 28 years old, Russ participated in a landmark exercise physiology study, in which world-class runners including Steve Prefontaine and Frank Shorter were assessed for measures such as $\dot{V}O_2$max and muscle fiber type. A biopsy of Russ's calf muscle showed that his slow-twitch fiber type composition was 90 percent, likely a reason for his success at the longer races.

In general, athletes who have a relatively high percentage of fast-twitch fibers are better suited for sprinting and middle-distance races (800 meters to the mile), whereas those with a high percentage of slow-twitch fibers will reach their potential in the longer races (3,000 to 5,000 meters). However, genetics doesn't completely determine a distance runner's fate. Through sound training, athletes can compensate for genetic weaknesses. In addition, as a result of many years of well-targeted training, some muscle fibers can actually convert their contractile and metabolic properties from one type to another.

Anaerobic Fitness Counts, Too

Let's get back on track with our attempt at the high school mile record. Suppose you've got an optimal ratio of slow-twitch to fast-twitch muscle fibers and that, through training, you've developed supreme aerobic fitness. At 800 meters into the race, you're on pace for the record, with a split of 1:56 for boys and 2:11 for girls. Although you're running comfortably and feeling strong, sustaining the pace over the next lap will definitely be challenging. Even for world-class runners, the pace from 800 to 1,200 meters in a mile race is fast enough to activate a lot of fast-twitch muscle fibers and require a fair amount of energy produced through the anaerobic pathway. Reaching the bell lap on target pace will be something like walking a tightrope strung over a river of lactic acid. Whether you balance on the tightrope or fall into the river partly depends on your anaerobic fitness.

When small amounts of lactic acid are produced, the substance is easily cleared through the bloodstream. Lactic acid is transported from the muscle cells where it was produced to other muscle cells, the liver, and the heart. All of these tissues can use lactic acid in processes that re-form ATP. This might seem puzzling if you've heard that lactic acid is the culprit in causing muscle fatigue. Lactic acid is actually a valuable energy source, but it does cause fatigue at a threshold at which its production rate exceeds its rate of clearance from the muscles. As running intensity increases, every runner reaches this so-called *lactate threshold*.

Many distance training programs emphasize running at speeds corresponding to the lactate threshold. For young runners, a sample workout might be a 20- to 35-minute run at a pace 30 seconds to 1 minute per mile slower than their 1-mile personal record. Over time, physiological adaptations to this training increase the lactate threshold, enabling runners to sustain faster paces before lactic acid begins to accumulate. One key adaptation is the development of new capillaries, tiny blood vessels that deliver oxygen to muscle cells. New capillaries and more oxygen enable a greater amount of aerobic energy to be produced, thereby reducing the need for anaerobic energy and the potential for lactic acid accumulation. Newly formed blood vessels are also involved in clearing lactic acid away from muscle cells and into the bloodstream.

Recovery and Sleep: Keys to Gaining Fitness

For running performance to improve as a result of training, a two-phase cycle must be repeated over time. In the first phase, the body's physiological systems are overloaded, or stressed, by demanding workouts. Then, in the second phase, the body restores its spent energy and rebuilds its physiological capacities to higher levels. With this overload–rebuilding cycle in mind, consider a critical point: adaptations to training that improve running performance don't occur *during* workouts. Instead, they happen *between* them through restorative processes. These include the formation of new red blood cells and hemoglobin molecules to carry more oxygen to the muscles. In rest and recovery periods between demanding workouts, the body also makes new protein molecules to strengthen muscle fibers and form enzymes for more efficient energy production.

Some of the body's most important restorative processes and adaptations to training occur during sleep. For example, during stages of deep sleep, the brain's pituitary gland releases large amounts of growth hormone, which is required for rebuilding muscle tissue, forming new red blood cells, synthesizing proteins for energy production, and supporting immune function. Studies have demonstrated that growth hormone production is suppressed in animals and humans deprived of sleep (Morris, Aeschbach, and Scheer, 2012). Moreover, studies consistently show that many physiological and performance capacities decline in athletes who don't get sufficient amounts of sleep (Halson, 2014).

Experts agree that most adolescents need about 9 to 10 hours of nightly sleep. At least on school days, most teens have no choice but to wake up early. So, to get enough sleep, they need to go to bed early. Of course, with demands of homework and interests in social activities and hobbies, many teens like to stay up late. Also, in adolescence, the body's circadian rhythm, or biological clock, undergoes a characteristic shift that delays signals to sleep until later at night. For young runners who are committed to performing at their best, insufficient sleep simply isn't an option. Through discipline, sacrifice, and excellent time management skills, serious runners ensure that they get enough nightly sleep to enable their bodies to restore energy and build performance capacities to higher and higher levels. Given the many daily demands on young student-athletes, good time management skills are especially important. In the words of Jumbo Elliott, the legendary coach at Villanova University from the 1950s through the 1980s, to be successful, runners must "live like a clock."

During the school year, athletes will know that they're getting enough sleep if they can wake up on their own and if they feel alert throughout the day. If they need an alarm to wake up or find themselves dozing in class, they need to go to bed earlier to ensure sufficient sleep. Here's more advice for developing good sleep habits for optimal performance and health:

- Don't drink caffeinated beverages in the hours before bedtime.

- On weekdays, set a nightly schedule that allows enough time for homework and minimizes television and Internet time.

- Set an alarm to remind yourself to go to sleep.

- Remind friends and family members to respect your sleep schedule as a valuable part of your training program.

- Sleep in on weekends, or take naps to catch up on any lost sleep during the week.

Conserving Energy Through Sound Technique

If you were walking a tightrope over a raging river, a single wrong step or movement might lead to a fall. Likewise, counterproductive movements in the running stride can topple you into the river of lactic acid. Consider a runner whose right arm crosses in front of his body, well past an imaginary midline that divides the two sides of his chest. As a result of this crossing action, the runner's torso rotates to the left with every stride. To correct the imbalance, the runner has to use muscles that aren't involved in a sound running stride. The extraneous muscle contractions use oxygen that could otherwise be used by the primary muscles that propel the runner's body upward and forward. If we measured this runner's oxygen consumption during a race, it would be higher than that of a competitor who is running at the same pace but has better form. Exercise physiologists refer to this as *running economy*. Poor running economy, which is linked to flawed technique and a lack of neuromuscular skill, taxes the aerobic system and causes runners to rely more heavily on anaerobic energy, which leads to early fatigue. We'll talk more about technique and running economy in chapter 5.

Bell Lap Physiology

The bell has just rung as we fast-forward to the 1,200-meter mark of our mile race. To make it interesting, imagine that you've slipped behind record pace by around 2 seconds. Now you'll need to run the last 400 meters in 56 seconds (boys) or

Dressed for Running Success

As you learn more about the physiology of distance running, you'll appreciate that many factors can affect performance by affecting the body's physiological systems. A great example is the clothing that runners wear in various weather conditions. Take the case of a runner who is overdressed, wearing a long-sleeve heavy cotton T-shirt and full-length tights on a hot and humid day. As the runner's core temperature rises and the clothing traps the heat, the circulatory system shunts extra blood away from the working muscles to the skin. This promotes cooling through the evaporation of sweat. In this scenario, however, the working muscles are deprived of essential oxygen-rich blood and fuel for energy. Also, when the body overheats, its energy-making proteins lose their shape and function, which further hurts performance. Of course, the extra sweating can lead to dangerous dehydration. That's why on hot and humid days it's always best to wear light, loose tops made of synthetic materials that "breathe," or enable body heat to escape into the environment. Local and online running stores sell moisture-wicking clothes, which are ideal for warm weather.

On cold days, if the core temperature is lowered too much, blood is diverted away from working muscles to the trunk. Again, this effect robs the muscles of essential energy. So, extra layers of warm clothing are necessary to trap body heat and redistribute blood flow to the muscles. In addition, runners who aren't dressed warmly enough on cold days shiver, which wastes precious energy. The best advice for dressing on cold days is to wear a few layers of clothing and remove them as the body warms up.

A new trend in running clothing is compression gear, or tight-fitting garments made of elastic material that applies pressure to the skin and muscles. The most common compression garments worn by distance runners are knee-length stockings, shorts, and arm sleeves. Advocates of compression gear claim that it improves performance through various physiological mechanisms. They say, for example, that compression stockings work like pumps to accelerate blood flow from the lower extremities, through the veins, and back to the heart. In theory, this effect would increase cardiac output and deliver oxygen-rich blood to the muscles at a higher rate. Another claim for compression gear is that it enhances the contractile force of the muscles.

Studies of the effects of compression garments on distance-running performance have produced mixed findings, and potential psychological (placebo) effects haven't been discounted (Born, Sperlich, and Holmberg, 2013). At the time this book was published, no reputable studies were available on the effects of compression garments on running performance in children and adolescents. Until evidence clearly shows that compression clothing improves performance and has no negative health effects, we'll refrain from recommending it for young runners.

63.6 seconds (girls). To start your finishing kick, you'll need to recruit more fast-twitch muscle fibers, which means that even more lactic acid will be produced. The challenge now is to swim or sink. In the muscles and bloodstream, this challenge is met by clearing and buffering, or neutralizing, lactic acid.

The body's buffering system uses chemicals called *bicarbonates*, which are transported into the bloodstream from the liver and kidneys. Bicarbonates increase the body's pH, reducing its acidity. Remember that the acid part of lactic acid causes muscle fatigue by limiting the activity of energy-catalyzing enzymes and interfering with the process of muscle contraction. The chemical reaction for buffering lactic acid produces carbonic acid (H_2CO_3). The bloodstream transports this substance from the muscles to the lungs, where it breaks down into carbon dioxide and water. Carbon dioxide is a strong stimulus for ventilation, which explains why you're breathing so hard as you start your last-lap kick.

Whether you will be able to sustain the kick to the finish depends partly on how effectively your body produces and buffers lactic acid. Your body must generate lactic acid at high rates (because you need it to make ATP), buffer it, and then expel it as carbon dioxide. These capacities are developed through training that stresses the anaerobic pathway. Specifically, high-intensity interval training, which raises lactic acid to high levels and challenges the body to withstand its fatiguing effects, leads to increases in anaerobic enzymes and levels of bicarbonates (see table 2.2). We give lots of details on training methods for developing anaerobic fitness in chapter 7.

Now you're on the backstretch of the bell lap, with 200 meters remaining in our imaginary mile race. You've made up those 2 seconds lost on lap 3. But now, suddenly, it seems as if someone has shackled heavy weights to your legs and arms. Your brain is stridently commanding your legs to push forcefully off the ground, to lift your knees higher, and to swing your arms powerfully. But the communication lines are jammed with fatigue. Of course, you need supreme physiological fitness to maintain the sprint to the finish. Now, more than ever, sustaining the pace and maintaining your form are also matters of the mind. It'll take every scrap of your willpower, concentration, and courage to amplify the brain's commands to your muscles to keep generating powerful contractions and to maintain good sprinting form.

As you round the last curve, now with 100 meters to go, you might find that your supreme mental effort overcomes your feelings of physical fatigue. Suddenly, your arms and legs are unshackled, and you've broken through to a new level of energy and speed. Have you noticed that at the end of world-class distance races, the winners often cross the finish line looking as fresh as they did at the starting line, in jubilation, with ear-to-ear smiles on their faces? That's what we envision for you as you cross the finish line of our fantasy mile, setting a new U.S. high school record!

Striding Ahead

We've reached the finish line of our short course on running physiology. Along the way, perhaps you've experienced the vicarious thrill of setting a U.S. high school record in the mile run. The best reason for learning physiology is to apply it to training programs, which we do throughout part II. Before we get there, however, we extend our lesson in physiology to matters of nutrition. In chapter 3, you'll learn about optimal intakes of the body's main energy sources—carbohydrate, fat, and protein—as well as other nutrients such as vitamins and minerals.

3

Optimal Nutrition

In the years that have passed since we were competitive young runners, we've seen many new national and world distance records set in events from 800 meters to the marathon. Given our interests in exercise science, we naturally wonder why today's athletes are running so much faster than the record holders of our heyday. No doubt, advances in training methods partly explain the differences. Today's runners also have better gear, such as more efficient high-performance shoes. Another factor, which has gained much deserved attention in contemporary sport, is nutrition and diet. In the old days, very few distance runners paid careful attention to what they were eating. How things have changed! Based on advances in the field of nutrition science, we now know that the types and amounts of foods runners eat, as well as the fluids they drink, can have a huge impact on performance. Indeed, we suspect that better nutrition has played a big role in the dramatic lowering of running records over the last few decades.

In this chapter we explain why optimal nutrition is so important for young runners, and we offer guidelines for a healthy performance-enhancing diet. The chapter also covers some controversies involving fad foods and dietary supplements. We weigh in with our recommendations based on research evidence and expert advice. Along the way we answer these questions:

- How many calories should runners consume in their daily diet?
- What proportions of the diet should come from carbohydrate, fat, and protein?
- Are vitamin and mineral supplements necessary?
- What's the best fare for prerace and postrace meals?
- Do runners need special sport drinks, or is water best for rehydration?
- What are the nutritional keys to performing at the highest levels while also maintaining optimal health?

Nutrition, Diet, and Performance

Ric's state cross country championship race started early—7:30 a.m. To get a little extra sleep, he skipped breakfast that morning. Because of prerace jitters, he also didn't eat much the day before, only a small cheeseburger for an early dinner. Feeling completely sapped of energy right from the start, Ric wound up finishing almost a minute slower than he had expected to run on the 5K course.

Melinda usually takes a few sips from her water bottle between classes. But on the day of a big track meet, Melinda forgot to bring her water bottle to school, and she didn't think to use the water fountains. At 400 meters into the 1,600-meter race, the clock showed 80 seconds, which was Melinda's goal pace, but her effort and building fatigue made the pace feel more like a 75 or 76.

Alicia had a great summer of training in preparation for her senior cross country season. From June through August, she ran almost 500 miles (805 km), averaging about 40 miles (64 km) a week. Over that time she also lost 9 pounds (4 kg), which she attributes to going on a vegetarian diet. Starting in mid-September, Alicia just didn't feel right. She was tired all the time, had trouble concentrating in school, and couldn't train—even an easy warm-up jog drained her energy.

Each of these stories has the same unfortunate ending: the runners fall short of their potential and risk negative health outcomes as a result of oversights in nutrition and diet. For Ric, not eating breakfast before the competition resulted in low blood glucose. This energy source is essential for brain and muscle function. When we fast, glucose is released into the bloodstream from the liver, where it is stored as glycogen. The liver can store only a small amount of glycogen, which is broken down to maintain blood glucose levels, even during sleep. After an overnight fast, liver glycogen and blood glucose levels fall, especially when the daily diet is low in carbohydrate. Recall from chapter 2 that carbohydrate-rich foods include breads, cereals (grains), pastas, legumes, fruits, and vegetables.

For Melinda, forgetting to drink water led to dehydration, which affects blood volume and circulation. The main components of blood are plasma, which is mostly water, and red blood cells. When the body becomes dehydrated, the concentration of red blood cells increases. This thickening of the blood slows the transport of oxygenated red blood cells to the working muscles, forcing muscle cells to function anaerobically, which results in early fatigue. Dehydration also severely impairs the body's capacity to cool itself through sweating. As you learned in chapter 2, a high core temperature slows energy production because heat breaks down energy-making enzymes.

The doctor's diagnosis for Alicia was iron-deficiency anemia. Along with this bad news came the order to stop running for at least three months—the rest of the cross country season—to allow her body's iron levels to return to normal. Iron plays an important role in forming hemoglobin, which transports oxygen in the blood, and myoglobin, which transports oxygen in the muscles. When iron levels fall, the body has difficulty supplying oxygen to muscle cells, which explains Alicia's general loss of energy and her inability to train without becoming exhausted. When Alicia started her vegetarian diet, she eliminated the best sources of iron: red meat, chicken, and fish. A vegetarian diet doesn't cause anemia, especially if it includes plant foods that contain iron, such as breads, grains, legumes, and certain vegetables and fruits. As we explain later in this chapter, however, running can lower the body's iron levels. Some runners, especially those on vegetarian diets, may need to take iron supplements to prevent anemia.

These three cases are common examples of how poor nutrition and diet can negatively influence running performance and health. Let's talk now about positive approaches to nutrition and diet that lead to the best outcomes for young runners. We begin by introducing the concept of energy balance, which is critical for knowing how much food young runners need to eat.

Daily Calorie Needs

One of the most important nutritional goals for distance runners is to eat enough food to replenish calories burned through training, other daily activities, and basic metabolic (energy-making) processes. When energy intake falls short of energy needs, runners of all ages are at increased risk for unhealthy weight loss, illness, injury, and poor performance. This condition of negative energy balance is especially dangerous for children and adolescents because of their high energy needs for normal growth and maturation. When energy intake exceeds the body's needs, the result is a positive energy balance. In extreme cases, performance suffers as a result of the extra accumulation of body fat.

How many calories do young runners burn daily? Researchers from Iowa State University sought to answer this question by estimating daily calorie expenditure in 20 male and 8 female competitive runners who ranged in age between 10 and 19 years (Eisenmann and Wickel, 2007). The runners' average age was 16.7 years. These were very fit endurance athletes, judging from the researchers' measurements of their $\dot{V}O_2$max (68 and 56 ml/kg/min for the boys and girls, respectively) and low body fat (10.4 and 17.7 percent for the boys and girls, respectively). In the study, the runners rated and recorded their activity levels every 15 minutes over a three-day period. They used a scale of 1 (physically inactive) to 9 (most vigorous physical activity). From the activity scores, the researchers performed calculations to estimate the runners' total daily energy expenditure, accounting for calories spent in training, other physical activities, and basic metabolic processes.

The researchers found that the average total daily energy expenditure was 2,467 calories for the girls and 3,609 calories for the boys. There was, however, a wide range of energy expenditures. For the girls, values ranged from 1,843 to 3,050 calories per day. For the boys, the range was 2,306 to 6,442 calories per day. The variation across runners can be explained by differences in size, training loads, and genetic factors that influence metabolism. The take-home message from this study is that young runners burn and therefore need a lot of calories. They must eat full meals, and maybe even some snacks, to replenish 2,467 to 3,609 calories in a day.

Carbohydrate Intake

In chapter 2 we discussed the role of carbohydrate as a fuel for distance running. Let's review the main points:

- Carbohydrate is a key source of energy for ATP production in 800- to 5,000-meter events.
- The body's carbohydrate stores—blood glucose and liver and muscle glycogen—are very limited, especially in less mature youth.
- Muscle glycogen stores can decrease over several days of intense training if they are not replaced through carbohydrate-rich foods.

Given that carbohydrate plays a key role in providing energy for 800- to 5,000-meter races, it's no surprise that sport nutritionists advise middle- and long-distance runners to eat a high-carbohydrate diet. For competitive adult runners, many experts recommend that 55 to 70 percent of total daily calories come from carbohydrate. Unfortunately, research on carbohydrate intake for young runners is lacking. For good health in normally active youth, major nutrition organizations commonly suggest that carbohydrate make up 50 to 70 percent of total calories. Another set of guidelines for athletes is presented as grams of daily carbohydrate relative to body weight expressed in kilograms (to calculate body weight in kilograms, divide the weight in pounds by 2.2). Among adult endurance athletes, a high-carbohydrate diet has 7 to 10 grams of this energy source per kilogram of body weight per day. Among young athletes, recommended daily carbohydrate intakes generally range from 6 to 9 grams per kilogram of body weight.

Table 3.1 presents ranges of suggested carbohydrate intake for 12- to 18-year-old runners. These values are based on carbohydrate accounting for 50 to 70 percent of total daily calories, or 6 to 9 grams per kilogram of body weight. The values are also based on estimates of daily energy expenditure among normally active adolescents, which were calculated through extensive research conducted by the Food and Nutrition Board of the U.S. Institute of Medicine. We've adapted the estimates to add energy required for running 3 to 6 miles (4.8 to 9.7 km) per day.

As a guide to understanding the table, focus on the first row, which shows values for a 12-year-old girl who weighs almost 92 pounds (42 kg) and runs 3 miles (4.8 km) a day. As shown in column 4, her estimated total energy requirement is 2,458 calories per day. To calculate how many calories should come from carbohydrate, we first apply the suggested range of 50 to 70 percent of the runner's total calorie requirement. Of the 2,458 daily calories, 1,229 to 1,721 should be carbohydrate (2,458 calories $\times$ 0.50 = 1,229 calories; 2,458 calories $\times$ 0.70 =

Table 3.1 Ranges of Recommended Carbohydrate Intake for Young Runners

Age	Gender	Reference weight in kg (lb)	Total daily calories	ESTIMATED DAILY REQUIREMENTS Carbohydrate (calories, based on 50-70% of total caloric intake)	Carbohydrate (grams, based on 6-9 g per kg per day)
12	Girls	41.6 (91.6)	2,458	1,229-1,721	250-374
12	Boys	40.5 (89.2)	2,703	1,352-1,892	243-365
13	Girls	45.8 (100.9)	2,556	1,278-1,789	275-412
13	Boys	45.6 (100.4)	2,893	1,447-2,025	274-410
14	Girls	49.4 (108.8)	2,609	1,305-1,826	296-445
14	Boys	51.0 (112.3)	3,104	1,552-2,173	306-459
15	Girls	52.0 (114.5)	2,937	1,469-2,056	312-468
15	Boys	56.3 (124.0)	3,588	1,794-2,512	338-507
16	Girls	53.9 (118.7)	2,943	1,472-2,060	323-485
16	Boys	60.9 (134.1)	3,727	1,864-2,609	365-548
17	Girls	55.1 (121.4)	2,928	1,464-2,050	331-496
17	Boys	64.6 (142.3)	3,801	1,901-2,661	388-581
18	Girls	56.2 (123.8)	2,911	1,456-2,038	337-506
18	Boys	67.2 (148.0)	3,838	1,919-2,687	403-605

Adapted from estimated energy requirements derived from *Dietary Reference Intakes for Energy, Carbohydrate, Fiber, Fat, Protein, and Amino Acids*, published by the National Academy of Sciences (www.nal.usda.gov/fnic/DRI//DRI_Energy/energy_full_report.pdf). Estimates of total daily caloric requirements were obtained by adding 300 calories (for 12- to 14-year-olds) and 600 calories (for 15- to 18-year-olds) to the estimated energy requirements of normally active teenagers. The additional 300 and 600 calories roughly estimate the energy expended in running 3 and 6 miles (4.8 and 9.7 km) per day.

1,720.6 calories). Column 5 of the table shows these amounts. The last column lists suggested ranges based on the guideline of 6 to 9 grams of carbohydrate per kilogram of body weight per day. A 12-year-old girl who weighs 41.6 kilograms (91.6 lb) should consume approximately 250 to 374 grams of carbohydrate per day (41.6 kg × 6 g per kg = 249.6 g; 41.6 kg × 9 g per kg = 374.4 g).

Keep in mind that the values in table 3.1 are only suggested ranges. Use them as general guidelines, rather than as strict prescriptions, for getting a sense how much carbohydrate-rich food young runners may need to eat. If you have access to an exercise physiology or sport nutrition laboratory in your area, you might be able to get accurate individual assessments of daily calorie expenditure and carbohydrate needs. More practically, though, runners can judge their dietary needs by regularly monitoring body weight, energy levels, and general health. They might try experimenting with various levels of carbohydrate intake, within the ranges in table 3.1, to see how their bodies respond and whether they perform better at certain levels.

To figure out the amount of carbohydrate in a diet, study the nutrition fact labels on food packages. As another guide, tables 3.2 and 3.3 list the carbohydrate contents of various foods in both grams and calories. Note that 1 gram of carbohydrate contains 4 calories. The foods are grouped by type of carbohydrate, complex or simple. Complex carbohydrates (table 3.2), named for their long chains of glucose molecules, are in starchy foods, grain products, and most vegetables. Simple carbohydrates (table 3.3) make up sugary foods and fruits. Both forms provide glucose for muscle activity; however, complex carbohydrates and fruits are usually healthier because they are found in foods that are rich in vitamins, minerals, and fiber. These nutrients are usually stripped away from processed foods such as candy and doughnuts. For this reason, experts recommend that no more than 10 percent of total caloric intake come from highly processed sweets.

Using tables 3.2 and 3.3, let's add up the grams and calories of carbohydrate in a high-energy breakfast:

2 whole-grain pancakes = 28 grams (112 calories)

2 tablespoons syrup = 30 grams (120 calories)

1 banana = 28 grams (112 calories)

1 cup orange juice = 26 grams (104 calories)

1 cup low-fat milk = 12 grams (48 calories)

124 grams (496 calories)

Based on this sample breakfast, which provides 496 calories (124 grams) from carbohydrate, let's calculate its contribution to the daily carbohydrate intake of a 16-year-old male runner who weighs 60.9 kilograms (134.3 lb). You can see from table 3.1 that his recommended needs are at least 365 grams of carbohydrate daily. If you do the math, you'll discover that the sample breakfast supplies about 34 percent of his suggested daily carbohydrate intake. Keep in mind that these values are intended as general guidelines.

Table 3.2 High-Carbohydrate Foods: Complex Carbohydrates

Food	Serving size	Grams of carbohydrate	Calories from carbohydrate
BREAD, CEREAL, PASTA, AND RICE			
Bread, whole wheat	1 slice	12	48
Bagel, cinnamon raisin	1 (3 1/2 in. diameter)	39	156
Flour tortilla	1 (8 in. diameter)	20	80
Pancake	1 (5 in. diameter)	14	56
Waffle, frozen, ready-to-heat	1	13	52
Cereal, ready to eat, Cheerios	1 cup	22	88
Cereal, ready to eat, Honey-Nut Cheerios	1 cup	46	184
Oatmeal, instant, maple and brown sugar	1 packet	31	124
Spaghetti or macaroni, cooked	1 cup	40	160
Rice, white, cooked	1 cup	45	180
VEGETABLES			
Broccoli, cooked	1/2 cup	4	16
Carrot, raw	1	7	28
Corn, frozen	1/2 cup	21	84
Lettuce, iceberg	1 cup	1	4
Peas, green, frozen	1/2 cup	11	44
Potato, baked	1	43	172
BEANS AND NUTS*			
Baked beans, canned	1/2 cup	26	104
Black beans, cooked	1/2 cup	20	80
Refried beans, canned	1/2 cup	19	76
Almonds, dry roasted	1 oz	6	24
Peanuts, dry roasted	1 oz	6	24
Sunflower seeds	1 oz	7	32
SNACKS*			
Popcorn	1 cup	6	24
Potato chips	1 oz	15	60
Tortilla chips	1 oz	18	72

*These foods are high in carbohydrate, but they can also be high in fat and sodium.

Table 3.3 High-Carbohydrate Foods: Simple Carbohydrates

Food	Serving size	Grams of carbohydrate	Calories from carbohydrate
FRUITS AND FRUIT JUICES			
Apple	1	21	84
Banana	1	28	112
Cherries	10	11	44
Grapes	10	9	36
Orange	1	15	60
Pear	1	25	100
Raisins	1/3 cup	38	152
Orange juice	1 cup	26	104
Grape juice	1 cup	38	152
Apple juice	1 cup	29	116
DAIRY PRODUCTS			
Milk, low fat (2%)	1 cup	12	48
Yogurt, plain	1 cup	16	64
Yogurt, fruit	1 cup	43	172
DRINKS			
Sport drinks	12 oz	16	64
Soft drinks	12 oz	38	152
BREAKFAST SWEETS			
Honey	1 tbsp	17	68
Syrup, pancake	1 tbsp	15	60
Jams and jellies	1 tbsp	13	52
Table sugar	1 tbsp	4	16
SWEET SNACKS			
Chocolate candy	1 bar (2 oz)	34	136
Chocolate chip cookies, store-bought	4	28	112
Doughnuts, glazed	1	27	108

Fat Intake

As discussed in chapter 2, the contribution of fat to total energy needs during running increases as the pace slows. So, fat plays a major role in fueling low- to moderate-intensity training runs and longer races. Recall also from chapter 2 that middle- and long-distance runners whose bodies can burn a large amount of fat are at an advantage. Fat is a highly concentrated source of energy: 1 gram of fat contains about 9 calories, which far exceeds the energy in 1 gram of carbohydrate (4 calories) and 1 gram of protein (also 4 calories). In addition, when the muscles burn fat, the body's limited stores of carbohydrate are spared. Carbohydrate sparing is important in distance running because it delays the fatigue caused by glycogen depletion. Fat is also an essential nutrient for the normal processes of growth and maturation, including the development of growth hormones.

Unlike carbohydrate, the body stores fat in abundant amounts. In healthy non-athletic teens, fat makes up 12 to 15 percent of body weight in boys and 21 to 25 percent in girls. Studies show that teenage distance runners have body fat values as low as 8 to 12 percent for boys and 12 to 16 percent for girls. A runner who weighs 60 kilograms (132 lb) and whose body fat content is only 12 percent has enough energy from fat stores to fuel about 600 miles (966 km) of slow running! Of course, an excess amount of fat wastes energy because it's dead weight that makes the muscles work harder to transport the body.

Evidence-based guidelines are lacking for how much fat young runners should eat. However, nutrition experts generally suggest that children and adolescents get 20 to 30 percent of their total daily calories from fat. Based on this range, table 3.4 presents general recommendations for daily fat intake in calories and grams. As shown, a 17-year-old boy who runs 6 miles (9.7 km) a day would need to eat about 760 to 1,140 calories (84 to 127 g) of fat per day. Again, these are only estimates—individual differences in energy requirements can be substantial. Nonetheless, these estimates are useful for gaining insight into how much food young runners may need to eat from the various energy sources.

Table 3.4 Recommended Fat Intake for Young Runners

Age	Gender	Reference weight in kg (lb)	Total daily calories	Fat (calories, based on 20-30% of total caloric intake)	Fat (grams per day)
12	Girls	41.6 (91.6)	2,458	492-737	55-82
12	Boys	40.5 (89.2)	2,703	541-811	60-90
13	Girls	45.8 (100.9)	2,556	511-767	57-85
13	Boys	45.6 (100.4)	2,893	579-868	64-96
14	Girls	49.4 (108.8)	2,609	522-783	58-87
14	Boys	51.0 (112.3)	3,104	621-931	69-103
15	Girls	52.0 (114.5)	2,937	587-881	65-98
15	Boys	56.3 (124.0)	3,588	718-1,076	80-120
16	Girls	53.9 (118.7)	2,943	589-883	65-98
16	Boys	60.9 (134.1)	3,727	745-1,118	83-124
17	Girls	55.1 (121.4)	2,928	586-878	65-98
17	Boys	64.6 (142.3)	3,801	760-1,140	84-127
18	Girls	56.2 (123.8)	2,911	582-873	65-97
18	Boys	67.2 (148.0)	3,838	768-1,151	85-128

Estimates of total daily caloric requirements were obtained by adding 300 calories (for 12- to 14-year-olds) and 600 calories (for 15- to 18-year-olds) to the estimated energy requirements of normally active teenagers. The additional 300 and 600 calories roughly estimates the energy expended in running 3 and 6 miles (4.8 and 9.7 km) per day.

Table 3.5 lists the fat content of some common foods. Note, for example, that dairy products such as cheese and ice cream have a high fat content. Runners who often get more than 30 percent of their daily calories from fat should consider switching to nonfat or low-fat dairy products. As for meat, even lean beef and pork contain a lot of fat. Low-fat alternatives are chicken and fish, but if these foods are cooked with butter or oil, fat content skyrockets. For example, the fried fish sandwich with cheese from a fast-food restaurant has around 29 grams of fat. The fish itself may have only 1 or 2 grams of fat, but the oil in which it's fried contains about 15 grams of fat per tablespoon. A carbohydrate-rich food that hides a lot of fat is granola. The fat content of the cereals in table 3.5 ranges from 1 to 17 grams; many granola cereals are at the high end of this range. To avoid consuming unwanted fat, athletes should read the nutrition fact labels on cereal boxes carefully.

Like carbohydrate, fat comes in various forms, some of which are healthier than others. Saturated fat and cholesterol are found primarily in animal products such as beef, bacon, and dairy foods. Research has historically shown that people who eat a lot of these fats have high rates of heart disease. According to many nutrition experts, no more than 10 percent of daily fat should come from saturated sources. The rest should come from foods that are high in unsaturated fat, such as vegetable oils (canola, corn, safflower, and olive), soy, and fish. Eaten in moderation, unsaturated fat is good for your heart, other organs, and many physiological functions, including the immune system's response to disease. Research even shows that a healthy form of fat, called *omega-3 fatty acids*, can reduce inflammation and promote faster recovery from strenuous training. Foods that have large amounts of omega-3 fatty acids include fish, flax seeds, nuts, and various oils.

Protein Intake

When the body has adequate amounts of carbohydrate and fat, it uses very little protein for fuel during running. Only in cases of extreme, unhealthy glycogen depletion and starvation does protein metabolism occur on a large scale. Nevertheless, the runner must replenish protein on a daily basis because it is continually broken down in the body. Protein is necessary for normal physiological functions, including energy metabolism as well as the growth and repair of muscle tissue. As discussed in chapter 2, muscle fibers are made of protein, so athletes require this nutrient to rebuild and strengthen muscle tissue broken down in training. Protein also makes up hemoglobin and myoglobin, which are critical to endurance performance because they transport oxygen to muscle cells. Even the enzymes that spark reactions in the energy pathways are composed of protein.

Protein is made up of compounds called *amino acids*. Twenty amino acids are required to build protein. Although the body can synthesize 11 of these by itself, the remaining 9, called the *essential amino acids*, must be consumed in the diet. The best protein sources are animal products such as lean meat, fish, poultry, eggs, and milk. Animal sources of protein are considered complete because they contain all of the essential amino acids. Many plant foods are also good sources of

Table 3.5 Fat Content in Common Foods

Food	Serving size	Grams of fat	Calories from fat
BREAD, CEREAL, PASTA, AND RICE			
Bread, whole wheat	1 slice	1	9
Bagel, cinnamon raisin	1 (3 1/2 in. diameter)	1	9
Cereal, ready to eat, frosted wheat squares	1 cup	1	9
Cereal, ready to eat, granola	1 cup	17	153
Oatmeal, instant, maple and brown sugar	1 packet	2	18
Spaghetti or macaroni, cooked	1 cup	1	9
Rice, white, cooked	1 cup	0.5	4.5
DAIRY PRODUCTS			
Milk, 2%	1 cup	5	45
Milk, whole fat	1 cup	8	72
Yogurt, whole fat	1 cup	7	63
Yogurt, low fat	1 cup	3	27
Cheese, cheddar	1 oz	9	81
Cheese, cream	1 tbsp	5	45
Butter	1 tbsp	12	108
Ice cream	1/2 cup	12	108
MEAT, POULTRY, FISH, BEANS, NUTS, AND EGGS			
Ground beef, broiled (15% fat)	3 oz	16	166
Pork chop, broiled	3 oz	11	99
Chicken breast, skinless, broiled	4 oz	5	45
Fish, tuna, canned in water	3 oz	2	18
Fish, cod	3 oz	1	9
Baked beans, canned	1 cup	1	9
Almonds, dry roasted	1 oz	14	126
Peanuts, dry roasted	1 oz	14	126
Peanut butter	2 tbsp	16	144
Eggs	1	5	45
SNACKS			
Popcorn, oil-popped	1 cup	3	27
Potato chips	1 oz	9	81
Tortilla chips	1 oz	7	63
Chocolate chip cookies, store-bought	4	10	90

Pointers for Parents

Parents are in the best position to ensure positive nutrition habits and outcomes for young runners. Here are a few pointers in support of this all-important role:

- **Watch for signs of suboptimal nutrition.**

  Examples of suboptimal nutrition include sharp declines in weight or an accumulation of extra body fat—signs that your child's overall calorie intake may need adjustment. Keep an eye out also for dry lips and skin, which signal dehydration. Excessive, long-lasting fatigue may indicate shortages of key vitamins or minerals.

- **Keep the coach in the loop.**

  Parents, coaches, and young runners must work together where nutrition is concerned. The coach needs to know about your child's regular diet as well as any planned changes. For the best outcomes, some dietary changes demand corresponding modifications of the training program.

- **Account for dietary differences among family members.**

  A case in point is when, for heart health, mom or dad is on a diet low in calories, fat, and sodium. The young runner in the family may need extra amounts of these nutrients. The solution is a salt shaker on the runner's side of the dinner table, along with side dishes of calorie-rich foods.

- **Be a positive nutrition role model.**

  In teaching children and adolescents about healthy nutrition habits, what parents practice is often more important than what they preach. Be a positive role model for your child by eating fresh, nutritious foods and expressing your lifelong value of nutrition for good health.

- **When in doubt about diet, consult your family physician.**

  This advice is especially important when your child and you are concerned about his or her weight. If you both agree that better health and performance would result through weight gain or loss, your son or daughter and you should talk with your doctor about safe and effective dietary guidelines. If your doctor is not an expert in this area, ask for a referral to a nutrition specialist, such as a registered dietitian with a sport background.

protein, but they are incomplete, or lacking in one or two essential amino acids. Even so, vegetarian runners can get a complete supply of essential amino acids by combining protein sources, or by eating a variety of plant foods including beans, nuts, and whole-grain products such as corn, rice, bread, and pasta. For runners going the vegetarian route, we strongly suggest consulting a registered dietitian, preferably one who specializes in sport nutrition, for guidance.

For active adolescent boys and girls who aren't training, the recommended daily allowance (RDA) for protein is 0.85 to 0.95 grams per kilogram of body weight.

A person who weighs 59 kilograms (130 lb) thus needs approximately 50 to 56 grams of protein per day. The RDA is a liberal standard that an athlete can easily meet on a diet that includes meat. One 3-ounce (85 g) serving of beef, chicken, or fish contains 20 to 24 grams of protein (see table 3.6). Add a serving of macaroni (7 grams of protein) topped with 1 ounce (30 g) of cheese (7 grams of protein)

Table 3.6 Protein Content in Common Foods

Food	Serving size	Grams of protein	Calories from protein
BREAD, CEREAL, PASTA, AND RICE			
Bread, whole wheat	1 slice	2	8
Bagel, cinnamon-raisin	1 (3 1/2 in. diameter)	7	28
Cereal, boxed, ready to eat, frosted wheat squares	1 cup	6	24
Cereal, boxed, ready to eat, crisp rice	1 cup	2	8
Oatmeal, instant, maple and brown sugar	1 packet	4	16
Spaghetti or macaroni, cooked	1 cup	7	28
Rice, white, cooked	1 cup	4	16
DAIRY PRODUCTS			
Milk, 2% fat	1 cup	8	32
Yogurt, whole milk	1 cup	8	32
Cheese, cheddar	1 oz	7	28
Cheese, cream	1 tbsp	1	4
Ice cream	1/2 cup	3	12
MEAT, POULTRY, FISH, BEANS, NUTS, AND EGGS			
Ground beef, broiled (15% fat)	3 oz	22	88
Pork chop, broiled	3 oz	24	96
Chicken breast, skinless, broiled	3 oz	24	96
Fish, tuna, canned in water	3 oz	20	80
Fish, cod	3 oz	20	80
Baked beans, canned	1 cup	12	48
Black beans, canned	1 cup	15	60
Almonds, dry roasted	1 oz	6	24
Peanuts, dry roasted	1 oz	7	28
Peanut butter	2 tbsp	8	32
Eggs	1	7	28
SNACKS			
Potato chips	1 oz	2	8
Tortilla chips	1 oz	2	8
Chocolate chip cookies, store-bought	4	2	8

along with a cup of milk (8 grams of protein), and the total of 42 to 46 grams of protein approaches the recommendation for a normally active adolescent who weighs 59 kilograms (130 lb) in just one meal.

Growing runners, who are constantly breaking down muscle tissue in training, may need slightly more protein than their normally active peers. For adult runners, protein balance may require between 1.0 and 1.8 grams per kilogram of body weight per day. Evidence is lacking to guide specific recommendations for young runners. However, some sport nutrition experts advise that young athletes need as much as 1.6 grams of dietary protein per kilogram of body weight. Although

Sample Menu for a 14- to 15-Year-Old Male Runner

Total calories: 3,300
Percentage from carbohydrate: 60
Percentage from fat: 25
Percentage from protein: 15

Breakfast	1 1/2 to 2 cups Cheerios (ready-to-eat cereal)
	2 slices whole-grain toast with 2 tsp margarine and 2 tsp jam
	1 banana
	12 oz orange juice
	1 cup skim milk
Morning snack	1 bagel
	1 apple (or other fruit)
	Water
Lunch	Chicken sandwich (3 oz skinless baked chicken breast, 2 slices whole-grain bread, lettuce, mustard)
	1 small bag of potato chips
	1 slice of cantaloupe (or other fruit)
	1 carrot
	12 oz of a sport drink (e.g., Gatorade)
Afternoon snack	1/2 cup canned fruit or 1/4 cup dried fruit (e.g., raisins)
	6 graham crackers (3 in. square)
	Water
Dinner	Cheeseburger (3 oz lean ground beef or turkey, whole-wheat bun, tomato and lettuce slices, 1 slice cheese, ketchup, and mustard)
	1/2 cup baked beans
	Large salad (2 cups lettuce or mixed greens, 1 cup mixed vegetables such as tomatoes, cucumbers, carrots, peppers, mushrooms, 2 tbsp low-fat salad dressing)
	Iced tea (decaffeinated)
After-dinner snack or dessert	1 cup low-fat fruit yogurt
	6 vanilla wafers

Note: If breakfast and dinner meals are too much food for one sitting, the athlete can substitute a sandwich, fruit, or vegetable for a snack.

young runners may very well have higher protein needs than normally active youth, they don't need to take protein supplements such as powders. They can easily meet their extra protein needs by eating a well-balanced diet that contains enough calories to replace those burned in training.

So far, this chapter has covered a lot of information about carbohydrate, fat, and protein. To put it all together, we've designed a sample menu to meet the energy requirements for a 14- to 15-year-old boy who runs about 5 miles (8 km) per day or who does other forms of training that demand as much energy. The total number of calories in the sample menu is 3,300, and the breakdown is 60 percent from carbohydrate, 15 percent from protein, and 25 percent from fat.

Other Key Nutrients: Vitamins, Minerals, and Water

In addition to the three energy sources, food contains other important nutrients— namely, vitamins, minerals, and water. These nutrients are not directly used to fuel muscle contraction. Instead, they perform vital physiological functions such as catalyzing reactions in the energy pathways, supporting nutrient and oxygen transport to the working muscles, promoting growth and healing, and protecting against disease. This section addresses these nutrients and their contributions to distance-running performance.

Getting Your Vitamins and Minerals

Vitamins are organic compounds found in meats, fruits, vegetables, and dairy products. Distance runners need to get enough of these nutrients because they play a

Should Runners Take Vitamin and Mineral Supplements?

Because vitamins and minerals are critical to good health and athletic performance, many people believe that they should take supplements of these nutrients. However, most nutrition experts agree that young athletes do not need vitamin and mineral supplements if they eat a complete, balanced diet. No strong scientific evidence exists to prove that runners can improve performance by taking extra doses of vitamins and minerals. In fact, the body simply excretes excessive amounts of most vitamins and minerals. For example, vitamin C and the B-complex vitamins are transported in water in the body. These and other water-soluble vitamins are eliminated in the urine when the daily intake exceeds the body's requirements. In contrast, the fat-soluble vitamins—A, D, E, and K—are stored in body fat. These vitamins can be toxic when consumed in excessive amounts (several hundred percent of the RDA). Although a balanced diet is the best approach, most sport nutrition experts see no harm in taking a generic multiple vitamin and mineral supplement that does not exceed 100 percent of recommended daily allowances (RDA; the information labels on these products list the percentages of the RDA they offer).

Kimberly Mueller, MS, RD, CSSD

Fuel Factor Nutrition Coaching
San Diego, California

An elite marathoner, registered dietitian, and board-certified specialist in sport dietetics, Kimberly Mueller has extensive experience counseling distance runners on nutrition strategies that enhance endurance, facilitate optimal recovery, and protect against performance staleness. Kimberly is well known for her clinics and contributions to several books on sport nutrition. She is the author of *The Athlete's Guide to Sports Supplements*.

Ian Kucerak/Edmonton Sun QMI Age

What do you see as the main areas for improvement in the typical young runner's diet?—Recommendations obviously vary from case to case, but I find that many young athletes fail to consume adequate calories not only to support the demands of training but also to promote normal growth. The lack of sufficient calorie intake can be especially prevalent among female adolescent runners. They may feel pressure to conform to a media-driven perception of an ideal body type, and they may also be influenced by what they personally perceive to be an ideal weight or look for high levels of running performance. Restriction of calories can not only stunt growth and hurt performance but also increase the risks for nutritional deficiencies, stress fractures as well as other injuries, and illness. Therefore, it is important for coaches and parents to educate young runners not only on desirable food choices, but also on the volume of calories needed to support their growth, health, and performance.

What advice would you offer to parents of young athletes who eat too much junk food?—Inevitably, kids will be exposed to empty calories, or what we commonly call junk food, when they are outside the house. So, a first step for parents is to avoid bringing junk food into the house and to make healthier selections of foods available instead. Parents can encourage healthy diet choices also by being actively involved in preparing nutritious foods. One suggestion is to blend up a simple fruit smoothie for the runner to drink immediately postworkout and before dinner. You might blend 1 cup of unsweetened almond milk with 1/2 cup of low-fat Greek yogurt, 1 banana, and 1 cup of berries. By having the drink ready after practice, the parent helps avoid invasion of the cupboard for less nutritious snacks, which may otherwise spoil the runner's appetite for dinner. Another suggestion is to offer low-fat chocolate milk and a banana in a cooler upon picking up the athlete from practice.

Should young runners take vitamin or mineral supplements?—Recommendations vary from runner to runner, but in general, a young athlete who consumes a balance of whole foods does not need to take vitamin and mineral supplements. One exception is that certain vitamins and minerals may be needed in supplemental form if lab results from a physician indicate deficiencies. For example, if blood work shows deficiencies in iron or vitamin D, supplements should be taken under the direction of a qualified health professional.

What foods do you recommend for prerace meals?—Runners should focus on easy-to-digest, low-fiber carbohydrates such as rice- or corn-based cereals, plain bagels, plain pasta, white rice, white bread, melons, bananas, pulp-free juices, sport drinks, energy bars, pretzels, and potatoes. I also recommend small amounts of protein, between 10 and 20 grams, for the prerace meal. An hour of digestion time should be allowed for every 200 to 300 calories consumed.

What advice would you offer coaches and parents of young runners who are concerned about their weight?—Rather than targeting and emphasizing the tricky subject of weight, it's best for coaches and parents to offer sufficient education on making healthy food choices. For example, coaches might invite a registered dietitian to provide a nutrition clinic for the team early in the season. With guidance from a qualified nutrition expert, the coach can also put together a packet of nutrition information to give each athlete at orientation. For information on maintaining a healthy body weight, as well as many other topics on sport nutrition, I recommend that parents, coaches, and young runners refer to the excellent free handouts on the Academy of Nutrition and Dietetics website (www.eatright.org).

---

major role in energy production. For example, several of the B-complex vitamins speed up the metabolism of carbohydrate and fat. Vitamins play other roles, too. Vitamin C, which is found in many fruits and vegetables, strengthens bones and connective tissue. Some research shows that this vitamin also protects the body against infections and common colds by boosting the immune system. Vitamin B_1 (thiamine), which is found in meats, grains, and nuts, helps form hemoglobin. Other vitamins, such as vitamin D, are essential for young runners because they contribute to normal growth. Found in dairy foods and eggs, vitamin D plays a major role in promoting bone growth.

Minerals are inorganic elements found in water, vegetables, and animal foods. Minerals help build bones, form enzymes, transmit neural signals, and produce muscle contractions. For young runners, one of the most important minerals is calcium, which promotes bone growth and helps muscle contraction. Good sources of calcium include dairy products, vegetables, and whole-grain foods. Another important mineral for runners is iron, which is important in forming hemoglobin in red blood cells. Iron is found in red meats, green vegetables, eggs, nuts, and whole grains. If dietary intake of iron is insufficient, distance runners can easily suffer low iron and hemoglobin levels. This is because iron can be depleted through sweating, and hemoglobin can be lost as red blood cells are broken down through the repetitive stress of the foot strike during the running stride.

Adolescent girls lose iron through menstruation as well. Some studies show that more than 50 percent of young female runners do not consume the recommended daily allowance for dietary iron, which is 15 milligrams per day for 14- to 18-year-old females. Extreme iron deficiency, as described at the beginning of the chapter with Alicia, can result in anemia, a debilitating condition in which red blood cells and hemoglobin reach dangerously low levels.

Female Athlete Triad

Risks of injury and illness come with the territory of competitive distance running. Few runners get through any season without at least a slight muscle strain or a head cold. On the positive side, these sorts of minor setbacks can teach runners important lessons such as warming up properly, getting enough sleep, and eating nutritious food. However, some risks of running are more extreme and can have long-term negative effects on performance and health. For girl runners, one of these risks is the female athlete triad. This medical condition comprises three inter-related disorders: deficient energy availability, irregular menstrual function, and low bone density. In the first of these disorders, the body lacks the energy reserves needed for normal functions. Among runners, this dangerous state can result from intentionally or unintentionally restricting calorie intake, overtraining, or both. Second, irregular menstrual function is categorized by (1) primary amenorrhea, or delayed menarche; (2) secondary amenorrhea, in which menstruation ceases for three or more consecutive months; or (3) oligomenorrhea, in which menstrual cycles occur more than 35 days apart (Nattiv et al., 2007). In the third disorder of the triad, bone density, which has to do with the mineral composition of the bones (primarily calcium and phosphorous), is below normal age-specific levels.

Studies have revealed high rates of female athlete triad disorders in young distance runners. In one study of adolescents, researchers measured bone density in 90 distance runners and 93 athletes in nonendurance sports (Barrack, Rauh, and Nichols, 2010). Low bone density was observed in significantly more runners (39.8%) than nonrunners (10.0%). An especially disturbing finding among the runners was that bone density was similar in 13- and 14-year-olds and 17- and 18-year-olds. This suggests that younger runners with the disorder may not accumulate enough bone mass to reach normal levels in late adolescence. This is a serious health problem because approximately 50 percent of lifetime bone development normally occurs during adolescence. The low bone density associated with the female athlete triad increases risks for bone injuries, including stress fractures, as well as bone diseases such as osteopenia and osteoporosis in later life.

Compared with age-matched nonathletes, young female athletes, including runners, also have higher rates of abnormal menstrual function. This condition has been reported in approximately 20 to 50 percent of adolescent athletes. The female hormone estrogen plays a central role in menstrual function and in bone and cardiovascular health. Estrogen levels are abnormally low in many athletes who are affected by one or more triad components. Although the long-term effects of menstrual dysfunction and low estrogen levels have not been studied in young runners, experts have raised concerns about the potential risks of infertility and cardiovascular disease associated with the triad.

Although various factors can contribute to the female athlete triad, experts view deficient energy availability as a central culprit. Although this state can result from overtraining, often the main cause in young female runners is related to diet, especially a chronic state of insufficient calorie intake. This condition may stem from unintentional dietary restriction in athletes who aren't aware of their daily energy needs or who skip meals because of their busy daily schedules. Some female runners, however, voluntarily limit their calorie intake because they believe that being leaner will improve their performance. In extreme cases, low energy availability results from disordered eating behaviors such as fasting, using diet pills, and binge eating followed by vomiting.

Preventing the female athlete triad begins with a nutritious diet in which daily calorie intake matches energy needs. Support for prevention through diet comes from a good study of nutritional factors that reduce the risks of stress fractures in young adult runners (Nieves et al., 2010). The researchers asked 125 competitive female runners (ages 18 to 26) to complete a food frequency questionnaire and, over an average period of nearly two years, to report whether they experienced a stress fracture. Seventeen of the 125 runners had at least one stress fracture during the follow-up period. The researchers found significantly lower rates of stress fractures in women who reported higher daily intakes of calcium, skim milk, whole milk, and dairy products. With every additional cup of skim milk consumed per day, the risk of fracture was 62 percent lower, and each additional serving of dairy products was associated with a 40 percent reduction in fracture risk.

Leading medical organizations recommend that physicians screen adolescent female athletes to determine whether they are at risk for the female athlete triad during yearly preparticipation examinations. An organization called the Female Athlete Triad Coalition (www.femaleathletetriad.org) has developed a screening instrument that is endorsed by organizations including the American Academy of Family Physicians, the American Academy of Pediatrics, and the American College of Sports Medicine.

For runners who develop one or more of the triad components, optimal treatment approaches depend on the underlying causes. For example, young athletes who have disordered eating behaviors should be guided to psychologists or other health professionals with training in this field. In extreme cases of menstrual irregularity or low bone density, pharmacological therapy may be required to restore normal function and avoid negative long-term health outcomes.

Staying Hydrated

For normally active youth, experts estimate that daily fluid needs are 7 cups for 9- to 13-year-old girls, 8 cups for 9- to 13-year-old boys, 8 cups for 14- to 18-year-old girls, and 11 cups for 14- to 18-year-old boys (1 cup is 8 oz or 0.24 L). Compared with nonathletic youth and adult runners, young runners have extra needs for fluid intake. They sweat more than their nonathletic peers, and their bodies are less efficient in cooling than the bodies of adult runners. When fluids are available, most young athletes, without any encouragement, drink enough to avoid dehydration. However, coaches should insist on more fluid intake if runners show signs of dehydration, including dry lips, sunken eyes, and muscle cramps. Runners should increase their fluid intake if they notice that they are urinating infrequently or if their urine is dark yellow. Coaches absolutely must make provisions to have water available at every training session and competition.

Following are general guidelines for meeting the fluid needs of young runners. Given specific circumstances, including weather conditions and individual differences in sweating rates, modifications will be necessary.

- Two hours before training or competition: 18 to 24 ounces (0.53 to 0.71 L) of water.

- During training: 5 to 9 ounces (0.15 to 0.27 L) of water every 15 to 20 minutes.

- During competition: In 800- to 5,000-meter races, runners do not need to drink fluids if they are sufficiently hydrated before the start.

- After training and competition: 16 to 24 ounces (0.47 to 0.71 L) of water or a sport drink for every pound (0.5 kg) of weight lost.

Water is usually the best drink for young runners, but in some cases sport drinks that contain a 4 to 8 percent solution of carbohydrate and electrolytes are advised. For example, runners who lose their appetite for solid foods after intense workouts

Will Beetroot Juice Help You Beat the Competition?

When a healthy vegetable is hailed for its performance-boosting effects, the running world takes notice, as indeed it should. That's what happened a few years back when a few studies showed that endurance athletes performed better after consuming whole beetroot or drinking beetroot juice versus taking a placebo (Cermak, Gibala, and van Loon, 2012; Murphy et al., 2012). Along with many vitamins and minerals, beetroot juice contains nitrate, a compound that exists naturally in the body. Nitrates are known to have positive effects on blood vessel function, muscle contraction, and energy production. Many studies have now been published on beetroot juice for endurance performance (see Hoon et al., 2013, for a review of these studies). Although the results have been mixed, some evidence points to small physiological and performance improvements for adult cyclists and runners.

As of this book's publication date, no guidelines are available for how much beetroot juice runners should drink or when, in relation to training sessions and races, to drink it. Most important, no studies have been published on how the juice affects performance in young runners. We do know that beetroot juice is a nutritious natural food. So we encourage everyone who likes it and can afford it (it's expensive) to drink it. However, we're not convinced that beetroot juice is an essential food for optimal performance in young runners.

and races can begin to replace their glycogen stores with sport drinks. In addition, runners who don't like water may not rehydrate their bodies adequately. They are likely to drink more fluid in the form of flavored sport drinks.

Energy for Competition: Prerace and Postrace Meals

It's an unfortunate but fairly common occurrence for runners to race poorly because of what they have or have not eaten in the hours before competition. Like Ric, athletes who skip a meal on race day may experience low blood sugar, general exhaustion, and muscle fatigue, even before the race starts. In addition, eating too late before a race or eating the wrong kinds of foods can cause an upset stomach.

In general, distance runners should eat a high-energy meal about two to four hours before competing, in which approximately 60 percent of the calories come from carbohydrate. For morning races, breakfast foods (cereal with milk, toast and jelly, and pancakes or waffles with syrup) can be ideal. It's okay to include small amounts of fat and protein, such as butter and bacon, for taste. For afternoon or evening races, some runners prefer a plate of plain pasta because it has a high carbohydrate content and digests easily. Beyond this guideline, the best advice is to go with what works best. Runners should take note of the foods that they ate before the races in which they felt and performed best. Then, they should stick with those foods for their prerace meals in the future.

Diet composition plays an important role in recovery, especially after longer races (3,000 to 5,000 meters). The primary goal of the postrace meal is to replenish depleted glycogen, so it should be high in carbohydrate. In addition, the postrace meal should include protein to rebuild damaged muscle and to re-form enzymes in the energy pathways. The normal runner's diet, which we discussed earlier, is generally sufficient for the postrace meal, but some experts contend that the timing is critical. They point out that glycogen resynthesis occurs faster when athletes eat a high-carbohydrate meal within two hours of exhausting training or competition.

Striding Ahead

Before moving on to the psychological side of running in chapter 4, let's recap some key take-home messages about nutrition, diet, and performance.

- Because carbohydrate is the main energy source in events from 800 to 5,000 meters, it should make up a large part of the young runner's diet, approximately 50 to 70 percent, or 6 to 9 grams per kilogram of body weight.

- As long as runners eat a balanced diet with adequate amounts of fruits and vegetables, they don't need to supplement with vitamin and mineral pills.

- Coaches should ensure that sufficient water is available at all training sessions and competitions.

- The ideal prerace meal, which runners should eat about two to four hours before competition, is high in carbohydrate. The postrace meal should be high in carbohydrate and protein.

- Drastic measures to change weight and body composition can negatively affect performance and health. Parents and coaches should consult a physician or professional nutrition expert for sound strategies and should closely supervise runners who want to lose or gain weight.

4

Champion Psyche

Chapter 2 covered the physiology of distance running while lead-ing you through an imaginary attempt at the U.S. high school record in the mile run. Let's go back to the starting line of that race, this time shifting our focus to the psychology of distance running. How will your emotions, thoughts, and tac-tical plan affect your performance in this record-setting effort? What aspects of mental fitness are essential to fulfill your potential? And how will you overcome the negative emotions and thoughts that might arise when your body starts to fatigue? We answer these questions in this chapter, which covers the all-important mental side of distance running.

Powerful Mind–Body Connection

Recall the scenario from our fantasy mile race: It's a perfect day to challenge the high school record in the mile run—great weather, a fast track, a first-rate field, and a packed stadium abuzz with excitement and anticipation. The announcer has just introduced the field, and the starter has called the runners to the line. Take a moment to visualize yourself there, feel your emotions, and note the thoughts run-ning through your mind. Imagine that you're supremely confident in your ability and highly motivated to meet the challenge at hand. Your attention is focused on exactly the right cues. Instead of being distracted by the crowd and your competi-tors, you're feeding off their energy. Maybe you're a little nervous, but that's okay. The butterflies in your stomach are a sign that you really care about this race and want to do your best. And, like a good warm-up, a little nervousness will even prepare your body for meeting its energy needs.

But what if your jitters aren't in control? After all, you're about to run the big-gest race of your life. If you succeed, you'll be the new national record holder in the mile run. There are thousands of people in the stands, including friends and family members. (Did we mention that this race is being broadcast on national TV?) Maybe some doubts are creeping into your mind as you question whether you're truly prepared for the challenge. Trying desperately to cast aside your doubts, you remind yourself to concentrate. But what should you concentrate on? In your exhaustive effort to concentrate, you've completely forgotten your race strategy, and you feel your muscles tightening. Those prerace jitters are now registering on a seismic scale. You're so nervous that you're literally shaking in your spikes. Your heart is racing, and you notice that you can't catch your breath. Your body is starting to waste the precious energy that you'll need for your bell lap sprint. In this scenario, you've gone from psyched up to psyched out. Although you're still standing on the starting line with your competitors, you might as well be 100 meters behind before the race even begins.

We do apologize for setting such a negative scene on the starting line of your fantasy run for the mile record, but our intentions are good. We've highlighted an all-too-common situation in which young runners in peak physical condition fall short of their potential because they lack high levels of mental fitness. The challenges of mental training for distance running truly parallel those of physical training. As you learned in chapter 2, physical training involves boosting aerobic power, building anaerobic capacity, fine-tuning technique, and sharpening speed. Among other objectives, training to develop mental fitness involves boosting motivation and willpower, building confidence, fine-tuning concentration, and sharpening racing tactics. Especially for young distance runners, these qualities of mental fitness are highly trainable, and they have a major impact on performance.

Boosting Motivation and Willpower

Everyone who has tried it knows that competitive distance running demands high levels of motivation and willpower. Strong motivation, or the deep desire to succeed, is a product of well-defined goals and a thirst for experiencing the satisfaction that comes with achieving them. Motivation for running also stems from a sense of truly enjoying the activity and recognizing its personal value. Strongly motivated runners naturally have great willpower, which is demonstrated in a fearless commitment to defying fatigue and challenging themselves completely in training and during races.

To optimally motivate young runners, coaches must first understand each one's reasons for participating and then tailor training programs and coaching styles accordingly. Another important challenge for coaches and parents alike is to inspire values that motivate young runners to participate for the best reasons— the intrinsic reward of the satisfaction that comes from dedication, hard work, and self-improvement. Sport psychologists tell us that extrinsic awards, such as trophies, ribbons, and other prizes, are usually less effective at increasing motivation than intrinsic rewards. Nevertheless, when they accompany intrinsic rewards, prizes can motivate athletes by reminding them of the satisfaction that comes with success. A T-shirt for completing a summer training program, a letter jacket for making the varsity team, and even a certificate for setting a new personal record (PR) can be good motivators.

Building Confidence

Confidence is obviously an essential element of mental fitness for distance running. The opposite of confidence, self-doubt, is a barrier that keeps athletes from setting high goals and challenging themselves in training and competition. Three keys to building confidence are reinforcing positive beliefs in their abilities, defusing self-doubt when it arises, and designing daily training programs to ensure success.

Sometimes, the simple act of reminding ourselves, through self-talk, that we're capable of achieving our goals can boost self-confidence and keep self-doubt in check. And through regularly expressing and reinforcing their confidence in young athletes, coaches and parents play critical roles in cultivating this aspect of mental fitness. Encouraging words from teammates and friends can also have a big influence on a runner's confidence. Runners especially need their coaches, parents, and friends to help repair the emotional wounds when training and racing aren't going so well. Lost confidence can be regained with friendly reminders that a bad race is just a temporary setback and that many opportunities for success are just around the corner.

Perhaps more than anything, however, unshakable self-confidence results from a consistent history of success. Athletes who have achieved high goals despite challenging circumstances in the past have little or no doubt about their ability to do so in the future. Remembering that success breeds confidence is absolutely critical for training young distance runners. In upcoming chapters on designing effective training programs, you'll see many examples of this principle in action. For now, let's consider how confidence can be cultivated by setting goals and planning daily training sessions to ensure gradual improvement over a single cross country or track season.

A sure sign of a well-designed program is that runners peak, or have their best performances, at the end of the competitive season, when championship meets are held. To set the stage for gradual improvement and a string of successes that build momentum, early-season goals should be relatively easy to achieve. For instance, the first few races of each season might be devoted to accomplishing technical and tactical goals. As the season progresses, runners should view each race as a stepping-stone to the ultimate goals of PRs or high finish places in championship meets. Taking this approach, runners will build higher and higher levels of confidence as the season progresses. The confidence gained from performing well at a season's end will then carry over to the start of the next season.

Setting Goals for Training

In daily training sessions, young runners must learn that success doesn't mean finishing ahead of teammates or setting new PRs. Instead, success means running

Pointers for Parents

In their everyday roles, parents naturally provide psychological and emotional support for their children. Extending this support to their children's running is just a matter of understanding the basics of the sport's mental challenges. Here are a few key pointers to guide the way:

- **Tune into what motivates your child.**

  To best help your young runner develop mental fitness, you need to know her motivations for participation. How much is she inspired by competitive success versus other motives such as health reasons or the enjoyment of spending time with teammates? When you know what truly motivates your child, you can tailor your support for the best psychological outcomes.

- **Encourage goal setting.**

  Even runners whose main motives aren't competitive should have goals for competition. Along with the coach, you can help your young runner set and achieve appropriate goals. They should be specific, measurable, and challenging, but achievable through smart and demanding training. Express interest in your child's time goals for various track events or the finish places he's shooting for in cross country meets. Learn about what it really takes—in terms of training, diet, and lifestyle—for your child to accomplish his performance goals. (See chapter 8 for details on setting optimal training and seasonal racing goals.)

- **Be a role model for mental fitness.**

  Through competitive running, your child has priceless opportunities to develop psychological qualities that are essential for happiness and success in life. You can reinforce these qualities at home through your actions. Let your child see your willpower and dedication in parenting and your daily work. When you face disappointment in failing to achieve your goals, demonstrate self-confidence and a strong commitment to working harder and smarter to achieve them. Above all, be a role model for positive emotions such as appreciation, joy, and excitement.

- **Push 'em to safe limits.**

  In chapter 1 we described potential health risks of distance running for children and adolescents. We also recognized that most young runners slow down or stop long before they reach their physical limits. However, for young athletes who are primarily motivated by competitive success, major psychological breakthroughs often come from finding out just how far they can push themselves. So it's okay to encourage your child to put more effort into training and competition as long as the coach and you are mindful of situations that pose risks of injury.

- **Praise processes and products.**

  Praise can have a very positive effect on the psychological development of children and adolescents. However, the best outcomes often depend on praising young athletes' work processes and products rather than the athletes themselves. For example, the message "You're a great runner" will have far less impact than "You ran a great race because you followed your plan to pace yourself evenly."

at the assigned pace and effort to accomplish prespecified goals for a given day. For this to happen, coaches must clearly communicate daily training objectives and how to meet them.

Let's say an easy 3-mile (4.8 km) run is planned for a Tuesday, the day after an intense interval workout. The coach intends for Tuesday's session to be a recovery run. Before the session, the coach must make clear to the athletes that if they push themselves and run too fast, they won't achieve the day's training goal. They need to understand that the confidence they might gain from running hard in the recovery session will likely be short-lived, because if they don't recover properly, they won't have the energy to complete upcoming high-intensity workouts.

Coaches should provide plenty of feedback during and after workouts so that runners know whether they've accomplished the daily training goals. This feedback includes talking about whether runners hit their split times in interval sessions, going over videos of technique with individual runners, and reviewing charts that show individual athletes' training progressions over time.

Perfecting Concentration

A major aim of mental training is to gain some control over emotions and thoughts by focusing attention—in other words, by concentrating. Coaches commonly tell runners to concentrate, but what does this really mean? What, exactly, should runners concentrate on? It's not a simple question if you consider the many cues (objects and sensations) that compete for the distance runner's attention. Sport psychologists categorize these cues by whether they are located outside (external cues) or inside (internal cues) the body (see table 4.1).

The key to good concentration in distance running is to focus on the right cues at the right moments. Think of this skill as adjusting the focus on a beam of light. The beam can be adjusted in direction and width. Runners vary the direction of attention by focusing on internal or external cues, and they vary the width by focusing narrowly on a few cues or broadly on many cues. So, a runner with a narrow-internal style of concentrating might focus only on her technique, excluding other internal and external cues. In contrast, a runner with a broad-external

Table 4.1 Focusing Attention

Internal cues	External cues
Running form	Position in relation to competitors
Feelings of fatigue and other body sensations (breathing intensity, muscle tightness, or sensations of core temperature)	Feedback from the coach (split times or instructions to change racing strategy)
Visual and muscular feedback about pace and effort	Demands of the course (upcoming turns, hills, or changes in terrain)
Thoughts about racing strategies	Spectators' cheers

Mindfulness Training

Elite athletes have a special ability to focus their attention. They are keenly aware of what's going on inside and outside their bodies and minds. By attending to the most relevant cues, elite athletes are able to dampen distractions and neutralize negative thoughts. A popular term for this quality of mental fitness is *mindfulness*. Recognizing its value, coaches and athletes in many sports have recently begun to incorporate mindfulness training into their programs.

As an example of mindfulness training for runners, consider a day planned for a moderately paced 25-minute run with the physiological goal of maintaining aerobic fitness. Let's add the mental training goal to develop the skill of mindfulness. We'll divide the 25-minute run into five 5-minute segments, each devoted to focusing attention and awareness on a specific set of internal or external cues. The instruction for the first 5 minutes is to maintain awareness of your breathing. Without any attempt to control it, just sense the feelings of rhythmic inhalations and exhalations. Listen to the sound of your breath, and take mental note of its relative ease or difficulty. You might also attend to the feeling of muscles contracting and relaxing in your chest and lower torso. Again, the goal is just to maintain awareness of your breathing rather than to control it in any way.

For the next 5 minutes of the 25-minute run, direct your attention to the muscles of your shoulders, neck, and face. These muscles aren't involved in the propulsive action of the running stride, so excessive tension in them is counterproductive and wastes energy. Scanning your shoulder, neck, and facial muscles, become aware of any tension. A key instruction in mindfulness training is to avoid negative judgments and knee-jerk reactions. So, if you sense extreme tightness in your shoulders, feeling that they are rising up toward your ears, a good initial response is to just mentally note the sensation. You might say to yourself, "Tightness in shoulders." This response will prevent a common negative reaction—"Oh no, my shoulders are tight like knots. My form is falling apart completely, and I must be slowing down. I'll be lucky to make it to the finish line." A more skillful response, after noting the tightness, is to calmly make the adjustment of lowering your shoulders and feeling the muscles relax.

For the third 5-minute segment, direct your attention to your arm movements. Are your arms swinging back and forth in the direction your body is heading? Or, do you feel a twisting action that causes your arms to move across the front of your body? You might also focus on the sensation of your hands brushing lightly against the sides of your shorts. Again, the primary objective is to gain a heightened sense of awareness. This is an essential first step to making adjustments, if necessary.

During the next 5 minutes, focus on your foot strike and the actions in the muscles and joints of your lower legs. Pay special attention to the position of your feet on landing. Which part of your shoe strikes the ground first—heel, midsole, or toe? Next, feel the action at your ankles as your feet push off the ground. As you'll learn in chapter 5, running performance strongly depends on efficient foot strike patterns and actions of the lower leg muscles and joints.

For the last 5 minutes of the mindfulness training run, shift your attention to external objects and events. Become aware, for instance, of the running form and breathing sounds of your teammates. This is great practice for races, when noting these cues in your competitors will help you make tactical decisions such as when to surge or start your finishing kick. It's also good to practice sharpening your awareness of cues in the external environment such as upcoming turns, hills, and changes in terrain. This awareness also guides tactical decisions.

When done properly, mindfulness training develops the abilities to flexibly shift attention to where it's needed at any given time, to deepen awareness to what's going on in the present moment, and to make appropriate adjustments in form, pacing, and tactics. In addition, mindfulness training naturally suppresses distractions and prevents negative thoughts from taking over.

approach might open his focus to include other competitors, his coach's instructions, and the encouragement of spectators.

Mental fitness demands the ability to quickly adjust the direction and width of the attention beam as needed. For example, on the approach to a steep hill in a cross country race, the focus should be internal and narrow. To concentrate on good technique, the athlete might focus on the feelings of the legs extending while pushing forcefully off the ground. After settling into good hill-running form, the athlete might open the focus to include external cues such as the distance to any runners in front or to the next turn. Concentrating only on technique could result in missing a competitor breaking away and surging up the hill.

Concentration is greatly influenced by what sport psychologists call *arousal*, which refers to the level of mental energy. When mental energy is low and the runner is not very psyched up, the attention beam widens and it's difficult to focus on important cues. In contrast, when mental energy is too high, the attention beam narrows and can't easily change direction, so the runner can miss important cues. The Goldilocks principle applies to tweaking levels of mental energy for optimal concentration: not too passive, but not too psyched up. Coaches should carefully observe the mental energy levels of their athletes to give feedback for good adjustments.

Preparing With a Positive Mind-Set

The mental side of distance running is all about creating conditions that lead to good performance. This involves preparing for training and competition with a positive mind-set, which means an attitude focused on good results. Cultivating a positive mind-set runs much deeper than shallow optimism or wishful thinking. Instead, it demands the use of disciplined mental training methods and strategic planning.

Visualizing Success

An especially powerful mental training method, one that really accentuates the positive, is visualization. This involves mentally rehearsing oneself in competition. Here's how to perform visualization: In a quiet setting, either lying down or sitting, close your eyes and imagine yourself on the starting line of your next race. Feel your body relaxing and sense your strong motivation and self-confidence. In your mind's ears, so to speak, hear the starter's commands and, in your mind's eyes, see yourself beginning the race in a good position. Mentally see, hear, and feel yourself moving through each stage of the race, as if you were actually running it. The objective is to visualize positive outcomes and success in carrying out strategies to achieve them. For example, you might visualize yourself running with good form, hear the voice of your coach calling split times you're shooting for, and feel yourself gaining energy for a strong finish. Another effective approach is to play mental movies of your best races from the past. By practicing visualization several days a week for only 5 or 10 minutes at a time, you can build a strong, positive mind-set.

Studying the Competition

For elite runners, a big part of mental preparation is studying competitors to identify their strengths, weaknesses, and preferred racing tactics. Way back in 1977, one of this book's authors (Larry Greene) won the Florida high school championship in cross country by developing a race plan to capitalize on his strengths and attack the strategic weaknesses that he had observed in the other leading contenders across the state. Larry had strong pacing skills, but he lacked natural sprinting speed and was often outkicked at the end of races. By observing his main rivals in previous races, and through detailed planning with his coach, Larry suspected that the leaders in the championship race would start very fast, slow significantly in the middle, and finish with a strong kick. So he developed a plan to pace himself early, catch the leaders by the halfway point of the 3-mile (4.8 km) race, and surge hard for the next half mile to break the field. Anticipating that he might slow over the last half mile of the race, Larry aimed to gain at least a 10-second lead by that point. The strategy worked like a charm. Larry wound up winning the race by 6 seconds.

In addition to learning about their competitors, mentally prepared runners study the conditions and, in cross country, the demands of the courses. In the state cross country meet, for example, Larry expected a fast early pace because the race fell on an uncharacteristically cool day in Central Florida. He knew that the field would be energized by the good weather conditions. Having reviewed the course the day before the race, Larry picked a pivotal point at which to start his surge, coming out of a gulley where he anticipated the other leaders would slow.

In preparing their teams for local cross country races, coaches should schedule demanding training sessions on the courses. For away meets that require staying overnight, the team should arrive early enough the day before the race to walk or jog the course and note its challenges.

Knowing the course helps runners anticipate changes in attention focus as the race unfolds. For example, a runner who knows that a steep 400-meter hill is close to the finish line will be prepared to gather her strength and concentrate on her best technique when the time comes. By knowing the course, runners can also prepare by visualizing their performance on it.

Relying on Familiar Routines

To promote a positive mind-set in preparing for training sessions and races, good runners rely on familiar routines that have worked well for them in the past. An example is eating prerace meals that always provide good energy and don't upset the stomach. It's also helpful to develop a consistent prerace warm-up routine, which might include jogging for a specific number of minutes, going through a set sequence of stretching exercises, or running the same number of strides. Runners can make their routines familiar by performing them regularly before training sessions, especially those that simulate the physical and mental demands of competition. As practiced by many professional runners, consistent warm-up routines are great for focusing attention and avoiding worries about race preparation.

Racing Tactics

Stacy is an elite runner whose only racing tactic is to lead the pack from the start. Front running works perfectly in small dual meets in which Stacy is superior to her competitors. She opens up a huge lead and holds on to win, even though she slows in the final stages. In championship races against runners of comparable ability and fitness, however, the strategy often backfires. Try as she might, Stacy can't break away from her competitors. The pack's jostling, an unfamiliar experience, distracts her and weakens her concentration. When she can't shake the other runners as the race progresses, she begins to doubt her ability to win. Finally, when the pack begins to kick, Stacy can't respond—she doesn't have a finishing kick because she never practiced one.

Stacy's experience points to the importance of developing a repertoire of well-tested and effective racing tactics through physical and mental training. Successful racing means choosing the best tactics for a given situation, taking into account, among other things, fitness level, goals, the ability and tactical approaches of competitors, the weather, and course conditions (in cross country). The following sections consider the tactics runners need to master: even pacing, negative-split pacing, racing for time, and racing for place.

Racing for Time

Racing for time involves setting and adjusting the pace to reach intermediate distances on target for a final goal time. It's a tactic that all young runners should practice from the time they start training. Beginners need to learn to run their

Gregory A. Dale, PhD

Duke University
Durham, North Carolina

Dr. Greg Dale is a professor of sport psychology and
sport ethics at Duke University, where he serves as
the director of the Sport Psychology and Leadership
Programs. A member of the sport psychology staff
for USA Track & Field, Dr. Dale has written several
books, including *It's a Mental Thing! 5 Keys to
Improving Performance and Enjoying Sport* and *101
Teambuilding Activities: Ideas Every Coach Can Use
to Enhance Teamwork, Communication and Trust.*

Courtesy of Gregory Dale.

**Which qualities of psychological fitness
and health are most important for young
distance runners to develop?**—Two qualities
that come to mind are perspective and confidence.
I always respect the dedication and discipline of runners. But they can be pretty tough
on themselves when their practices and competitions don't go well. So, we need to help
young runners develop a good perspective on their sport. This means learning to view
each workout and race as a step in a journey to their long-term goals. Coaches need to
understand that each runner is on an individual journey and shouldn't be compared with
others. Another absolutely critical quality is confidence. A runner can have a great week
of training going into a race but not necessarily feel confident.

**What are some practical methods for building confidence in young
runners?**—I encourage runners to keep training logs and to record mental aspects in
them. For instance, before each day's training, they can write down a few goals or focus
cues. Then, after practice, they can evaluate whether they were successful. In this way,
runners will see factors that are linked to their success. They can then rely on these
factors in difficult parts of training and competition. This is a way to build confidence.
Coaches need to help runners understand that confidence is not a gift that other people
can give them. The more athletes stop looking to others for encouragement, and the
more they look inwardly for confidence, the more secure they will be.

Confidence comes from knowing that you're prepared. When runners have trained
properly, and when they eat and sleep right, they feel more confident. But they need to
stop and really think about their good preparation. Confidence also obviously comes from
past success, which should be defined in terms of achieving process goals such as having
a certain mind-set or following a race plan. Self-talk is another key to building confidence.
I try to get athletes to talk to themselves as they would talk to a teammate they respect.
You wouldn't tell a teammate, "Your legs are heavy and your training didn't go well this
week, so you're going to have a bad race today." Instead you would focus on what's
positive and relevant. Last but not least, sometimes you have to fake it until you make it.
That means acting and carrying yourself in a way that reflects confidence.

What advice do you offer parents who want to be involved in their children's training?—Early on, parents need to be their children's advocates, sometimes scheduling events for them and perhaps talking with coaches for them. But, by middle school, parents should act more as consultants. By this time, kids need to start taking ownership, and parents should be there to offer advice if their children ask for it. If there's a question about training, for instance, middle school and high school kids should be talking to the coach directly. What a great life lesson it is for a child to talk with coaches and other people in supervisory roles about their concerns.

If a child asks for advice, parents can role-play, taking the perspective of the coach and letting the child practice communicating certain questions or concerns. It's important for parents to understand that if they're continually questioning the coach and the training program, they're planting seeds that contribute to a lack of confidence in their kids. Parents also need to let their kids know that they support them unconditionally. They shouldn't judge their kids based on performance. And they need to give their kids space when competitions don't go well.

How can cross country coaches inspire a strong sense of teamwork?— The most important advice for coaches is to spend time developing a culture of teamwork. It has to be a priority. There's a great saying: "Culture will eat strategy for lunch every day." A team won't reach its full potential if the coach doesn't develop a healthy team culture in which the athletes are working together, supporting each other, and holding each other accountable. A good team-building exercise is to tape a piece of paper on each athlete's back, and then have teammates write something that they appreciate or respect about each person on the paper. When runners are struggling with confidence or doubt the impact they're having on the team, that piece of paper, posted inside their locker, can be valuable for reinforcing that they're doing a good job. Another exercise that teaches athletes to be honest and accountable for each other is to pair athletes and have them tell each other one thing they do great and one thing they can do better to help the team be more successful.

---

own races rather than blindly following someone else's plan. Moreover, racing for time emphasizes pacing skill, which helps beginners avoid starting too fast or too slow. Finally, runners who master this tactic experience a boost in mental fitness. When the stopwatch shows that they have achieved their time goal or set a new PR, they gain confidence and motivation for future races.

To race for time, the coach and athlete decide on a goal time that is challenging but achievable considering the athlete's current fitness level, the point in the competitive season, and other factors such as the weather. Let's say that Michelle's goal is to run 5:24 for 1,600 meters, which calls for averaging 81 seconds for each 400-meter split. If Michelle were to run at an even pace, her splits would be 81 (400), 2:42 (800), and 4:03 (1,200). Physiologically, even-paced running is advantageous because it restrains runners from going out too fast and fatiguing. However, especially in events from 800 to 3,000 meters, the energy and excitement at the start of a race often make it difficult to run the first lap at an even

Mastering the Skill of Pacing

In distance running, pacing means controlling effort and speed to achieve time goals, or splits, for successive segments of a run. All elite runners are highly skilled at pacing. They tune their attention to sensory signals from their eyes, muscles, and joints—signals that provide information about how fast they are running. To decide whether to maintain pace, speed up, or slow down, the best runners continually process these sensory cues, relating them to perceptions of their effort, energy level, and fatigue. Pacing is partly a cognitive, or thinking, skill. To achieve time goals in track races, for example, runners must memorize split times for intermediate distances and, after hearing actual splits called out, perform calculations to determine whether they are on or off the target pace.

Two key factors that determine pacing skill are age and experience. Over time and through trial and error, most young runners naturally improve their ability to control effort and speed. However, given the complexity of the skill, mastery of pacing requires purposeful and focused training.

As an example for beginners, consider a simple but effective track workout of 10 × 100 meters with a 100-meter walk or jog between runs. We'll set the target time as the athlete's goal pace for 3,200 meters. Consider a runner whose season goal for this race is 12:00, which averages 22.5 seconds per 100-meter split. In the training session, if he runs 25.4 seconds on the first 100-meter repeat, the coach will give feedback to speed up on the next one. If the second repeat is 21.8 seconds, the athlete will know to go a little slower on the third repeat. The athlete will develop pacing skill by paying attention to his effort and speed, relating these cues to the coach's feedback, and making adjustments to hit his goal time more consistently. There are lots of creative variations to this workout. For example, the coach can give 50-meter splits so that the athlete must make pacing adjustments during each 100-meter repeat. Or, before getting the coach's feedback, the athlete can be challenged to estimate his time. More suggestions for training sessions that focus specifically on developing pacing skill are provided later in this book.

pace, so Michelle might set her splits in these ranges: 79 to 80 (400), 2:41 to 2:43 (800), and 4:03 to 4:04 (1,200). If the leaders set out at a pace of 74 seconds for the first 400, Michelle will have to let them go. If Michelle's early pace is on target but faster than her competitors', she'll have to run in front. Most important, she'll have to concentrate on running her own race while staying aware of what her competitors are doing.

Another approach to racing for time is to run negative splits, which means covering the last half of the race faster than the first half. Physiologically, this tactic works well because it helps runners avoid early fatigue. Psychologically, negative-split running is a knockout strategy, especially in longer events when inexperienced runners start too fast and slow dramatically as the race progresses. Athletes who run negative splits can count on catching and blowing by their competitors, gaining confidence and energy with every runner passed.

If you study the splits for most record-setting performances by professional distance runners, you'll see a consistent pattern of even-paced running early on and blazing fast finishes. Figure 4.1, a great example, shows the 1-kilometer splits from the world-record performance in the men's 5,000-meter run, set by Ethiopian Kenenisa Bekele in 2004. Bekele's finishing time was 12:37.35, which averages 2:31.47 for each kilometer. From the first to last kilometer, Bekele ran 2:33.24, 2:32.23, 2:31.87, 2:30.59, and 2:29.42. Notice that each kilometer was faster than the previous one, and the difference between kilometers 1 and 5 was only 3.8 seconds. If you watch videos of this race on the Internet, you'll see Bekele gaining momentum and energy with every passing lap. For longer races on the track, his pacing strategy is a perfect model for young runners to emulate.

There's one important caveat to racing for time: runners must be flexible, even to the point of abandoning the plan midway through a race. Consider a scenario in which a runner is on perfect pace early in the race, running with the leaders, and feeling better than ever. The leaders begin to surge, and the runner must decide whether to stay on his goal pace or cover the break. If he completely ignores the competition and focuses only on his planned splits, he might miss a great opportunity to challenge himself for a major breakthrough. When he's feeling good in the middle of a race, he might experiment with forgetting about split times and focusing on competing. He must keep in mind, though, that most of the time, runners feel strongest in the late stages of the race when they have paced themselves early on.

Young runners won't learn pacing skills by themselves. Coaches must teach these skills and provide training experiences to reinforce them. As a first step, runners should learn the splits required to achieve their time goals. Coaches can hand out pacing charts such as table 4.2 and quiz athletes to make sure that they've memorized their splits. In chapter 8 we'll show how to integrate methods for developing pacing and tactical skills into race-specific sessions such as aerobic and anaerobic interval training.

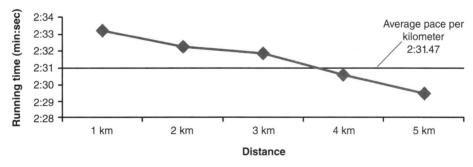

Figure 4.1   Kenenisa Bekele's 1-kilometer splits for his world record in the 5,000 meters, set on May 31, 2004, in Hengelo, Netherlands.

Table 4.2 Pacing Chart

Meters									
100	200	400	800	1,000	1,500	1,600	3,000	3,200	5,000
:15	:30	1:00	2:00	2:30	3:45	4:00	7:30	8:00	12:30
:15.5	:31	1:02	2:04	2:35	3:52.5	4:08	7:45	8:16	12:55
:16	:32	1:04	2:08	2:40	4:00	4:16	8:00	8:32	13:20
:16.5	:33	1:06	2:12	2:45	4:07.5	4:24	8:15	8:48	13:45
:17	:34	1:08	2:16	2:50	4:15	4:32	8:30	9:04	14:10
:17.5	:35	1:10	2:20	2:55	4:22.5	4:40	8:45	9:20	14:35
:18	:36	1:12	2:24	3:00	4:30	4:48	9:00	9:36	15:00
:18.5	:37	1:14	2:28	3:05	4:37.5	4:56	9:15	9:52	15:25
:19	:38	1:16	2:32	3:10	4:45	5:04	9:30	10:08	15:50
:19.5	:39	1:18	2:36	3:15	4:52.5	5:12	9:45	10:24	16:15
:20	:40	1:20	2:40	3:20	5:00	5:20	10:00	10:40	16:40
:20.5	:41	1:22	2:44	3:25	5:07.5	5:28	10:15	10:56	17:05
:21	:42	1:24	2:48	3:30	5:15	5:36	10:30	11:12	17:30
:21.5	:43	1:26	2:52	3:35	5:22.5	5:44	10:45	11:28	17:55
:22	:44	1:28	2:56	3:40	5:30	5:52	11:00	11:44	18:20
:22.5	:45	1:30	3:00	3:45	5:37.5	6:00	11:15	12:00	18:45
:23	:46	1:32	3:04	3:50	5:45	6:08	11:30	12:16	19:10
:23.5	:47	1:34	3:08	3:55	5:52.5	6:16	11:45	12:32	19:35
:24	:48	1:36	3:12	4:00	6:00	6:24	12:00	12:48	20:00
:24.5	:49	1:38	3:16	4:05	6:07.5	6:32	12:15	13:04	20:25
:25	:50	1:40	3:20	4:10	6:15	6:40	12:30	13:20	20:50
:25.5	:51	1:42	3:24	4:15	6:22.5	6:48	12:45	13:36	21:15
:26	:52	1:44	3:28	4:20	6:30	6:56	13:00	13:52	21:40
:26.5	:53	1:46	3:32	4:25	6:37.5	7:04	13:15	14:08	22:05
:27	:54	1:48	3:36	4:30	6:45	7:12	13:30	14:24	22:30
:27.5	:55	1:50	3:40	4:35	6:52.5	7:20	13:45	14:40	22:55
:28	:56	1:52	3:44	4:40	7:00	7:28	14:00	14:56	23:20
:28.5	:57	1:54	3:48	4:45	7:07.5	7:36	14:15	15:12	23:45
:29	:58	1:56	3:52	4:50	7:15	7:44	14:30	15:28	24:10
:29.5	:59	1:58	3:56	4:55	7:22.5	7:52	14:45	15:44	24:35
:30	:60	2:00	4:00	5:00	7:30	8:00	15:00	16:00	25:00

Rows show minutes and seconds for even-paced running across standard track distances.

Racing for Place

Racing for time and maintaining an even pace aren't always useful strategies, especially in cross country. Instead, sometimes the best tactic is to aim for a certain finish place. Let's say Brad's goal is to place in the top 25 of a cross country race. Brad has to know the demands of the course and plan how much effort to put into various segments of the race. During the race, he has to gauge his success by his position relative to his competitors. If Brad finds himself running with the lead pack and the pace feels too fast, he'll have to slow down. Or, if he isn't even in the top 50 by the middle of the race and he's feeling good, he'll have to pick up the pace. With feedback from the coach about his place as the race unfolds, Brad can make adjustments to ensure that he doesn't wind up at the finish line with too much or too little energy left.

Racing for First Place

Runners whose goal is to finish in first place might use one of several strategies including front running, surging, and kicking. The first strategy, front running, is a double-edged sword—it can cut competitors by breaking their spirits and shaking their confidence, but it can cut front runners if they wield it improperly. Front runners must be supremely fit and confident that they can cover the distance alone. Another option is to use a surging tactic, in which the runner speeds up over segments of the race to shake up competitors and break their confidence. The runner must plan the surge to catch the competition off-guard and to convince them that she is in control of the race.

Another strategy for winning races is kicking. Kickers feed off the energy and momentum of the other runners by tucking themselves in the pack in the early stages of the race. Then, in the final stages, they use their fitness and speed to sprint away from their competitors. Runners should practice starting their kicks at various distances from the finish line. For example, a runner who lacks basic speed might experiment with a long, controlled sprint 400 to 600 meters out. A runner with good speed might wait until the last 100 to 200 meters to start an explosive sprint.

Experimentation is the key to mastering racing strategies. Runners who can't adapt tactics to a variety of competitive situations limit themselves to performing well only when the conditions suit them. In addition, using the same plan race after race can get boring and limit motivation. Runners who are skilled at many racing strategies have the potential for superior performance every time they toe the starting line. And it's fun to try different approaches on a regular basis.

Striding Ahead

Distance runners must be mentally fit to reach their potential. The elements of mental fitness are willpower and motivation, self-confidence, a flexible attention style, and pacing and tactical skill. The most important point, though, is that mental fitness can be improved with training. This improvement depends on carefully planned training and racing experiences that go beyond simply conditioning the body's physiological systems. Indeed, every training session should be geared toward developing mental as well as physical fitness. When we discuss the details of training design in part II, we suggest ways to integrate methods for developing mental fitness. First, let's cover one more fundamental topic: running technique, or form.

5

Form Fundamentals

Athletes in most sports devote a great amount of training to improving technique, or the optimal form for carrying out movement skills. Right-handed golfers work on keeping a straight left arm during the swing, basketball players spend hours perfecting the follow-through of the jump shot, and high jumpers practice their over-the-bar technique by performing specialized drills. Technique is important for distance runners, too, because it has a major impact on energy costs and injury risks. In designing training programs, however, many coaches don't give form the attention it deserves. A common misconception is that running isn't like other "technical" sports because its movement patterns are "natural" and can't be refined through learning and practice. In this chapter we show why form matters, and we offer pointers for improving it to achieve the goals of better performance and injury prevention.

Good Form = Good Performance

Picture yourself in the middle of a 3,000-meter race on a 400-meter track. You're rounding the curve and coming onto the home straightaway. In technical terms, your objective is to cover the next 100 meters on target pace, spending the least amount of energy possible. To get to the next curve, your most efficient path will be along a straight line, clearly drawn by the track's lane lines. So, to be most efficient, your whole body must move forward, and your limbs—including your feet, shins, thighs, hands, and arms—must move in the *straight-ahead* direction. Now imagine that, for some odd reason, you decide to take a few backward steps. To do so, you'll need to bring your whole body to a complete stop and then start backpedaling. After deciding that backward running isn't the way to go, you stop your body again and reaccelerate to go forward. Another 30 meters down the track, you get the strange urge to zigzag. So you start swerving sideways, crossing three or four lane lines at a time. Of course, this is an extreme example, one that wouldn't actually happen in a race. But it serves to make a point: movements in the wrong direction slow runners down and waste precious energy. Over the course of a 3,000-meter race, a runner can take several thousand steps. Even subtle movements in the wrong direction can add up to hurt performance.

To reinforce the message that form matters, let's consider the effects of two fairly common flaws in the technique of inexperienced young runners: overstriding and ragdoll arms. Both negatively affect performance by increasing the energy cost of running, which speeds up the physiological processes that cause fatigue, such as glycogen depletion and lactic acid accumulation. Overstriding occurs when the foot strikes the ground far in front of the center of gravity, which is the most concentrated point through which gravity acts to pull the body to the ground. The runner's center of gravity is located just above the center of the pelvis. In over-striding, the front leg has a propping and braking effect on the body (see figure 5.1). Although not as extreme as stopping and backpedaling, the action halts the runner's forward momentum and costs the muscles extra energy to reaccelerate the body to push off the ground. Later in the chapter, we offer advice for correct-ing the flaw of overstriding.

As the name suggests, ragdoll arms flap around loosely in all directions. In young runners who lack core strength in their trunk, abdominal, and low back muscles, the arms often cross the body's midline, which causes the upper body to twist. It might not be as bad as swerving across a track's lane lines, but this counterpro-ductive sideways movement is costly. Through core-strengthening exercises and specialized drills, described later in the book, young runners can correct the flaw of ragdoll arms and thereby improve their racing performance.

Figure 5.1 Overstriding, an energy-wasting technical flaw.

Technique and Injury Prevention

In addition to improving running economy and performance, good technique is essential for preventing injuries. With every foot strike, the runner's body is subjected to forces two to three times its weight. Given the repetitive nature of the running stride, a flawed movement pattern can greatly stress muscles, bones, tendons, and ligaments. A case in point is overstriding. As shown in figure 5.1, the first part of the foot to hit the ground in overstriding is the heel. Immediately after heel strike, the force of impact moves like a shockwave through the lower leg bones and joints. The sudden braking and jarring action transmits a great amount of force to the knee and hip joints, which can injure them.

The risk of injury is especially high when poor technique is coupled with structural abnormalities, most notably misalignment of the foot, shin, thigh, and pelvis. When the leg bones aren't vertically aligned, the muscles and joints bear more stress on one side than the other, which can lead to joint or connective tissue injuries. A technically sound stride helps to ensure that no one muscle group or joint structure is excessively overloaded.

To understand how structural abnormalities and flaws in technique can cause injuries, let's look at the biomechanics of the foot and lower leg upon foot strike (see figure 5.2). In a normal landing the foot hits the ground and pronates, or rolls inward at the ankle joint (see figure 5.2*a*). Slight pronation is beneficial because it lowers the whole foot to the ground and helps cushion the impact. Excessive pronation, however, pulls the foot out of alignment with the lower leg (see figure 5.2*b*). This stresses the arch, Achilles tendon, and connective tissue supporting the ankle and knee joints. Runners with flat feet or low arches, knock knees, and weak ankles tend to overpronate and as a result are at risk for injuries such as stress fractures of the foot and shin, plantar fasciitis (arch pain), Achilles tendinitis, and runner's knee.

Another biomechanical flaw during foot strike is excessive supination, or outward rolling of the foot (see figure 5.2*c*). Supination, which follows pronation in

Figure 5.2   Foot strike positions: *(a)* normal, (b) excessive pronation, and (c) excessive supination.

a normal landing, puts the foot into position for a forceful push-off. Upon landing, some runners supinate without allowing the foot to pronate and absorb impact forces. This causes undue stress on the lateral side of the ankle, knee, and hip joints. Runners who supinate excessively suffer injuries such as iliotibial band syndrome (lateral knee and hip pain), Achilles tendinitis, and calf muscle strains.

Bone and joint structure is largely determined by genetics. For runners with structural abnormalities, improving technique isn't a simple matter of changing patterns of limb movement. Instead, these athletes may require special gear and training methods. Take the case of runners who have flat feet and who pronate. They may benefit from a motion-control running shoe designed to support the arch and prevent the foot from rolling inward. To avoid injury, runners who pronate excessively may need orthotics, which are shoe inserts made from shock-absorbing materials that guide the foot through its most efficient and least stressful movement pattern. Runners whose legs aren't perfectly aligned can improve their technique and reduce their injury risk by performing special stretching and strengthening exercises. We describe some of these exercises in chapter 6. Parents of young runners with noticeable structural misalignment and joint instability should consult a sport doctor for further guidance on proper gear and exercises to avoid injuries.

Breaking Down the Stride Cycle

Just around the corner, we present 10 technique tips. To apply them in training sessions, coaches need to develop a sharp, analytical eye for the running stride. The two major phases of the stride are the stance and the swing. The stance phase consists of the actions that occur while the foot is in contact with the ground, whereas the swing phase consists of the actions that occur when both feet are off the ground and the body is airborne. To guide our description of these two phases, we refer to the sequence of four photos in figure 5.3, which shows a runner moving through half of a stride cycle, beginning with the right-foot landing and ending with the left-foot takeoff.

The stance phase begins when the foot contacts the ground and ends with the pushing-off action that propels the body into flight. The subphases of the stance are landing (see figure 5.3a), midsupport, and takeoff (see figure 5.3b). When watching a runner in the landing subphase, the coach should focus on foot position as well as the extent of flexion, or bending, of the ankle, knee, and hip joints. When evaluating foot position, the coach should check for whether the runner has a neutral landing or whether she pronates or supinates (a video of the runner from behind is necessary to check this). Foot placement from the side is checked to determine whether the runner is overstriding. In a separate evaluation of the landing subphase, the coach needs to watch how much the leg joints flex immediately upon foot strike to check for excessive lowering of the hips on landing, a common flaw in young runners' technique.

An instant after landing, the hips pass over the foot and the takeoff subphase begins. The body is propelled upward and forward as the driving leg pushes

Figure 5.3 The phases of a stride cycle: (a) landing, (b) takeoff, (c) follow-through, and (d) forward swing.

against the ground, exerting force in a backward, downward direction (see figure 5.3b). The coach should direct attention to the runner's ankle, knee, and hip joints during this subphase to assess the degree of extension, or straightening. As running speed increases, these joints should extend to a greater degree, reflecting a more forceful pushing-off action.

After pushing off the ground, the leg begins the swing phase, preparing for another landing in a sequence of three subphases: follow-through, forward swing, and foot descent. Figure 5.3c illustrates the follow-through of the right leg after it pushes off the ground. Soon after takeoff, the extended leg should bend at the knee so that the foot remains close to the body, creating a shorter lever in the trailing leg. In the forward-swing phase (see figure 5.3, *c* and *d*), the foot should move forward and up toward the buttocks. At the end of the forward swing, appropriate knee height depends on running speed. A higher knee lift promotes faster running by increasing stride length. After the knee reaches its peak height, the foot-descent subphase begins. This action should be a rapid lowering of the thigh with little movement at the knee joint.

Technique Tips

Is there a single ideal form that all runners should aim to imitate? Most experts agree that the answer is no. For proof, next time you watch elite distance runners racing in a pack, pay close attention to the various features of their technique. Compare and contrast the posture of their upper bodies, the length of their strides, how high they lift their knees, and how extensively they swing their arms. You'll see for yourself that there is no overall technique that distinctly characterizes the best runners. In fact, drastic changes in form to match some notion of an ideal style can actually worsen aspects of performance such as running economy. However, most elite runners share form features that do predict better performance and lower risks of injury. In designing training programs for young runners, coaches should include methods that enhance these key features, which we highlight in the 10 technique tips that follow.

1. Relax muscles that aren't active in the running movement. Whereas baseball coaches give the instruction to keep an eye on the ball, and golf coaches advise their athletes to keep the head down, cross country and track coaches are famous for telling distance runners to relax. But when coaches don't specify what they mean, tired runners can easily mistake the cue to relax for slowing down. They may loosen muscles all over the body, including the arm and leg muscles that generate propelling force. If runners relax everything, they reduce

Using Video to Evaluate Technique

Evaluating strengths and weaknesses in running technique is a challenge because running involves so many body parts moving rapidly at the same time. Seeing flaws such as overstriding and insufficient ankle extension is difficult because they occur so quickly. The solution to this problem is using video to record technique sessions, interval training, and races. A smartphone video camera is perfect for this purpose. During the recovery periods in an interval session, for example, the coach and runner can view the video in slow motion, pausing at critical points in the stride cycle. After identifying aspects of form to improve, the athlete can make necessary adjustments as the workout continues.

Pointers for Parents

Maybe more than anyone else on the young runner's team, parents need to know about running shoes. With countless brands to choose from and costs that can skyrocket, moms and dads are naturally sensible about focusing on the essential features of their kids' footwear. Here are a few pointers to guide parents in helping young runners find the best shoes to maximize performance and reduce the chances of injury:

- **Study before you shop.**

  The subject of running shoes is so complex that entire books have been written on how to choose them. One of the best educational resources is *Runner's World* magazine, which regularly publishes guides to new products. On its website, *Runner's World* has helpful articles and tools for choosing shoes to match individual characteristics, such as body weight and foot type. You'll find other great learning resources on the websites of the American Podiatric Medical Association (www.apma.org) and the American Academy of Podiatric Sports Medicine (www.aapsm.org).

- **Visit a good local running store.**

  If you live near a store that specializes in running gear, you're likely to find expert staff who can answer questions and provide good advice on footwear. The best local running stores have treadmills and video equipment for biomechanical analysis to guide shoe selection. Although you can expect to pay more for shoes at running specialty stores, you'll get the best quality, advice, and service.

- **Prepare to go shopping.**

  If you're going shopping at a local running store, have your child bring a current pair of shoes. The sales staff may have suggestions based on patterns of wear. Make sure also to bring the type of socks and insoles or orthotics your child wears when running.

- **Ask about product features.**

  The experts recommend replacing running shoes after 300 to 500 miles (483 to 805 km). So, young runners who average 30 miles (about 48 km) a week might need three to five pairs of shoes per year. Considering that a good pair of running shoes can cost $100 or more, you'll certainly appreciate how important it is to shop smartly. Here are some key questions to ask sales staff before you buy a pair of running shoes: How is the shoe designed for your child's foot type? How durable is the outersole (bottom of the shoe), and does it have good traction for the surfaces your child will run on? Does your child need a cushioned midsole? How many miles can you expect before the midsole loses its shock absorption? Does your child need a motion-control shoe, or is a "minimalist" shoe an option? (See the sidebar on the barefoot running debate later in this chapter.)

- **Check for comfort and optimal sizing.**

  These days, marketing and peer pressure to buy the most stylish products can influence the young runner's wish list for shoes. Of course, style doesn't top the

(continued)

Pointers for Parents *(continued)*

list of parents' priorities. When shopping for shoes, make sure your child tries on several pairs and goes for test runs around the store to compare them. Check for pinching, poking, or rubbing, and ensure that the foot isn't sliding back and forth or slipping out of the heel. Experts recommend that the space between the longest toe and the shoe's end should be approximately 1/2 inch (1.3 cm), or about the width of an adult's index finger.

the contractile force produced by the leg muscles, shorten the stride, decrease stride frequency, and slow down. It's important for runners to eliminate tension in the muscles that don't contribute to the running movement, because tension in these muscles is counterproductive. At the same time, they must maintain a high level of contractile force in the prime movers. So, coaches instructing runners to relax should be specific about the part of the body that looks tense, such as the shoulders or hands.

2. Keep the body in an almost upright position, squaring the shoulders and holding the head level. Good form is characterized by a stable, straight posture of the upper body, without energy-wasting turning and swaying motions. In good posture, the upper body leans forward slightly and the shoulders are squared so that the arms can swing freely to counteract hip rotation. The head is level without turning or bobbing, and the eyes are focused 20 to 30 meters ahead. One of the most important factors for maintaining good body position is core strength, or strength in the abdominal and back muscles that support the hips and spine. In addition, good posture requires a conscious effort to avoid slouching and excessive upper-body movement. Coaches can help runners focus on posture by cuing them to pull their shoulders back if they're slouching, to run tall, and to imagine being pulled upward by a rope attached to the top of the head.

3. Drive the arms and legs in the direction you want the body to go. Arm movements should be coordinated with the legs to balance the body and counteract rotational forces. Figure 5.4 illustrates the importance of good arm action. As the runner's right knee lifts in front of the body, the hips naturally rotate right to left. To offset the turning action of the hips caused by lifting the right knee, the left arm moves forward, stabilizing the upper body. The runner maintains balance when the left arm moves in sync with the right leg, and vice versa. When evaluating arm action, focus on where the movement occurs. To minimize unnecessary motion of the upper body, the arms should swing naturally at the shoulder joint rather than opening and closing at the elbow joint, which should be kept at about a 90-degree angle. The runner should also focus on the direction and range of arm movements. Although the hands may pass slightly in front of the body, they should not cross over an imaginary vertical line that divides the body into right and left halves. The best range of arm movement varies with running speed. At fast paces, the arms should move vigorously, with the hands passing the hips on the downswing and coming up even with the shoulders on the upswing.

Figure 5.4 Proper upper-body posture and arm action make for more efficient running.

Upon striking the ground and during the takeoff subphase, the foot should point straight ahead rather than turn inward or outward. Runners who have a natural toe-in or toe-out foot position may have difficulty positioning their feet straight. Trying to change foot placement in these athletes isn't a good idea because it might cause a painful twisting at the knee and hip joints. When changes in technique cause joint pain, it's best to let the runner use the style that feels most comfortable.

4. Settle into your own natural stride length and frequency. Unless runners are obviously overstriding or taking short, choppy steps, they should not consciously alter their strides when running at a constant pace. With training and experience, most runners naturally choose a stride length and frequency that optimize performance. Coaches should, however, keenly observe how runners accelerate in midrace surges and sprint finishes. For the distances over which young runners race, often the best strategy for speeding up is to consciously increase stride length by generating greater propulsive force in the takeoff subphase. Mastering this technique requires training to enhance strength, flexibility, and neuromuscular skill. Chapter 6 covers key methods for improving these elements of fitness.

5. Minimize downward sinking and upward bouncing. When the runner's foot contacts the ground and as the body moves over the foot, the coach should keep an eye on the head and hips. Do they stay at about the same height throughout

Jay Dicharry, PT, SCS

Bend, Oregon

Jay Dicharry is an internationally recognized expert in the biomechanical analysis of running and other sports. An active clinician and researcher, Dicharry has coached athletes at local and national levels. He is an instructor in the USA Track & Field Coaching Education program and is the author of *Run Like an Athlete: Unlocking Your Potential for Health, Speed and Injury Prevention.* In his unique approach to working with distance runners, Dicharry aims to identify and correct imbalances in body posture and control to improve performance and prevent injuries.

Courtesy of Jay Dicharry.

What developmental factors influence form and the training needs of young distance runners?—Coaches especially need to be aware of the adolescent growth spurt—the period when young athletes are experiencing rapid limb growth. They now have these new long levers, but it takes a while for their muscle and tendon strength to catch up. During this transition, it's important to avoid overloading the body. Training should be focused on keeping the body healthy and allowing it to adapt appropriately. Anytime you're moving properly, you're putting the least amount of stress on the body. So for adolescents during the growth spurt, we need to emphasize proper body control and patterns of movement.

What flaws in form do you commonly see in young runners?—Two common problems are overstriding and poor postural alignment. In overstriding, the foot lands way too far forward, and often the knee collapses. Correcting this problem is all about getting the foot to land closer to the body. That's a rule of thumb that has held up over the years. As a cue for avoiding overstriding, I tell runners to imagine that they're on ice, which gets them to shorten their stride. People talk a lot about which part of the foot should land first—whether it's the rearfoot, the midfoot, or the forefoot. Actually, there is no proof that any one landing pattern is better than another for runners. But to improve performance and reduce injury risk, the key is to land with the foot close to the body—as close as possible for the speed you're running.

The other big problem is poor postural alignment. During periods of rapid growth, many kids have poor posture. A main reason is that they don't have enough strength to keep their bodies aligned properly. So they wind up in an arched or extended low back position, and their center of mass shifts backward. This position actually contributes to overstriding. You see this especially when kids get tired at the end of races. When you see an arch in the runner's back, that's a sign that postural development has been neglected. Conditioning runners to have better postural alignment means helping them develop awareness and good core strength. Kids need to learn the difference between good posture and bad posture, so that when they're tired, they know how to correct their alignment. You always want to have a neutral postural orientation.

What are the keys to good upper-body control and arm movement?— When you see poor upper-body form, usually it's not caused by an upper-body problem. Instead, it's due to a lack of stability in the lower body. In general, when you see runners with a wide arm swing, they have a lateral imbalance in the lower body. When you see a lot of crossover in the arms, runners usually have a rotational imbalance in their hips or feet. When you fix the lower-body instability, the upper-body movement improves. Take a runner whose arms cross over. The problem might actually be due to poor forefoot control or a lack of stability in the feet. The runner might land too far on the inside of the foot, which causes the arch to collapse. This then causes the knee to collapse inward, which leads to excessive rotation in the pelvis and spine. This lower-body rotation is the reason for the arms crossing over.

How can coaches recognize flaws in body control that lead to poor running form?—There are so many factors that can cause flaws in movement patterns. That's why it's so important to assess each runner to find the causes of poor form. If you identify the problems, you'll know how to fix them. I recommend a series of tests. As an example, for assessing foot control, have runners stand on one leg. Look for what they're doing as they stand. Do they keep the inside and outside of the foot on the ground? Or does the foot roll to the outside? Are they compensating because they don't have good control of the big toe? Or, does the foot constantly collapse inward because of a lack of strength? For both sorts of problems, we need to teach runners how to keep the forefoot and rearfoot stable on the ground. This involves developing awareness and reengaging control of the feet.

I also recommend doing a vertical compression test in which the athlete is standing and you push down gently on the shoulders. If the back buckles when you push down on the shoulders, the runner is standing in an overly extended position. The runner can actually feel the buckling, which is important for correcting the alignment problem. This requires moving the spine into a neutral position, which means making sure that the chest is over the pelvis. To make this adjustment, I cue runners to drop their ribs. This brings the body weight more to the middle part of the foot versus the back of the foot. This approach emphasizes body awareness and control more than form. Concentrating on the form, instead of what actually influences form, sometimes misses the boat.

---

the stance phase, or do they drop like an anchor? Sinking of the hips reflects a major technique flaw: excessive flexion at the knee and ankle joints. When the hips sink and the leg joints collapse immediately upon foot strike, the muscles have to expend considerable energy to correct the downward movement and raise the body. The cause of this sinking is leg weakness, lack of neuromuscular skill, or a combination of both. As you'll learn in upcoming chapters, runners can fix this flaw through strength training, such as circuit training and weight training, as well as technique drills that isolate the action of the leg upon foot strike, promoting rapid and forceful extension.

Coaches should also watch the runner's head and hips for excessive bouncing. This occurs during the takeoff subphase when too much vertical force is exerted against the ground. Bouncy runners benefit from technique drills that promote pushing off the ground in a more backward than downward direction.

6. When running at fast speeds, land on and push off the midfoot or forefoot. An effective stride begins with foot positioning upon landing. The part of the foot that touches the ground first depends on running speed. As the speed gets faster, foot strike should occur closer to the ball of the foot, the padded bony structure where the toes connect. In shorter races and fast interval sessions, the best technique is to strike first near the ball of the foot. The whole foot is then naturally lowered to the ground for an instant, allowing for slight pronation and shock absorption. During the takeoff subphase, midfoot and forefoot strikers forcefully push off from the front of the foot.

The best runners tend to be midfoot and forefoot strikers. That's why you often hear coaches cuing their runners to get up on their toes. Heel strikers typically spend too long on the ground, losing forward momentum when they have to roll into position for push-off. The arch, ankle joint, and Achilles tendon must be able to withstand considerable force in midfoot or forefoot striking, so heel strikers who want to convert should improve their strength and flexibility first. Some runners, particularly those with flat feet, have great difficulty landing on the front part of

Barefoot Running Debate

As we were writing this book, a lively debate about shoes and form was brewing in the running, scientific, and medical communities. Widely publicized, the debate paired shod running (*shod* means "with shoes") against barefoot running, raising intriguing questions about whether one is better than the other for injury prevention and performance success. The debate also involves so-called *minimalist footwear*, or shoes with a thin rubber sole to protect the bottom of the feet, and little or no cushioning or midfoot support.

Proponents of barefoot running contend that it's how humans naturally evolved to run over millions of years. Only since the 1970s have competitive distance runners trained in modern shoes with elevated heels, rigid arch supports, and cushioned midsoles. These features, say barefoot runners, can actually cause injuries by weakening muscles in the feet and lower legs, encouraging bad form, and dampening sensory feedback that is necessary to maintain stability and protect the leg joints. In contrast, runners who support shod running claim that the elevated heels and cushioned midsoles of modern training shoes reduce injury risks by protecting the feet and legs from high-impact forces. In addition, they say, running shoes are designed to stabilize the foot and lower leg to correct misalignments that can cause injury.

The debate has attracted leading scientists in various fields, including anthropology, biology, exercise physiology, biomechanics, and sports medicine. All agree that the issue is quite complex, defying any simple answer. And like shoe sizes, a single answer won't fit all runners. The experts tell us that arguments for or against barefoot running also involve the all-important factor of running form, especially patterns of foot strike. In the words of Harvard scientist Daniel Lieberman, "How one runs probably is more important than what is on one's feet, but what is on one's feet may affect how one runs" (Lieberman, 2012, p. 64).

Studies and common observation show that most runners are rearfoot strikers when wearing conventional training shoes (Hasegawa et al., 2007; Larson et al., 2011). That is, they land on the heel before the midfoot touches the ground. In contrast, most barefoot runners are forefoot strikers, landing first on the ball of the foot before the heel touches down. Why does running barefoot encourage forefoot striking? You can answer this question for yourself by taking off your shoes and going for a run on a hard surface using a rearfoot-striking pattern. You'll quickly experience sharp pain in your heel bones and jarring in your ankle and knee joints. So, like other barefoot runners, you may naturally transition to landing closer to the front of the foot. As a result of the compliance of the foot and lower leg during forefoot striking, skilled barefoot runners don't usually experience pain on landing.

How do the differences in foot strike during barefoot and shod running relate to injury risk? The answer involves forces that our bodies absorb when our feet strike the ground in running. In rearfoot striking, immediately after landing there is a sharp spike in the ground reaction force. Even with raised, cushioned heels, this jarring force is transmitted from the heel up through the leg, placing stress on the bones and joints. In forefoot striking, the force profile is smoother—there is no sharp spike after landing. As the hypothesis goes, barefoot running encourages forefoot striking, which reduces peak impact forces and thereby spares the leg bones and joints from excessive repetitive stress that can cause injury.

Another interesting observation is that stride length tends to be shorter in barefoot running than in shod running. A shorter stride with a higher cadence also characterizes forefoot striking, in which the foot lands closer to the body's center of gravity.

A shorter stride may reduce stressful forces on the knees and hips. However, the experts warn that in barefoot and minimalist running, the shift to forefoot striking loads greater forces in the calf muscles and Achilles tendon, posing risks of injury to these areas. In addition, runners who switch from conventional training shoes to minimalist shoes or barefoot running may be at risk of foot injuries, including stress fractures in the bones of the feet. And barefoot runners risk bruising, scraping, and cutting the skin.

Some studies have shown that oxygen costs are lower in barefoot or minimalist running than they are in shod running, although at the time this book was published, the question of whether barefoot running is better for overall performance was unanswered (Lieberman, 2012). No studies were available to determine how barefoot or minimalist running affects risks of injuries in young endurance athletes.

Weighing in on the debate, we believe that every runner needs at least two pairs of shoes. One is for longer training runs on relatively hard surfaces. The other, a pair of racing flats or spikes, is for shorter race-related training, including interval sessions,

(continued)

Barefoot Running Debate *(continued)*

and for competition. The shoes for longer runs on harder surfaces should have more cushioning and midfoot support than the flats or spikes. The amount of cushioning and support needed depends on several factors, including the runner's training experience and volume, limb and bone structure, and running form. Consider a 17-year-old who runs 60 miles a week, strikes on her heels, and pronates as a result of a genetic misalignment of the leg bones. A minimalist training shoe might cause lower-leg injuries in this runner. In contrast, for beginners who aren't running a lot of miles yet, a minimalist shoe might actually promote features of good technique, including the desired midfoot strike pattern, and prevent future injuries.

We don't recommend running long distances without shoes. However, low volumes of barefoot training can help young runners develop an efficient foot-striking pattern and overall running form. After aerobic training runs of 30 to 40 minutes, athletes can take off their shoes to do repeated 100- to 150-meter strides, or controlled sprints for developing speed and good technique. Coaches should take all precautions to avoid risks of bruising, scraping, or cutting the bottom of the feet. Young runners should go barefoot only on soft surfaces, such as grass fields or rubberized running tracks, from which littered sharp objects have been removed.

the foot. Because of the risk of injury, coaches should never force runners to alter their technique if the change doesn't suit their body structure or if it causes pain.

7. Avoid overstriding and passive landings—land with the foot close to the hips and moving backward. To increase stride length, some runners make the mistake of swinging the lower leg forward in a kicking action just before landing. This flaw is easily detected because the foot appears to be reaching out to the ground. Often, the result is overstriding, which we've defined as foot placement well in front of the hips, where the center of gravity is located. For a smooth and efficient style, the foot should land close to the hips.

Overstriding is linked to another technical flaw: forward movement or lack of movement of the foot as it strikes the ground. If the foot is moving forward upon landing, the ground returns force to the body in a backward direction, slowing the runner down. This is called a *passive landing*. In contrast, if the foot is already moving backward as it lands, the ground reaction force helps propel the body forward. This technique is called an *active landing*. A runner can develop the active landing skill through drills and conscious effort to "paw" the track, or bring the foot toward the body in the foot-descent subphase.

8. In the takeoff phase, extend the leg joints, especially the ankle. Imagine how little propulsive power runners would generate if they used only one joint in the takeoff phase. An effective stride requires the coordinated extension of the three major leg joints—ankle, knee, and hip. You can tell whether runners are achieving good ankle extension by whether their toes point downward as their feet leave the ground. For good knee and hip extension during fast running, you should be able to draw a diagonal line from the ankle joint to the hip joint when looking at the runner from the side. At slower speeds, however, runners do not need to completely straighten their leg joints.

9. Lift the knees to increase stride length and running speed. In the forward-swing subphase, knee flexion lifts the foot off the ground, and hip flexion brings the knee up in front of the body. Especially during fast running, lifting the knee high is critical because it brings the foot into proper position for the next landing and push-off. Runners who have poor knee lift tend to drop the foot to the ground too quickly after push-off. This shortens stride length by limiting the amount of time over which force can be produced by the opposite, driving leg. Several of the drills in chapter 6 are designed to increase knee lift.

10. Alter posture and stride mechanics for proper uphill and downhill form. On tough cross country courses, hill-running technique plays a major role. Going uphill, runners should try to maintain their rhythm and pace without straining. The main technical adjustment for uphill running is to lean slightly forward and to more forcefully extend the drive leg as it pushes off the ground. Arm action should also be more vigorous going uphill. Finally, the eyes should focus 20 to 30 meters ahead. When runners' eyes turn to the ground, it's a sure sign that the hill has defeated them.

Downhill sections allow runners to relax and maintain pace with relatively little effort. They should lean backward slightly and allow their strides to lengthen. The action should be controlled rather than reckless to avoid jarring that can cause injury. Good downhill runners have the strength and technique to use the hill to pick up speed and pass competitors.

Striding Ahead

To advise runners about what they should keep doing as well as what adjustments to make in their form, coaches must know how to diagnose strengths and weaknesses in technique. Following are features to watch for:

- Stable upper body
- Efficient arm movement
- Placement of the foot under the hips upon landing (avoiding overstriding)
- Fairly stiff leg joints upon landing (avoiding excessive flexion, or sinking, of the ankle, knee, and hip)
- Sufficient knee lift to match running speed
- Active landing
- Good extension of the leg joints in the takeoff subphase

Training to correct flaws in technique involves increasing flexibility with stretching exercises, improving joint stability with strength exercises, and refining movement patterns with technique drills. We discuss these methods in chapter 6.

Part II
Training and Racing Programs

Let's talk training! We begin in chapters 6 and 7 by describing training methods for developing foundational and advanced physical and mental fitness. Chapter 6 covers six foundational, or general, qualities of fitness: flexibility, mobility, strength endurance, neuromuscular fitness, technical skill, and cardiorespiratory fitness. Next, chapter 7 describes methods for developing four capacities that specifically prepare runners for competition: aerobic power, anaerobic fitness, race-specific physical fitness, and race-specific mental fitness. In these two chapters we describe many training methods for developing the 10 general and competition-specific fitness capacities. For each method we discuss the training load—that is, the appropriate intensity, volume (distance or duration), and frequency of training—and we illustrate with sample sessions for runners of various developmental levels.

Our goal for chapters 6 and 7 is to familiarize you with important details about the training methods. Then, in chapters 8 through 10, we walk you through the following five-step process for selecting and implementing the best methods to meet individual runners' needs:

Step 1: Assess initial fitness and training, racing, and health history (chapter 8).

Step 2: Set goals for racing and training (chapter 8).

Step 3: Map out macrocycles, or seasons of training and competition (chapter 9).

Step 4: Plan and implement training sessions (chapter 9).

Step 5: Evaluate and revise the program as necessary (chapter 10).

In part II you'll learn about periodization, a systematic process for designing comprehensive, progressive, and individualized training programs. Using periodization within our five-step process will enable coaches to tailor programs according to the varying competitive goals and levels of maturation, fitness, and running experience of their athletes. In addition, this approach helps coaches design long-term training programs that safely and progressively guide young runners to achieve their ultimate potential.

6

General Training

To reach their ultimate potential, distance runners need to perform high-volume and high-intensity training. In other words, they must cover long distances at fast paces, maximally stressing the physiological energy pathways. Especially for young runners, however, the ability to sustain such high-level training depends on a strong foundation, or base, of fitness. The main capacities that form this foundation are flexibility, mobility, strength endurance, neuromuscular fitness, technical skill, and cardiorespiratory fitness. In this chapter we describe 12 training methods for developing these foundations of distance-running fitness (see figure 6.1). We refer to these methods as general because they don't simulate the exact movements or the specific physiological and psychological demands of cross country and track racing. In addition, they don't necessarily require the high-intensity effort that racing demands. Instead, they build a base of fitness to support more advanced, race-specific training, which we cover in chapter 7. A strong base boosts the runner's potential to develop high levels of race-specific fitness and reduces injury risk. Because the general methods prepare runners for race-specific training, they are used more in the early phases of preparation and relatively less as the racing season draws near. (See chapter 9 for guidelines on how much general and race-specific training runners should do as a season progresses.)

The sample sessions presented in this and the next chapter are appropriate for most young runners. Given individual differences, however, we consider these sessions flexible guidelines. It's likely that some runners will find the sessions too easy and some will find them too difficult. Coaches should adapt the loads of these workouts to meet the specific abilities, needs, and training responses of their athletes.

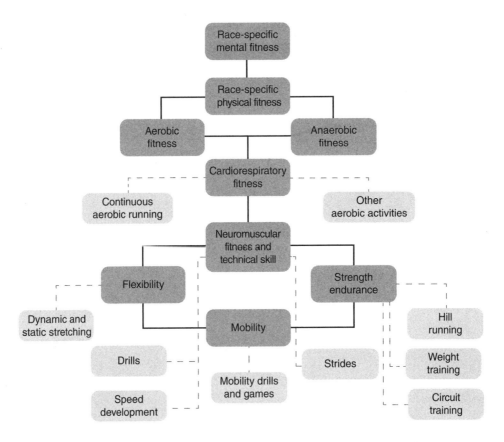

Figure 6.1 Training methods for developing general fitness capacities.

Developing Flexibility and Mobility

Flexibility is the capacity to move the limbs through a range of motion for optimally performing a given activity. Mobility is the skill of making coordinated movements in various planes, such as forward, sideways, and diagonally. Of course, running doesn't demand the extensive flexibility of sports such as gymnastics and figure skating, and the runner's limbs move mostly in one plane—in line with the forward direction. For these reasons, some distance coaches don't include training for flexibility and mobility. These capacities, however, are actually essential for young runners, especially for preventing injuries.

Distance running strengthens and tightens different muscle groups, sometimes causing imbalances on opposing sides of limbs and joints. Consider, for example, that runners don't lift their knees very high when covering long distances at relatively slow speeds. As a result, their hamstrings don't stretch much. Repetitive movement through such a limited range of motion can tighten the hamstrings, leading to strains and tears when athletes extend their stride for faster running in workouts and races. In addition, some runners have very tight calf muscles and experience calf strains and tears, as well as Achilles tendon injuries. These examples point to the need for stretching as a fundamental training method.

The stretching exercises in this chapter focus on muscle groups, such as the hamstrings, calves, and hip flexors, that tend to be tight in distance runners. Keep in mind, however, that athletes differ in terms of muscle tightness and the need for stretching. Some runners with loose joints and muscles can even injure their muscles and connective tissues by overstretching. Ideally, runners should be assessed for specific areas of tightness and imbalances by a qualified athletic trainer, physical therapist, or physician who specializes in sports medicine.

Dynamic and Static Stretching

Following is a routine of 13 stretching exercises for maintaining or improving flexibility. The first section shows dynamic stretches, which involve continuous movement of the limbs through sweeping ranges of motion around a joint. The second section shows static stretching exercises, which involve holding the position without movement. Follow these guidelines for performing the stretching exercises:

- Always warm up the muscles by jogging for 5 to 15 minutes before stretching.

- Perform dynamic stretches before static stretches. We recommend performing the stretching exercises in this book in the order they appear. The dynamic stretching exercises loosen up the joints and prepare the muscles for static stretching. The movements in dynamic stretching should be slow and gentle rather than fast and ballistic. Do 10 to 15 repetitions of each dynamic exercise.

- When performing static stretching, hold the position for 20 to 60 seconds, without rocking or bouncing. Stretching should never be so vigorous that it causes quivering or pain in the muscles.

- Use the same stretching routine for both training and racing. A familiar stretching routine helps you stay comfortable and relaxed during the prerace warm-up, when competitive anxiety can make it difficult to concentrate on proper preparation. Spend at least 10 minutes stretching, and never rush the routine.

- Stretch before and after training. Many runners think of stretching only as a pretraining and prerace activity, but stretching after training and racing is essential for maintaining flexibility and preventing injuries.

Arm Reach and Swing

Extend the arms above the head and then swing them downward in a wide, sweeping action.

Head Roll

Slowly roll the head in a circle, gently stretching the neck muscles. Perform repetitions clockwise, and then switch to counterclockwise.

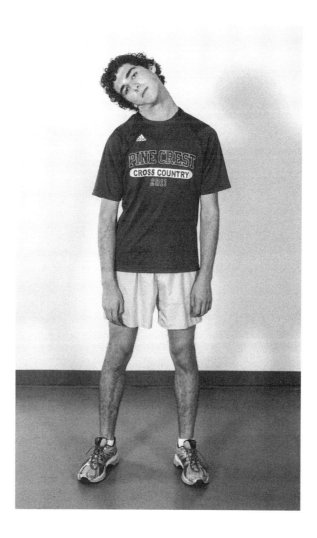

Torso Twist

Stand with the feet slightly wider than shoulder-width apart. With arms extended to the sides, turn the upper body from side to side.

Hip Circle

Make a slow circling action with the hips, gently stretching the groin and hip muscles. Perform repetitions clockwise, and then switch to counterclockwise.

Leg Swing

With the left foot firmly planted and the left leg straight, gently swing the right leg from the hip. Keep the right leg straight, and extend backward as far as possible without straining. Swing the leg forward until it is parallel to the ground. Complete repetitions for the right leg, and then repeat with the left leg.

DYNAMIC STRETCHES

Ankle Swing

Pointing the foot downward, make a slow circling motion, gently stretching the muscles and connective tissue around the ankle. Repeat with the other foot.

Warming Up and Cooling Down

Several of the training methods in this chapter are best applied as parts of warm-up and cool-down routines for training sessions and races. Here is a sample 30-minute routine for warming up that incorporates stretching, technique drills, and strides:

- 10 to 15 minutes of easy jogging
- Dynamic stretching
- 5 × 100-meter strides (working down from 5,000-meter race pace to 800-meter race pace)
- Static stretching
- Technique drills

This warm-up routine serves several important physiological functions that prepare the runner for training and racing. The jogging revs up the body's aerobic machinery by increasing heart rate and blood supply to the muscles, the stretching loosens the joints and muscles for optimal stride mechanics, and the 100-meter strides and technique drills prime the neuromuscular system for the upcoming fast running. Warming up is also an important part of psychological preparation for races because it helps runners focus on a familiar routine rather than worrying about the competition.

The sample warm-up has elements that runners can also use for cooling down after races and intense training sessions. Cool-downs should include 10 to 15 minutes of easy jogging followed by dynamic and static stretching.

Iliotibial Band Stretch

With the left hand against a support, place the left leg behind the right leg, with the left foot 8 to 12 inches (20 to 30 cm) to the outside of the right hip. Gently lower the left hip, stretching the lateral side of the left thigh, where the iliotibial band runs from the hip to the knee. Repeat for the right leg.

Hip and Butt Stretch

Lie on your back and cross the right knee over the body's midline. Repeat the stretch with the left leg.

Groin Stretch

Sit with the soles of the feet together and use the elbows to press down on the inner thighs.

Hamstring Stretch

Reach forward, keeping the legs straight. Don't strain to touch the toes.

Back Stretch

On all fours, tighten the abdominal muscles and arch the back, like a cat.

Quad Stretch

Holding on to a support with the left hand, pull the right foot up and back. Repeat for the left leg.

Calf and Achilles Tendon Stretch

Plant the left foot firmly behind the right foot and bend at the left ankle by pushing downward with the shin. Repeat on the right leg.

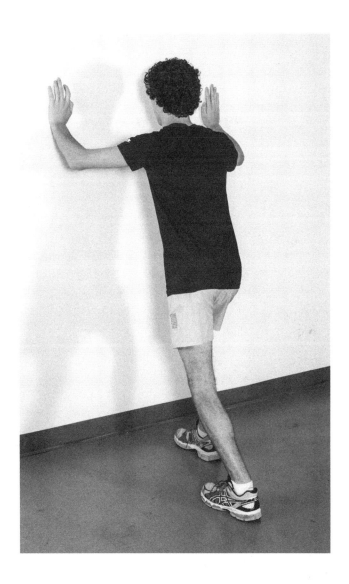

Drills and Games for Improving Mobility

The main reason for training to improve mobility is to strengthen the muscles and connective tissue that surround the joints to prevent injuries. Runners who lack mobility are at risk for ankle and knee sprains when training and racing on uneven surfaces. Poor mobility can also lead to injury when the primary muscles used for running become fatigued, activating weak and untrained supplemental muscle groups. Mobility training is a way to condition these supplemental muscles.

Formal drills, such as side shuffles, backward running, and cariocas, are good for improving mobility. For young runners, however, we suggest games such as basketball, soccer, flag American football, and keep-away. Games are best because they not only involve moving in various planes but also are fun. One of our favorite mobility games is ultimate Frisbee, which is a mixture of rugby and American football without the tackling. A 15- to 20-minute session of ultimate Frisbee once or twice a week during the early phases of preparation is a great way to improve mobility while also developing a base of cardiorespiratory endurance.

How to Play Ultimate Frisbee

Ultimate Frisbee, or ultimate, for short, is a noncontact game that two teams play on grass. In official games, each team has seven players. For purposes of training and fun, athletes can simply be placed on two teams. The object of the game is to score goals by throwing a Frisbee to teammates and advancing it across the opposing team's goal line. The Frisbee can advance only by passing, so the player who catches it is not allowed to take any steps. However, the game has plenty of running and movement in various planes as players try to get clear of defenders to catch the Frisbee. If the defense intercepts the Frisbee, that team becomes the offensive team and tries to score. The Frisbee also changes possession when an offensive player drops it, or when it hits the ground on an incomplete pass.

An official field is 70 by 40 yards (64 by 36.5 meters), but the field can be adjusted according to the number of players and training objectives. A longer and wider field challenges runners to cover more distance and can even promote the development of anaerobic fitness.

To prevent injuries, coaches should stress that ultimate is a noncontact game.

Developing Strength Endurance

The term *strength* refers to the ability to exert maximal muscular force, as you would do if you were bench pressing a heavy barbell one time. Strength is largely determined by the cross-sectional area and mass of the muscles. The importance of absolute strength in athletics depends on the sport. Offensive linemen in American football obviously need large muscles and extraordinary strength to successfully block defensive opponents. In contrast, distance runners don't need extraordinary strength because they don't exert maximal force in every running stride. Runners don't need large, bulky muscles; instead, they need a combination of strength and endurance (or *strength endurance*) to produce moderately high levels of muscular force over long periods of time. This capacity is essential for delaying fatigue, maintaining good running form, and preventing injuries.

Strength-endurance training requires working the muscles against greater loads than they normally have to resist. Because the objective is to gain a combination of strength and endurance, the training load is critical. Runners develop strength endurance using relatively light resistive loads and a fairly large number of repetitions. The combination of low resistance and high repetitions allows them to perform the exercise for a long time to gain endurance in addition to strength. This is in contrast to the high-resistance, low-repetition method used to develop maximal strength and gain muscle mass. We recommend three methods of strength-endurance training for distance runners: circuit training, weight training, and hill running.

Circuit Training

Circuit training consists of a series of strength-endurance exercises organized in a sequential pattern that is called a *circuit*. The stations of a circuit can be arranged on the infield of a track, in a gymnasium, at a park, or wherever space permits. Table 6.1 presents sample circuit training sessions for runners of various developmental levels. The sample sessions in this part of the book present guidelines for training during the early phases of the preparation period—in other words, when training first begins at the start of a season. We illustrate progression over time by showing sample sessions for beginners, intermediate runners, and advanced runners. In this chapter we don't provide detailed guidelines for progression within a single season, from the preparation period to the competition period. We only briefly address such within-season progression for each method here. In chapter 9, we present more detailed guidelines on how to organize training across phases of preparation and competition within a single season.

The exercises for the sample circuit training sessions are illustrated on the following pages. As you read the instructions, keep in mind that proper technique is essential in circuit training because, although the exercises are partly intended to prevent injuries, they can actually cause injuries if performed incorrectly.

The exercises in the sample circuit training sessions stress the main muscle groups used in running. Each station includes an exercise for the arms, body core (abdomen and back), and legs. Exercises for the arms, core, and legs are ordered sequentially, allowing time for recovery before working the same body part again at the next station. Using the same muscle groups consecutively at a station can result in excessive localized fatigue. This fatigue reduces the number of repetitions the athlete can perform, limiting the gain in endurance.

Table 6.1 Sample Sessions: Circuit Training

Duration of session: 15-60 minutes
Intensity: Controlled rate of movement; >70% of HRmax
Frequency: 6-30 repetitions per exercise
Recovery: 20-30 seconds between exercises; 3-5 minutes between circuits

Sample Sessions for the Early Preparation Period

Exercise	NUMBER OF REPETITIONS		
	Beginner CA[a] = 12-14 TA[b] = 0-2	Intermediate CA = 14-16 TA = 2-4	Advanced CA = 16-18 TA = 4-6
Station 1			
• Push-up	10-12	14-16	18-20
• Curl-up	18-20	22-24	26-28
• Squat	18-20	22-24	26-28
Station 2			
• Partner-assisted chin-up	10-12	12-14	14-16
• Back extension	10-12	14-16	18-20
• Heel raiser	18-20	22-24	26-28
Station 3			
• Partner-assisted dip	6-8	10-12	14-16
• Leg extension	18-20	22-24	26-28
• Step-up with medicine ball	10-12 (each leg)	14-16 (each leg)	18-20 (each leg)
Station 4			
• Medicine ball chest pass	10-12	14-16	18-20
• Superman arm and leg raiser	10-12 (each side)	14-16 (each side)	18-20 (each side)
• Lunge	10-12	14-16	18-20

[a]CA = chronological age in years

[b]TA = training age in years

STRENGTH-ENDURANCE EXERCISES

Push-Up (Station 1)

With the back and legs straight, lower the body to the ground and then push up to the starting position.

Curl-Up (Station 1)

Begin by lying flat on the back. Keeping the chin tucked to the chest and the lower back flat against the ground, tense the abdominal muscles, and slowly raise the body by curling the trunk. Then gently lower the back to the ground.

Squat (Station 1)

Begin by standing tall with the feet planted slightly wider than shoulder-width apart and the arms outstretched in front. Slowly bend at the knees, hips, and ankles. Keep the back straight by tensing the abdominal and back muscles. Keep the chin up, parallel to the ground. At the end of the lowering movement, the angle formed by the lower and upper legs (behind the knee) should be 120 to 140 degrees. Hold a medicine ball or dumbbells in outstretched arms for extra resistance.

Partner-Assisted Chin-Up (Station 2)

With help from a partner, lift the body so that the chin rises slightly over the top of the bar. Slowly lower the body back to the starting position. The partner should provide enough help so that at least 12 repetitions can be performed before fatigue.

Back Extension (Station 2)

Lying facedown, hands behind the head, slowly raise the head and torso off the ground. Slowly lower the body to the starting position.

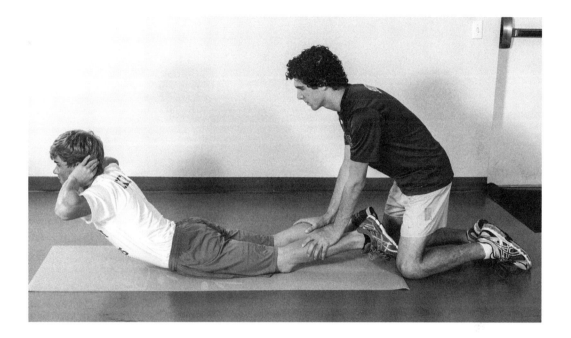

Heel Raiser (Station 2)

Starting with the heels flat on the ground and the balls of the feet on a two-by-four-inch (.051-by-.102-m) block of wood (or on the edge of a curb), raise the heels by standing on tiptoes. Lower the heels to return to the starting position.

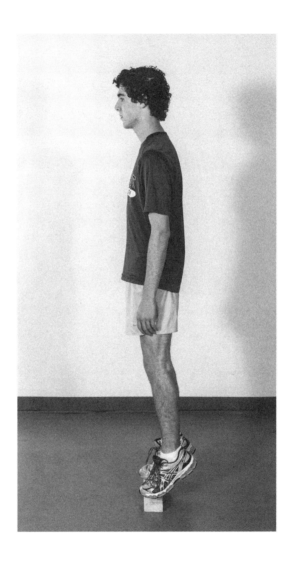

Partner-Assisted Dip (Station 3)

With help from a partner, raise and lower the body by bending at the elbows. Keep the back straight by tensing the abdominal and back muscles. The partner should provide enough help so that at least 12 repetitions can be performed.

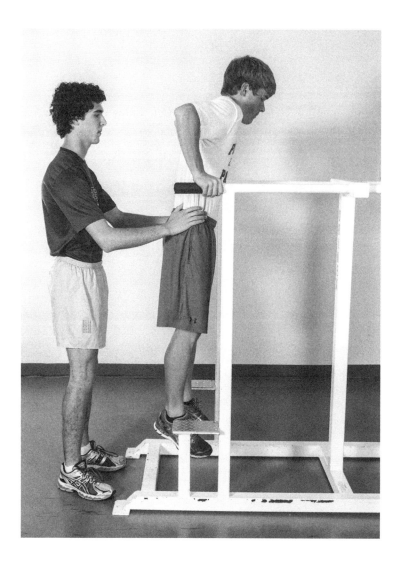

Leg Extension (Station 3)

Lie on your back, tensing the abdominal muscles. Slowly bring both knees to the chest, grasping them with the hands. Then, extend the legs straight out and hold them 4 to 6 inches (10 to 15 cm) off the ground for five seconds. Slowly lower the legs to the ground and repeat.

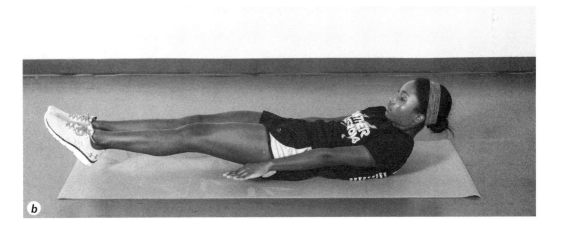

Step-Up With Medicine Ball (Station 3)

Begin with the left foot on top of a step or wooden box, high enough so that the thigh is almost parallel (but not beyond parallel) to the ground. Hold the medicine ball directly in front of the chest, arms fully outstretched. Keeping the back straight, step up onto the step or box, and then step down. Switch sides after completing the assigned repetitions with the left leg.

Medicine Ball Chest Pass (Station 4)

Throw the medicine ball as in a basketball chest pass, keeping the elbows out and extending the arms directly in front of the body. Partners should stand 6 to 8 feet (1.8 to 2.4 m) apart. The throwing action should be fast, but controlled.

Superman Arm and Leg Raiser (Station 4)

Lying facedown with arms and legs outstretched, lift the right arm and the left leg 4 to 6 inches (about 10 to 15 cm) off the ground and hold for three seconds. Lower the right arm and left leg, and then do the exercise with the left arm and right leg.

Lunge (Station 4)

With the right leg supporting the body, slowly raise the left knee, extend the left leg, and gently lunge forward. The left shin should be perpendicular, or just slightly beyond perpendicular, to the ground. From this position, raise the body and repeat the movement by lunging with the right leg. Use dumbbells or a weighted vest for extra resistance.

Most young runners enjoy circuit training because it adds variety to daily workouts, it's physically challenging, and it produces visible results, including enhanced muscle tone, improved posture, and a more powerful stride. Even so, it's important to be creative and change the circuit exercises over time. Although we recommend 8 to 12 exercises in a circuit, they can vary as long as they stress muscles used for postural support, driving the arms, absorbing impact forces, and propulsion. For example, to develop the calves, athletes can replace the heel raiser exercise with rope jumping. Instead of doing curl-ups for the abdominal muscles, they can do crossover sit-ups or crunches. For alternative exercises for the abdominal and back muscles, we suggest Pilates, which is an excellent form of exercise for developing core strength and good posture.

Depending on the type of exercise and the athlete's developmental level, the number of repetitions, performed at a controlled rate, will range between 10 and 30. Going too fast can result in sloppy technique, increasing the risk of injury. A 20- to 30-second recovery period between exercises at each station is short enough to keep the heart rate elevated, thereby ensuring an endurance training effect. Doing the exercises properly and keeping the recovery period short will elevate the heart rate to at least 70 percent of maximum throughout the session. To further promote the endurance effect, coaches can arrange the stations several hundred meters apart so that when athletes complete the exercises at a station, they have to run to the next station.

One complete circuit should take 15 to 20 minutes. At the start of a training season, runners should perform only one circuit per session. Over time they can work up to performing two or three circuits. A session of three circuits with a five-minute recovery between them can take an hour or more to complete. These workouts are demanding on the cardiovascular system and the muscles performing the resistance exercises, but they are extremely valuable for building a fitness base.

Many exercises that use the body weight as resistance are sufficient for developing strength endurance. However, conditioned intermediate and advanced runners can increase the intensity by doing circuit exercises with added resistance in the form of medicine balls, dumbbells, sandbags, ankle weights, or any object that creates an extra load. The added resistance should be light enough to allow the athlete to perform at least 15 repetitions with good technique before fatiguing.

Weight Training

As in circuit training, the objective of weight training for distance runners is to build strength endurance to improve performance and prevent injuries. Most of the principles and guidelines for circuit training apply to weight training. For example, the weight training load should be low in intensity and high in repetitions to develop muscular strength and endurance rather than pure strength.

Training Terminology

To better understand the sample training sessions presented in this and the next chapter, you'll need to know the following terms that describe the training load:

- *Volume* refers to the distance or duration of all or part of a training session. Volume can be expressed as the number of miles, kilometers, or minutes of a run or a strength-endurance session.

- *Frequency* refers to the number of times a repetition is performed in a training session. The frequency of repetitions must be designated when planning circuit training, weight training, and interval running workouts. For example, a session in which an athlete does four repetitions of a 600-meter run is written as 4 × 600 meters.

- *Intensity* refers to the amount of effort required to complete a repetition or a training session. When we describe training methods involving running, we define intensity by running time, pace per mile or kilometer, or percentage of maximal heart rate. To include its intensity, the preceding session might be further developed as 4 × 600 meters at 2:00 (for each 600). When we describe strength-endurance training methods (circuit and weight training), we define intensity by the load lifted. Athletes can increase training intensity by exerting more effort or by decreasing the recovery interval between repetitions during interval workouts.

- *Recovery* refers to the length of time between repetitions during interval training. We can add a recovery interval to complete our sample session as such: 4 × 600 meters at 2:00 with a 2:00 jog recovery. In this session, the athlete jogs for two minutes after each 600-meter repetition. Recovery can also be expressed as a ratio, relative to the duration of a repetition. For a session of 4 × 600 meters at 2:00, a 1:1 recovery period would last two minutes, a 1:0.5 recovery period would last one minute, and a 1:1.5 recovery period would last three minutes.

For intermediate and advanced runners, weight training can supplement circuit training as the training season progresses. Coaches must first make sure, however, that the weight training equipment is the appropriate size for youths. Weight machines in gyms and fitness clubs are usually sized for adults, and free weights on long bars may be too cumbersome and difficult for smaller athletes to control. If appropriately sized equipment is lacking, circuit training with added resistance, such as medicine balls and dumbbells, is an excellent means of developing strength endurance.

When properly sized, weight machines offer the advantage of isolating specific muscle groups. They also minimize the risk of injury because the path over which the movement occurs is controlled by pulleys and other mechanical devices. In contrast, free weights require considerable balance and technique to isolate key muscles and stabilize the movement. Because the technical demands are much greater for free weights, some experts recommend starting out on machines and progressing to free weights over time.

The sample weight training sessions in table 6.2 include exercises using both machines and free weights (see the exercises and instructions in this section). As in circuit training, weight training should stress the leg and arm muscles involved in the running movement and the core muscles that stabilize the torso. The exercise order should allow for recovery of a given muscle group before it is stressed again. For this reason, the sample sessions alternate exercises for the arms, body core, and legs. It's best to stress large muscles first and then small muscles. For variety, you can substitute the exercises in our sample sessions with others that target the same muscle groups.

Like circuit training, weight training can prevent injuries; however, injuries can occur if coaches don't supervise the exercises closely and provide instruction and feedback on technique. Some free weight exercises require spotters to help position the bar and to assist athletes if they have difficulty lifting the weights.

A concept called *repetition maximum*, or *RM*, guides coaches in determining the appropriate load of weight training for each athlete. For example, 12RM is the amount of weight an athlete can lift 12, but not 13, times without excessive straining and loss of form. To develop strength endurance, distance runners should perform 8 to 15 repetitions of each weight training exercise using a 10- to 15RM load. To determine how much weight to lift for, say, a 12RM, the athlete should start with a very light load that can be lifted at least 20 times. After resting for several minutes, he should increase the weight by 10 to 15 percent and perform the repetitions until fatigue sets in. The athlete should continue to repeat this process, with sufficient rest periods, until 12 repetitions is the highest number he can perform.

The lower end of the repetition range allows athletes to refine their lifting technique without becoming too fatigued. For example, an athlete who performs 10 to 12 repetitions of barbell squats with a 15RM load won't strain during the last few lifts. Athletes should never extend a weight training session to the point of compromising good technique. This can happen when deep fatigue sets in during exercises that involve many joints and require coordinating the whole body, such as barbell squats. When form breaks down, the risk of injury increases, so it's best to reduce the number of repetitions when still perfecting technique or when excessive fatigue sets in.

The year-to-year progression of weight training involves increasing the intensity, or the load lifted, by reducing the RM load over time. For intermediate runners, 15RM loads are appropriate because they are light enough to allow mastery of technique, yet heavy enough to increase strength endurance. The light load also reduces stress on growing bones in those who are still maturing. Advanced runners who are more physically mature and have learned the proper technique benefit from heavier weights, such as 10- or 12RM loads.

We recommend that runners not begin weight training until they have at least done 6 to 10 circuit training sessions over a period of three to four weeks. Circuit training builds a strength endurance base to prepare athletes for more intense weight training. In the beginning, the weight training session should include only one set. As the training season progresses, athletes may perform two or three sets. As the competitive season draws near and race-specific methods begin to be emphasized, the contribution of weight training to the total training load should decrease. Consider an intermediate-level runner who builds up to three sets of our sample weight training session (see table 6.2) twice a week by the end of the preparation period. Throughout the racing season, she might do only one set two days per week, which will maintain her strength-endurance base. The RM loads have to increase periodically as athletes gain strength endurance. It's important to keep detailed records of weight training workouts so that athletes can systematically increase their RM loads.

Table 6.2 Sample Sessions: Weight Training

Duration: 20-60 minutes
Intensity: 10- to 15RM; controlled rate of movement
Frequency: 8-15 repetitions per exercise
Recovery: 1-2 minutes between exercises

Sample Sessions for the Early Preparation Period

Exercise	Intermediate CA[a] = 14-16 TA[b] = 2-4	Advanced CA = 16-18 TA = 4-6
Bench press	12-15 reps at 15RM[c]	10-12 reps at 12RM
Abdominal crunch	10-12 reps at 15RM	12-15 reps at 15RM
Barbell squat	12-15 reps at 15RM	10-12 reps at 12RM
Overhead press	10-12 reps at 12RM	8-10 reps at 10RM
Good morning	10-12 reps at 12RM	8-10 reps at 10RM
Knee extension	12-15 reps at 15RM	10-12 reps at 12RM
Knee curl	10-12 reps at 12RM	8-10 reps at 10RM
Dumbbell arm pump	12-15 reps at 15RM	10-12 reps at 12RM
Barbell heel raiser	12-15 reps at 15RM	10-12 reps at 12RM
Lat pulldown	12-15 reps at 15RM	10-12 reps at 12RM

No sample workout is given for beginners because we recommend that runners with a training age of less than two years use circuit training rather than weight training.

[a]CA = chronological age in years

[b]TA = training age in years

[c]RM = repetition maximum (see text for explanation)

Bench Press

Lying on a bench with the feet flat on the floor, grip the bar so the hands are shoulder-width apart. Lower the bar to the upper chest in a controlled manner. Press the bar upward to the starting position. Do not raise the back or buttocks off the bench.

Barbell Squat

Stand with the bar resting on the shoulder blades, hands and feet spaced slightly greater than shoulder-width apart. Keeping the back as upright as possible, lower the body by bending at the hips, knees, and ankles. At the end of the lowering movement, the angle formed by the lower and upper legs (behind the knee) should be 120 to 140 degrees. Lift the body to the starting position, keeping the feet flat on the floor.

Overhead Press

Beginning in the same position as in the barbell squat, press the bar above the head until the arms are straight. Lower the bar slowly to the starting position. During the lowering and lifting movements, keep the feet flat on the floor.

Good Morning

Beginning in the same position as in the barbell squat, with the knees slightly bent, bend forward at the waist until the torso is almost parallel to the floor. Slowly raise the body back to the starting position. During the lowering and lifting movements, keep the back straight.

Knee Extension

Lift the weight by straightening the legs, holding for two seconds at the top. Slowly lower the weight to the starting position. During the lifting and lowering movement, keep the back flat against the seat.

Knee Curl

Contract the hamstring muscles to pull the heels toward the buttocks. To reverse the movement, straighten the legs in a slow, controlled manner.

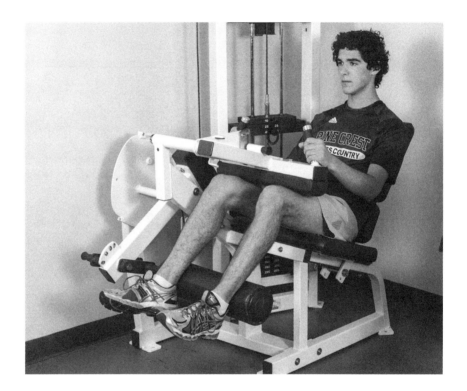

Dumbbell Arm Pump

Standing with one foot propped up on a bench or step, pump the arms rapidly using the same motion as in the running stride. Stand tall and keep the supporting leg straight, avoiding a sitting position of the hips.

Barbell Heel Raiser

Beginning in the same position as in the barbell squat, and making sure the feet point straight ahead, raise the heels by extending at the ankles and pushing down with the toes. Lower the heels to return to the starting position.

Lat Pulldown

Keeping the back straight and shoulders square, lower the bar, avoiding a jerking action. After bringing the bar under the chin, slowly extend the arms, to return the bar to the starting position.

Pointers for Parents

The general, foundational training methods featured in this chapter are emphasized during early phases of preparation for the upcoming competitive season. You might think of this time as the off-season. In U.S. high school cross country, for example, off-season preparation lasts from June through August, leading up to the start of the racing season in early September. For the summer months, the best coaches assign a comprehensive program that includes plenty of fundamental training. However, as a result of school regulations that restrict organized practices, summer jobs, family vacations, and other activities, coaches may not be able to meet with their athletes and supervise all of these sessions. So, parents can play valuable supportive roles during the off-season.

- **Encourage your child to train consistently.**

  When the competitive season is months away and young athletes have lots of opportunities for social and recreational activities, they may choose to skip foundational workouts. You can help by reminding your child that the base built through consistent off-season training determines the heights reached in upcoming competitions. The inspirational saying "Champions are made in the off-season" is especially true for distance runners.

- **Help with unofficial team practices.**

  If the coach is not allowed or available to organize and attend off-season practices, you can help in a variety of ways. You might take turns with other parents driving team members to parks for circuit training sessions or long runs. You can also prepare and deliver water coolers to practices arranged by team captains.

- **Enroll your child in multisport programs.**

  This pointer applies especially to the youngest runners and beginners, who benefit the most from developing all-around physical fitness. As we've mentioned, an ideal way to build foundational capacities such as mobility, flexibility, and strength endurance is to participate in other sports such as soccer, basketball, swimming, and cycling.

- **Keep your parenting role in mind.**

  Coaching supervision is essential for fundamental methods such as technique drills, weight lifting, and circuit training. If young athletes don't perform these methods correctly, they risk poor results and injury. So, when the coach is not available for off-season workouts, it may be tempting to assume the coaching role. This is usually a mistake, unless you have a strong coaching background as well as the coach's and team's support. Ideally, coaches should not assign highly technical workouts when they are not available to supervise. For less technical fundamental workouts, older and more experienced athletes should be on hand to guide teammates.

Hill Running

Several of the training methods described in this chapter have *crossover effects*—that is, they develop more than one general fitness capacity. For example, circuit training builds both strength endurance and cardiorespiratory fitness because its prolonged, continuous nature results in stresses to the skeletal muscles as well as the heart. One of the most complete crossover methods is hill running, which develops strength endurance, cardiorespiratory fitness, and technique. We focus on uphill running for developing strength endurance because it places an extra load on the leg muscles and requires more vigorous arm action than running on level ground.

As shown in the sample sessions in table 6.3, hill running to develop strength endurance is a form of interval training because it involves repetitions separated by recovery periods. The slope of the hill should be steep enough to force runners to alter their technique by using more vigorous muscle force than they would when running on level ground. The hill should not be so steep that it causes runners to strain and lose proper form. The distance of the hill should be fairly short, 200 to 400 meters. The session will still promote muscular endurance if runners take a short recovery between repetitions by jogging back down the hill. Even a short early-season session for a beginner, 6 × 200 meters, totals 2,400 meters of running when the downhill jog recoveries are included. The repetitions could even be extended another 50 to 100 meters on the flat, after the hill crests. In cross country, inexperienced runners tend to ease up when they get to the top of a hill, so if they practice holding the pace they'll gain a competitive advantage. Because the main objective of hill running is to develop strength endurance, the intensity should not highly stress the anaerobic system and cause fatigue from lactic acid accumulation. A guideline for intensity is to run at a pace that corresponds to a 3,000- to 5,000-meter race pace.

At the start of the preparation period, we recommend a low number of hill repetitions (five or six), even for advanced runners. The year-to-year progression for hill training in the sample sessions in table 6.3 features an increase in the

Table 6.3   Sample Sessions: Hill Running

Duration of repetitions: 200-500 meters
Intensity: Fast but controlled
Frequency: 5-10 repetitions
Recovery: Jog back to starting position
Total volume per session: 1,000-5,000 meters

Sample Sessions for the Early Preparation Period		
Beginner CA[a] = 12-14 TA[b] = 0-2	**Intermediate** CA = 14-16 TA = 2-4	**Advanced** CA = 16-18 TA = 4-6
5 or 6 × 200 m	5 or 6 × 300-400 m	5 or 6 × 400-500 m

[a]CA = chronological age in years

[b]TA = training age in years

distance of each repetition. Younger, less fit runners may have difficulty holding efficient form on long hills, so the coach can intensify the load by increasing the number of repetitions instead. A 16-year-old with three years of training experience might start a new season by doing 5 × 400-meter hills, and over the course of the preparation period, the session might progress to 10 × 400 meters.

Developing Neuromuscular Fitness and Technical Skill

In chapters 2 and 5, we emphasized the importance of sound running technique and its role in improving performance, conserving energy, and preventing injuries. Good running form is the product of precisely timed patterns of muscle activity and limb movement, which are controlled by the nervous system. So, technical skill and neuromuscular fitness are highly interrelated in running. These capacities can be improved through speed development (sprinting) training as well as technique drills and strides. For young runners, these methods are truly essential—both for learning to run efficiently and, when necessary, for breaking bad form habits before they become permanent.

Technique training typically fits into daily sessions as part of a warm-up routine or in combination with other fundamental training methods. An example is a warm-up that includes technique drills (described in the next section), followed by ten 100-meter strides for speed development, and ending with a 20-minute game of ultimate Frisbee for mobility and cardiorespiratory endurance.

Technique Drills

The sample sessions in table 6.4 include four technique drills for distance runners, which are illustrated in this section. These drills train the neuromuscular system to help runners develop the key characteristics of sound technique, including correct posture of the upper body, high knee lift, a powerful extension of the driving leg in the takeoff phase of the stride, a good pattern of dorsiflexion (closing) and extension (opening) at the ankle joint, and efficient arm action. An important element of any technique session is good feedback from the coach. Too often young athletes perform technique drills incorrectly, which reinforces inefficient and injury-risking movement patterns. Whenever possible, coaches should capture technique sessions on video to provide feedback on strengths and weaknesses. Fancy video equipment is not necessary—a smartphone will do the trick.

When performing technique drills, athletes should keep the upper body squared at the shoulders and bent very slightly forward at the hips. They should remember to "stand tall." This cue will engage the core muscles, keeping the spine in good alignment. With the chin parallel to the ground, the eyes should focus straight ahead. Practicing this posture helps avoid turning the upper body, flailing the arms, and using the inefficient stride mechanics that occur when the body slouches or leans too far forward or backward. Each drill also emphasizes a coordinated and vigorous pumping of the arms, in which the hands move up and down without crossing too far in front of the body.

Several of the drills, including high-knee marching, emphasize extending the driving leg during the takeoff phase of the stride and lifting the knees. These actions are necessary to increase stride length, which as we discussed in chapter 5 is an efficient way to surge or kick in middle- and long-distance races. Runners who can generate a great amount of propulsive force by extending the driving leg, and who can keep the leading foot off the ground by raising the knee high, naturally lengthen their stride. Those who are unable to quicken the pace by lengthening their strides are at a disadvantage.

The basic skipping drill develops sound technique of the lower leg and foot. This drill isolates the action at the ankle joint. A common flaw is keeping the ankle locked when the foot leaves the ground. As discussed in chapter 5, a good amount of the propulsive force in the running stride comes from extending the ankle joint. In the basic skipping exercise, the athlete keeps the knees fairly straight, forcing the muscles that extend the ankle to do all the propulsive work.

Table 6.4   Sample Sessions: Technique Drills

Duration of repetitions: 10-100 meters
Intensity: Fast but controlled
Frequency: 3-6 repetitions per drill
Recovery: Walk or jog back to starting position

	Sample Sessions for the Early Preparation Period		
Drill	Beginner CA[a] = 12-14 TA[b] = 0-2	Intermediate CA = 14-16 TA = 2-4	Advanced CA = 16-18 TA = 4-6
High-knee marching	3 × 20 m	3 × 30 m	3 × 40 m
Skipping	3 × 40 m	3 × 60 m	3 × 80 m
Butt kick	3 × 20 m	3 × 30 m	3 × 40 m
High-knee running	3 × 30 m	3 × 40 m	3 × 50 m

[a]CA = chronological age in years

[b]TA = training age in years

High-Knee Marching

This drill exaggerates walking (because both legs don't leave the ground at the same time) by demanding high knee lift and an extended driving action of the leg on takeoff. Begin by quickly raising the right knee to bring the thigh parallel to the ground. The right foot should be dorsiflexed, which means that the toe should be pulled toward the shin. The left leg should be straight, contacting the ground only with the ball of the foot and the toes. Keeping the right foot dorsiflexed, lower the leg, bringing the foot under the hip as the forefoot contacts the ground. The shoulders should be squared and the upper body should lean forward only slightly at the hips. The arms, kept at a 90- to 120-degree angle, should swing vigorously (as the right knee comes up, the left arm moves forward). Make sure the arms don't cross in front of the body. Continue the cyclic marching movement. A variation of this drill is high-knee running, which has the same technique, but it exaggerates the action of the driving leg so that both feet are off the ground. In high-knee running, the objective is not to move forward quickly, but to take many rapid, short strides by lifting the knees to parallel with the ground.

Skipping

Just as a child skips, land on the heel and quickly roll off the ball of the foot, accentuating the pushing-off action. The knees should be fairly straight, but not rigid. After pushing off and extending fully at the ankle joint, quickly pull the toe to the shin prior to landing. Swing the arms vigorously without crossing them in front of the body.

TECHNIQUE DRILLS

Butt Kick

Make a running motion with an exaggerated follow-through action in which the heel lightly touches the buttocks. The action occurs by bending the knee. Instead of lifting the knee in front of the body as in a normal stride, the knee and thigh remain vertical throughout the drill.

Speed Development and Technique Strides

Using the methods of speed development and technique strides, the athlete runs repeated strides over short distances of 100 to 150 meters. Strides are fast, controlled runs at race pace or faster. During these sessions, the coach identifies any areas for improvement in the runner's form and gives instructions for making corrections. To show you how technique strides can be used in individualized training, let's consider the runner who overstrides, has a passive landing, and brings his arms across the front of his body, causing rotation of the torso. Recall from chapter 5 that in a passive landing the foot moves forward or lacks movement as it hits the ground; in contrast, in an active landing the foot is moving backward as it hits the ground. A session for this athlete might involve 15 repetitions of a 150-meter stride with complete recovery between repetitions. To work on each flaw, the session can be divided as follows:

- 5 × 150 meters at 1,500-meter race pace, with the focus on correcting the overstride by planting the foot closer to the body
- 5 × 150 meters at 800-meter race pace, with the focus on an active landing
- 5 × 150 meters at a controlled sprint, with the focus on driving the arms in a straight line without crossing over the body's midline

As with drills, athletes should do technique strides when they are fairly well rested. Fatigue limits the ability to perform and thereby learn the correct motor patterns. However, coaches should pay special attention to runners' technique during high-intensity training sessions that cause fatigue, especially race-specific sessions (see chapter 7). After all, the objective of technique training is to apply it to racing situations when fatigue occurs. To keep runners focused on form during high-intensity training sessions and races, coaches should use the verbal cues and reminders we recommended in the technique tips in chapter 5.

Developing Cardiorespiratory Fitness

Cardiorespiratory fitness is the capacity of the heart and blood vessels to supply the working muscles with oxygen-rich blood. This foundation of fitness is essential for *endurance*, or the capacity to sustain moderate-intensity activity for a long duration. In this section we describe two training methods for developing cardiorespiratory fitness: continuous aerobic running and nonrunning aerobic activities.

Continuous Aerobic Running

To improve cardiorespiratory fitness, runners must train at a moderate intensity over relatively long periods of time. This form of training primarily stresses the aerobic energy pathways. The main training method is continuous running at a moderate intensity. The target pace for improving cardiorespiratory endurance won't necessarily feel fast, but it shouldn't feel like a jog either. Depending on the runner's developmental level and event specialty, as well as the phase of preparation for competition, the duration of running might vary from around 20 to 50 minutes, or approximately 3 to 10 miles (5 to 16 km).

In the sample sessions in table 6.5, we show the duration of continuous aerobic running in minutes rather than miles or kilometers. That's because the main objective for this form of training is to stress the cardiorespiratory system for a long time, regardless of distance. Also, for this form of training, when athletes run for time rather than distance, you don't have to measure all your courses. However, if you have set courses with known distances, or if your runners use GPS watches, it's perfectly fine to base your cardiorespiratory training on distance rather than time.

Table 6.5 Sample Sessions: Continuous Aerobic Running

Duration: 20-70 minutes
Intensity: 70-80% of HRmax

Sample Sessions for the Early Preparation Period		
Beginner CA[a] = 12-14 TA[b] = 0-2	**Intermediate** CA = 14-16 TA = 2-4	**Advanced** CA = 16-18 TA = 4-6
20-30 min at 70% of HRmax	30-40 min at 75% of HRmax	40-50 min at 80% of HRmax

[a]CA = chronological age in years

[b]TA = training age in years

Jay Johnson
Boulder, Colorado

Jay Johnson was a successful student-athlete at the University of Colorado, where he ran on the famed Buffaloes cross country team and earned a master's degree in kinesiology and applied physiology in 2000. Since then, Johnson has coached distance runners at the high school, college, and professional levels. In addition to his work as director of the Boulder Running Camps, Johnson writes for several running publications and designs training programs for endurance athletes at www.coachjayjohnson.com. In this interview, Johnson speaks about the importance of neuromuscular fitness and speed for young runners.

What is neuromuscular fitness, and why is it important for young distance runners?—The neuromuscular system is the nervous system integrating with the muscles and guiding their activity. Neuromuscular fitness is important in many aspects of distance running, including midrace surges and finishing sprints. For these demands, we want the young distance runner to develop a neuromuscular system capable of recruiting as many fast-twitch muscle fibers as possible. I often see runners with great times in cross country and for 3,200 meters on the track, yet they lack good 800- and 400-meter personal records (PRs). This disparity is partly due to a lack of metabolic fitness for the shorter races. But it can also be explained by the simple neuromuscular fact that, during practice, these athletes never recruit the muscle fibers to run faster than their 400- or 800-meter PRs. All young distance runners should regularly do speed development training that targets neuromuscular fitness.

What are your favorite methods for developing speed through neuromuscular fitness?—My favorite speed development workout, which my athletes do on a 400-meter track, has three parts. First, we start with three 150-meter in-and-outs, in which the athlete builds up speed for 50 meters, holds that pace for the next 50 meters, and then decelerates over the last 50 meters. In the middle 50-meter patch, we aim for a 200-meter PR pace. The recovery after each 150 is a 250-meter jog to the start line and the beginning of the next repetition.

Second, we do two or three 40-meter all-out sprints from a falling start. This couldn't be simpler: You stand up straight then lean forward until you're about to fall, at which point you break the fall and run as fast as you can for 40 meters. The recovery between these falling-start sprints is three to five minutes of walking.

The speed development workout ends with three or four 120-meter sprints at an 800-meter PR pace. I instruct my athletes to run into these repetitions by accelerating over 30 meters before they start the 120-meter sprints. The recovery is a 250-meter jog, as slow as necessary.

What are your views on plyometrics for young distance runners?—Plyometric exercises involve the quick coupling of an eccentric (lengthening) muscle contraction with a concentric (shortening) muscle contraction. Consider that sprinting is the most specific plyometric activity a runner can do. Sprinting has the quickest coupling of the lengthening and shortening of the various major muscle groups in the lower body.

So, through our speed development workouts, my athletes are really doing plyometric training.

Plyometric training also involves jumping and bounding exercises that train the neuromuscular system to react quickly and forcefully to the impact of landing in the running stride. To get the maximum benefit from these exercises and to avoid injury, distance runners must first have very good general strength. We develop this capacity through leg circuit training over two or three months before introducing plyometric jumping and bounding. In every plyometric workout, I watch my athletes very closely to ensure that they are performing the exercises correctly and safely.

Do you recommend stretching as a method for developing neuromuscular fitness?—Instead of traditional static stretching of the lower leg muscles, I view hip mobility exercises as elemental for all runners. We use the Wharton Active Isolated Flexibility (AIF) program for hip mobility, which coaches can learn about on the Internet. The exercises, which can be done standing or lying on the ground, take as little as five minutes. I assign daily AIF work for my athletes for neuromuscular fitness and injury prevention.

As shown in table 6.5, the low end of the range, 20 minutes, is suitable for beginners at the start of the season. The high end of the range, 50 minutes, is targeted to many advanced runners who specialize in 3,000- and 5,000-meter races and have gradually built up to this duration. Advanced runners, such as 17- and 18-year-olds who have been training for five years or more, may build up to long runs of 70 to 90 minutes over weeks of preparation for an upcoming season.

The pace for continuous aerobic running should elevate the heart rate to moderately high levels. Based on studies investigating cardiorespiratory adaptations to training in young athletes, we recommend a target range of roughly 70 to 80 percent of maximal heart rate (HRmax). For many adolescents, HRmax is in the range of 190 to 210 beats per minute (bpm). Runners can determine their HRmax by counting their heartbeats immediately after completing an all-out three- to five-minute run at an even pace. The result of this test can be used to gauge the training intensity for continuous aerobic running and for other running methods that we describe in chapter 7.

Consider, for example, a runner whose HRmax is 192 bpm. At the low end of our target range, which is 70 percent of HRmax, this runner would need to maintain a pace that raises her heart rate to 134 bpm (192 bpm × 0.70 = 134 bpm). At the higher end, 80 percent of HRmax, the pace would elicit a heart rate of 154 bpm (192 bpm × 0.80 = 154 bpm). The pace for continuous aerobic running sessions should feel faster than a jog but slow enough to carry on a conversation without labored breathing. It's a good practice to check every 20 minutes or so for whether heart rate is in the target range and to adjust the pace if it isn't (see Taking the Pulse to Count Heart Rate for instructions on how to measure heart rate).

Taking the Pulse to Count Heart Rate

The two photos in this sidebar show how to take your pulse, which is an echo of the heartbeat. The pulse can be felt in the wrist (radial artery) and the neck (carotid artery). To take your pulse at the wrist, place your right hand in your left palm, with the fingertips of your right hand on your left thumb. Slowly slide the first two fingertips along the edge of the thumb toward your wrist. Once your fingertips are on your wrist, feel for the pulse, count the number of beats for 15 seconds, and multiply by 4. To take your pulse at your neck, place the first two fingers of your right hand on your neck, level with your Adam's apple. Slide your fingers back until they are in the groove between your Adam's apple and the large muscle running down the front and side of your neck. Press gently to feel the pulse, count the number of beats for 15 seconds, and multiply by 4.

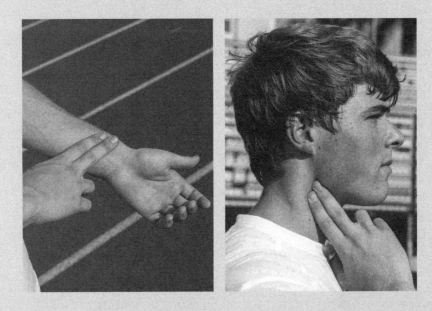

Another way to measure heart rate is to use a monitor that straps to the chest and digitally records the number of beats per minute on a wristwatch. Advancements in technology have made heart-rate monitors relatively inexpensive and easy to use.

When planning continuous aerobic running sessions, coaches should keep individual differences in mind. Beginners who have trained for less than one year may need to run at an 8:00- to 8:30-mile pace (5:00 to 5:17 per km) for optimal intensity. In contrast, advanced runners (training age of four years or more) may need to run at a 6:30- to 7:00-mile pace (4:02 to 4:21 per km) or faster to reach the threshold for improving cardiorespiratory fitness. If beginners try to keep up with advanced runners, their effort may exceed their threshold. In this case, anaerobic metabolism will kick in and fatigue will rapidly follow, causing the runner to slow or even stop. The result is that they won't achieve the objective of developing cardiorespiratory fitness.

The duration of continuous aerobic running should increase from year to year. As shown in the sample sessions in table 6.5, the advanced cross country runner's session (40 minutes) is twice as long as the beginner's (20 minutes), and the advanced runner works at the higher end of the intensity range. Even though a 13-year-old with one year of training experience might be able to handle 40 minutes or more, covering that distance goes against the principles of progression presented in chapter 1. If the 13-year-old has the motivation and potential for success throughout high school and perhaps beyond, his training volume should increase gradually over the years to ensure continued improvement and avoid injury or burnout.

Running duration should also increase over the course of a single training season. For example, over the first two months of the preparation period, beginning cross country runners might increase the duration of a run from 20 to 35 minutes. At the same time, these runners will have to quicken their pace because their aerobic conditioning will improve. Over a single training season, the pace required to keep the heart rate within 70 to 80 percent of maximum might be lowered by 30 seconds per mile (about 20 seconds per km) or more.

As often as possible, runs should be on soft surfaces rather than asphalt or concrete to avoid excessive jarring and stress to the leg muscles, connective tissue, and joints. It's also smart to run on different courses for variety and enjoyment. Every now and again, coaches might arrange to take the team for long runs in nearby parks or to the beach, mountain trails, dirt roads, or other natural settings in the area.

Nonrunning Aerobic Activities

Cardiorespiratory fitness emphasizes adaptations to the heart muscle rather than the body's other muscles. Therefore, any continuous, rhythmic activity that elevates heart rate to target levels is a suitable training method. As long as runners sustain a heart rate of 70 to 80 percent of maximum, they can improve their cardiorespiratory fitness by cycling, swimming, cross-country skiing, in-line skating, and so on. It's a great idea to include these nonrunning aerobic activities in the young runner's training program, especially in the early phases of preparation. Nonrunning methods add variety, making training fun and enhancing motivation. Because these methods stress many muscle groups, they also help young runners develop well-rounded fitness, which is important for avoiding injuries caused by the repetitive stress of running. Finally, in the unfortunate event of an injury that keeps the athlete from running, experience with nonrunning activities pays dividends. Injured runners who are familiar with training on a bicycle or in the pool are able to use these methods immediately to maintain aerobic fitness while their injuries heal.

Striding Ahead

General training methods build a foundation of fitness, conditioning the heart and vasculature, the muscles and connective tissue, and the neuromuscular system. Developing general fitness is the most important training objective for beginners and for runners of all developmental levels in the early phases of preparation for an upcoming racing season. A strong fitness base gives runners the strength and endurance to handle heavy loads of high-intensity, race-specific training methods. But the advantages go well beyond just preparing runners for more demanding training within a season. The fitness and skill developed through general training methods set the stage for success over an entire running career. Scientific principles and anecdotal evidence have convinced us that runners who incorporate methods such as circuit training, weight training, and technique drills have longer and more successful careers than runners whose training is based only on daily running. Runners who use the methods described in this chapter avoid injuries and are ultimately able to train at higher intensities because their bodies can withstand the stress. As we move on to discuss the higher intensity, race-specific training methods in chapter 7, don't lose sight of their relationship to the general methods covered here.

7

Race-Specific Training

The general methods covered in chapter 6 are described by the phrase *training to train*. These methods build a foundation of fitness for supporting the more advanced training required for the highest levels of success in competition. In this chapter we move on to these more advanced, race-specific methods. In other words, here we focus on *training to race*. This chapter presents training methods that closely simulate the physiological and psychological demands of competing in events from 800 to 5,000 meters. These methods are tempo running, aerobic intervals, anaerobic intervals, race-specific intervals, time trials, and pacing and tactical practice (see figure 7.1).

Race-specific training methods are guided by the principle of specificity, which states that physiological adaptations to training depend on the specific methods runners use. Consider, from chapter 6, the general training method of continuous aerobic running. It's perfect for building a base of cardiorespiratory fitness. But it's a relatively low-intensity form of training, which doesn't sufficiently stress the body to cause the physiological changes runners need to reach their competitive potential. For instance, continuous aerobic running doesn't condition the body to withstand the fatiguing effects of anaerobic metabolism and lactic acid accumulation. As a whole, the general training methods don't completely prepare runners for the physiological demands of racing. Complete preparation must include race-specific methods.

Here's another important point for understanding the principle of specificity: to race fast, runners must train fast. It's as simple as that. Keep in mind, however, that race-specific methods are more physically demanding than general methods, so they can pose greater risks of injury and burnout. Beginners, especially those who have not yet reached puberty, should start out with a low volume of race-specific training and slowly increase the load over time. For runners at all levels, volumes of race-specific methods should increase gradually through successive phases within a single season and across seasons. We echo this message in this

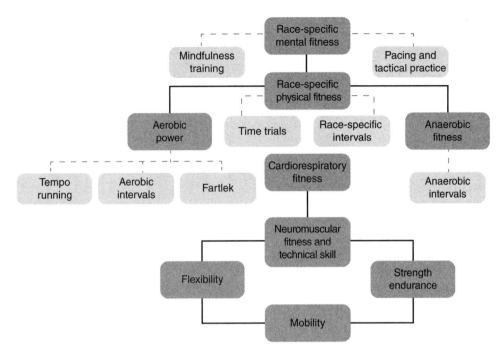

Figure 7.1 Race-specific fitness capacities.

chapter and in chapter 9, where we present guidelines for incorporating general and race-specific methods into the training program.

Developing Aerobic Power

As discussed in chapter 2, the most important physiological determinant of distance-running performance is an aspect of cardiorespiratory fitness called *aerobic power*, or the body's highest capacity to deliver oxygen to the working muscles and process it rapidly to form ATP. This section outlines three training methods—tempo running, aerobic interval training, and fartlek—for boosting aerobic power while also developing race-specific qualities of mental fitness such as willpower and pacing skill.

Tempo Running

Runners build aerobic power through training that raises the threshold at which lactic acid production begins to exceed its clearance in the muscles. In young runners this threshold typically occurs at a pace that corresponds to 80 to 85 percent of maximal heart rate, or HRmax. At this intensity runners can sustain the pace for a fairly long time before fatigue sets in. A highly fit 18-year-old, for example, might be able to run at 85 percent of HRmax for 40 minutes or more. This form of training is known as tempo running.

In this section we describe two approaches to the method: interval tempo running and continuous tempo running. We provide sample sessions for both methods in tables 7.1 and 7.2. Note that the sample sessions are recommendations for the early preparation period, or the first few weeks of a new training season. As the season progresses, the volume and speed of the workouts will increase. The following guidelines will help with setting the target intensity:

- The pace should elevate heart rate to roughly 80 to 85 percent of maximum. To make sure they are in the target range, runners can stop to take their pulse about one-fourth of the way through the run. Heart-rate monitors are helpful for tempo training because athletes can look at their watches for pulse readouts without having to stop.

- The pace should stimulate vigorous but not labored breathing. When it's done right, tempo training reaches an intensity that doesn't allow the runner to carry on a casual conversation.

- The pace should feel physically and mentally challenging, but at the end of the session, runners should be able to sustain the pace for another 6 to 10 minutes before having to slow down.

- For many runners the optimal pace is approximately one minute per mile slower than their current race pace for the mile run and 30 seconds slower than their pace per mile for 5,000 meters.

Using heart rate to determine intensity, runners can do tempo running anywhere, from flat dirt roads to rolling grassy hills to a 400-meter track. The main objective is to sustain a pace that keeps the heart rate at around 80 to 85 percent of maximum. Because tempo training involves fast but not all-out running, runners can be tempted to push the pace and compete with teammates. Two ways to keep this from happening are to group runners of similar ability or to start runners at staged intervals so that they run alone.

Interval Tempo Running

As shown in table 7.1, interval tempo training involves repetitions lasting from 3 to 10 minutes each. Between repetitions, for recovery, runners might jog somewhat briskly for 30 to 90 seconds. This recovery period provides a mental break during which runners can refocus their attention on maintaining pace and good form. Depending on the duration of each run, the number of repetitions ranges from 2 to 10. For example, a session for an intermediate-level runner starting to train for cross country season might be 4×4 minutes with a 60-second jog recovery between repetitions.

The interval method, which is less physically and mentally demanding than the continuous method, works especially well at the start of the training season, when runners lack the fitness, especially the mental fitness, to sustain fast-paced running without a break. Interval tempo running is also best for beginners who need to develop pacing and concentration skills.

Table 7.1 Sample Sessions: Interval Tempo Running

Duration of repetitions: 3-10 minutes per repetition
Intensity: 80-85% of HRmax; approximately 1 minute per mile slower than mile race pace
Frequency: 2-10 repetitions
Recovery: 30-90 seconds of brisk jogging
Total volume per session: Approximately 2-6 miles (3,200-10,000 meters)

Sample Sessions for the Early Preparation Period

Beginner CA^a = 12-14 TA^b = 0-2	Intermediate CA = 14-16 TA = 2-4	Advanced CA = 16-18 TA = 4-6
4 × 3 min with 60 s recovery, or 3 × 5 min with 90 s recovery	4 × 4 min with 60 s recovery, or 3 × 6 min, with 90 s recovery	4 × 6 min with 30 s recovery, or 3 × 8 min, with 60 s recovery

^{a}CA = chronological age in years

^{b}TA = training age in years

Continuous Tempo Running

Continuous tempo running is excellent for developing aerobic power as well as pacing skills and concentration. Interval tempo training isn't as good for developing these mental qualities because during repetitions runners might anticipate the upcoming recovery period and let up mentally. At the start of the training season—that is, in the early preparation period—we recommend 12 to 24 minutes of continuous running, depending on the athlete's development level and event specialty (see sample sessions in table 7.2). Of course, beginners should start at the low end of the range. More advanced runners who specialize in the shorter distances, particularly 800 meters, don't need to do as much tempo running as 5,000-meter runners do.

From season to season and year to year, the volume (time or distance) and intensity of continuous tempo running should increase. Because tempo running improves aerobic power by increasing the lactate threshold, target paces naturally

Table 7.2 Sample Sessions: Continuous Tempo Running

Duration: 12-40 minutes
Intensity: 80-85% of HRmax; approximately 1 minute per mile slower than mile race pace
Frequency: 1 repetition
Recovery: None
Total volume per session: Approximately 2-6 miles (3,200-10,000 meters)

Sample Sessions for the Early Preparation Period

Beginner CA^a = 12-14 TA^b = 0-2	Intermediate CA = 14-16 TA = 2-4	Advanced CA = 16-18 TA = 4-6
12-14 min at 80% of HRmax	14-18 min at 80% of HRmax	18-24 min at 85% of HRmax

^{a}CA = chronological age in years

^{b}TA = training age in years

Adding Variety to Interval Training Sessions

Many of the sample interval training sessions throughout the book have repetitions of a single duration or distance such as 4 × 2 minutes or 6 × 300 meters. We've given examples with the same duration of each repetition for simplicity. However, the duration and distance of repetitions can be altered to add variety. For example, an interval tempo session of 4 × 2 minutes might be changed to 1 × 3 minutes, 1× 2 minutes, and 1 × 3 minutes. The total duration is the same (8 minutes) and, for the most part, so is the physiological result and training outcome.

get faster over time. For example, at a training age of two years, a runner may require a pace between 7:00 and 7:30 per mile (4:21 and 4:40 per kilometer) to elevate his heart rate to 80 percent of maximum. After three or four years of training, his target pace may decrease to around 6:00 per mile (3:44 per kilometer).

The duration and speed of tempo running should also increase gradually throughout a single season, from early preparation through the start of competitions. Consider an example of a six-week period during cross country season in which a tempo session is held once per week. Over the first three weeks, a 16-year-old girl might progress from an interval session of 3 × 4 minutes to one of 3 × 7 minutes. Over the last three weeks, she might switch to continuous tempo running, increasing the duration from 16 to 22 minutes. An 18-year-old who has been training for five years might gradually progress from a 24-minute run to a 40-minute run over the first two months of training. Once runners can handle long repetitions—say, more than six minutes—it's often best to move from interval tempo running to the more demanding continuous tempo running.

Aerobic Intervals

Even though interval and continuous tempo running are fairly intense methods and are essential for boosting aerobic power and mental fitness, they don't maximally stress the aerobic system. To develop aerobic power to its fullest, runners have to train at paces at which their muscles consume oxygen at a near-maximal rate. The best method for meeting this objective is aerobic interval training. Interval training offers a physiological advantage over continuous running by allowing the body to experience an intense training stimulus for a longer duration.

Let's say that a 16-year-old runner with a training age of four years runs continuously at a pace that maximally stresses his aerobic system, eliciting $\dot{V}O_2$max. He might last for 8 to 10 minutes before slowing due to fatigue, and he might cover between 2,500 and 3,000 meters. Now consider the effect of repeating a series of three-minute runs at the same pace, taking a two- or three-minute recovery interval between repetitions. In this case, the athlete would be able to run considerably longer than the total of 8 to 10 minutes. He might be able to do six or more three-minute repetitions before fatiguing. So, he would be working at $\dot{V}O_2$max for

18 minutes and covering closer to 5,000 meters. The interval method extends the duration of running at high intensities.

Sample sessions for aerobic interval training early in the preparation period are shown in table 7.3. Note that the recommended intensity of running is close to 3,000- to 5,000-meter race pace, eliciting a heart rate that is 85 to 95 percent of HRmax. Many combinations of duration and frequency can have the desired training effect. Even numerous repetitions of very short runs, such as 20 × 100 meters with a brisk 50-meter jog recovery, can raise oxygen consumption to maximal levels for a long period of time. Our recommendation for aerobic interval training for distance runners, however, is to cover longer repetitions—600 meters to 1 mile. The longer repetitions are especially good for developing pacing skill along with aerobic power. At the start of the preparation period for track season, for example, intermediate-level 3,200-meter runners might do 800- to 1,000-meter repeats. The total volume of a session should range between 1,200 meters for beginners and 8,000 meters for advanced runners who specialize in the longer races.

Recovery periods in aerobic interval sessions are often expressed as a ratio of the run duration relative to the recovery duration. For a 1:1 run-to-recovery ratio, the recovery period lasts as long as the repetition. A runner who finishes a mile repeat in 5:42 should take 5:42 to recover before the next mile repeat. We recommend ratios of 1:0.5, 1:1, and 1:1.5 for aerobic interval training. If runners are so fatigued that they fail to achieve the goal pace on a repetition, the coach should lengthen the recovery period. While recovering between repetitions, runners should jog rather than walk or stand still. Jogging is thought to speed up recovery because the light muscle contractions move lactic acid from the muscles into the bloodstream.

The progression of aerobic interval training is similar to that of tempo running. This means gradually increasing the duration of repetitions and the total volume

Table 7.3   Sample Sessions: Aerobic Interval Training

Duration of repetitions: 600 meters to 1 mile
Intensity: 85-95% of HRmax; 3,000- to 5,000-meter race pace
Frequency: 2-10 repetitions
Recovery: Run-to-recovery ratios of 1:0.5, 1:1, or 1:1.5
Total volume per session: Approximately 0.75-5 miles (1,200-8,000 meters)
Sample Sessions for the Early Preparation Period

Beginner CA[a] = 12-14 TA[b] = 0-2	Intermediate CA = 14-16 TA = 2-4	Advanced CA = 16-18 TA = 4-6
2 × 600 m with a 1:1 recovery, or 2 × 800 m with a 1:1.5 recovery	4 × 800 m with a 1:1 recovery, or 3 × 1,000 m with a 1:1.5 recovery	4 × 1,000 m with a 1:1 recovery, or 3 × 1,200 m with a 1:1 recovery

[a]CA = chronological age in years

[b]TA = training age in years

per session. In addition, progression requires running at faster paces over a single season, from season to season, and from year to year. For example, beginners might set their target paces at 5,000-meter race pace, whereas advanced runners might set targets closer to 3,000-meter race pace. See chapter 9 for more specific examples of how aerobic interval sessions progress over the course of a season.

Often, the ideal venue for aerobic interval training is a simulation of the competition setting. After all, we're talking about *race-specific* training here! So, during cross country season, runners would do well to train on courses similar to the ones they race on. During track season, they should do aerobic intervals on a track or a flat, soft surface such as a dirt road or golf course fairway.

Fartlek

One more method for developing aerobic power is *fartlek*, which is a Swedish word meaning "speed play." Fartlek combines continuous and interval training in an unstructured format. As its name suggests, the method involves playful running, varying the pace and duration of repeated surges according to how one is feeling or how teammates are responding. Fartlek sessions are ideally held in natural settings, such as parks and forest trails. Runners training on their own might use natural landmarks to decide how long and fast to surge. If they feel like an all-out sprint to a tree 200 meters away, they should go for it. They might follow the sprint with a longer, controlled effort to reach a turn 800 meters down the trail. Fartlek is great for learning how to control pace and effort. Also, when the duration of a session exceeds 15 minutes and the surges are sufficiently fast (at least 5,000-meter race pace), runners can expect big gains in aerobic power. In addition, fartlek can be a lot of fun. A team of runners can take turns leading the surges without announcing when they'll begin and how long they'll go. Fartlek develops varied pacing skills and the mental toughness required to cover surges in races.

Sometimes, however, the unstructured nature of fartlek can be a drawback because the coach can't control the training load for each athlete. As a result, some runners may work too easy, or worse, some may work too hard. In a more structured version of fartlek, the coach dictates the duration of surges and recovery intervals by blowing a whistle. For example, during a continuous 25-minute run, one sharp blast of the whistle cues the runners to begin a surge at 1-mile race pace and to hold the pace until the next whistle sounds. Two sharp blasts signals surging at a 3,000-meter race pace, and three sharp blasts signals a 5,000-meter race pace. When the runners have surged long enough, the coach blows the whistle again to signal a recovery jog.

Developing Anaerobic Fitness

Races between 800 and 5,000 meters can max out the aerobic energy system, creating a significant demand for anaerobic energy. In an 800-meter race, for example, up to 40 percent of energy needs may be supplied through the anaerobic pathway

Pointers for Parents

Because this chapter focuses on preparing runners for competition, much of the information speaks directly to the concerns of coaches and the athletes themselves. Nonetheless, parents also play important roles in helping young runners train and compete to the best of their ability. Here are a few pointers that parents can follow to ensure positive outcomes of race-specific training and competition:

- **Add extra carbohydrate to postworkout meals.**

  From chapter 2, recall that as running intensity (effort and speed) increases, more glycogen—the body's storage form of dietary carbohydrate—is burned to fuel muscle contractions. Race-specific training takes intensity to the highest levels. As the competitive season approaches and the intensity of training increases, you can help your child recover faster by adding extra carbohydrate to postworkout meals (refer to chapter 3 for serving suggestions).

- **Invest in a pair of racing shoes.**

  For competitions, the only special gear that your child's school or club might not provide is a pair of racing shoes. They are lighter and less cushioned than training shoes, and they have less arch support. The bottoms of racing shoes are either flat or have spikes in the forefoot. Most elite distance runners wear spikes on grassy cross country courses and rubberized tracks. However, racing shoes can be expensive, and for most young runners, a good pair of racing flats will suffice for both cross country and track (refer to chapter 5 for more advice on buying running shoes).

- **Keep learning about competitive running.**

  If you want to be involved in your child's running, it helps to know about the competitive aspects of cross country and track. To learn more, you might read books and magazine articles about the racing strategies of professional runners. Or, watch world-class performances on television or on the Internet. As a spectator, you might be interested to learn how to calculate split times and figure out whether your child is on pace for setting performance goals. The more you learn about competitive running, the better position you'll be in to support your child.

- **Find out about your child's expectations and needs for support.**

  If you're a parent reading this book, you obviously want to fully support your child in achieving performance goals. Consider, however, that your willingness might not exactly match your child's expectations and needs. How much does your child want to share with you about goals for races and progress in training? The answer may depend on your child's main motives for running, which might not necessarily be oriented toward peak performance. Does your child want you to come to races? And are you welcome to cheer? Some young athletes get nervous when parents are in the stands, whereas others feel disappointed when their parents aren't there. The only way to know the answers to these sorts of questions is to ask your child. Opening up the lines of communication always results in the best outcomes.

(see table 2.1 in chapter 2). As discussed in chapter 2, all distance races require anaerobic energy to fuel midrace surges, uphill climbs, and finishing sprints. Under these conditions lactic acid accumulates rapidly, and unless the runner has trained her body to clear and buffer the lactic acid, she will fatigue and slow at critical points in races.

Anaerobic interval training conditions the body and mind to defy fatigue during maximal effort, such as an 800-meter race or a last-lap sprint in a longer race. Sometimes called *speed-endurance training*, anaerobic intervals emphasize running fast when really tired. The physiological effects of this method help the body buffer and clear lactic acid from the muscles. Because this form of training requires running close to maximal speed, sessions should be held on smooth and firm surfaces, such as a track or a level grassy field.

Table 7.4 shows sample anaerobic interval training sessions for the start of the preparation period. Repetitions range from 200 to 800 meters, depending on the athlete's development and event specialty. The number of repetitions in a session ranges from two to eight, and the total volume is relatively short, ranging between 600 and 3,200 meters. We recommend running each repetition 5 to 15 percent faster than race pace for 1,600 meters. If, for example, a runner's goal for 1,600 meters is 5:28 (an average of 82 seconds per 400 meters), he should run his 400-meter repetitions in 70 to 78 seconds. By training faster than race pace, runners develop a physical and mental sense of reserve speed. As a result, race pace will feel relatively easy.

Each repetition should exhaust the runner so that continuing for another 100 meters at the goal pace wouldn't be possible. Between repetitions, they should

Table 7.4   Sample Sessions: Anaerobic Interval Training

Duration of repetitions: 200-800 meters
Intensity: 5-15% faster than race pace for 1,500-1,600 meters; 100% of HRmax
Frequency: 2-8 repetitions
Recovery: Run-to-recovery ratios of 1:2-1:4
Total volume per session: Approximately 0.3-2 miles (600-3,200 meters)

	Sample Sessions for the Early Preparation Period		
Event specialty	**Beginner** CA[a] = 12-14 TA[b] = 0-2	**Intermediate** CA = 14-16 TA = 2-4	**Advanced** CA = 16-18 TA = 4-6
800 m	3 × 200 m, or 1 × 300 m and 1 × 200 m	4 × 200 m, or 2 × 300 m and 1 × 200 m	5 × 200 m, or 3 × 300 m
1,500 m to 1 mi	4 × 200 m, or 1 × 300 m and 3 × 200 m	3 × 300 m, or 2 × 300 m and 2 × 200 m	3 × 400 m, or 3 × 300 m and 2 × 200 m
3,000-5,000 m and cross country	3 × 400 m, or 2 × 500 m	4 × 400 m, or 2 × 600 m and 2 × 200 m	4 × 500 m, or 1 × 600 m and 3 × 400 m

[a]CA = chronological age in years

[b]TA = training age in years

take as much recovery as needed, jogging or walking, to be able to run the next repetition on target pace. As a general guideline, the run-to-recovery ratio ranges from 1:2 to 1:4. For example, in a session of 4 × 400 meters in which the runner covers each 400 in 70 seconds, the recovery period should last between 2:20 (1:2) and 4:40 (1:4). Although the repetitions should be exhausting, they shouldn't cause the runner's form to fall apart. If that happens, the coach should increase the recovery period to allow complete rest.

The sample sessions in table 7.4 show how anaerobic interval training progresses over time. From season to season and year to year, repetition distance and session volume should increase gradually. The most important element of progression is to run the repetitions at faster speeds. For example, at a training age of three years, a 15-year-old boy might be able to run 3 × 400 meters with five minutes of recovery in an average of 68 seconds. At age 17, the same athlete might improve his average to 61 to 62 seconds.

Anaerobic fitness training progresses within a season as the number of repetitions and the total volume of sessions increase. For example, intermediate-level 3,200-meter runners might start out with a session of 4 × 400 meters. As the competition period approaches, they might be able to handle 6 or 7 × 400 meters.

Developing Race-Specific Fitness: Putting It All Together

The fitness capacities described in this chapter and in chapter 6 are like individual building blocks of a large structure. Training to develop only one or a few capacities won't help runners build the all-around fitness needed for peak racing performance. Effective programs for young runners build each essential fitness capacity to its fullest—one by one. As you'll learn in chapter 9, most daily training sessions should concentrate on developing only one or two fitness capacities. Over time, the best programs gradually incorporate all of the methods in the right proportions for complete physical and mental fitness. On occasion, however, it's ideal to use training methods that stress many, or all, of the essential capacities simultaneously. These methods are race-specific interval training and time trials (practice races).

Race-Specific Interval Training

Race-specific interval training involves running at goal race pace over total distances similar to the athlete's event specialty. Each repetition should be relatively long, at least one-third of the race distance. Take the example of a runner with a goal of 4:45 for 1,500 meters. In a race-specific interval session, he might do 3 × 500 meters at goal pace (1:35 for each 500). Another sample session for this athlete is 2 × 700 meters in 2:13. In addition to running at goal race pace, these sessions are race specific because the recovery between repetitions is very short, only 20 to 60 seconds, or just enough time for the athletes to catch their breath and go again.

Preparing for Race-Specific Training Sessions

Race-specific training methods require special preparation because they are so demanding and essential for reaching the highest levels of fitness. Runners should take the necessary steps to restore a high level of energy at least a day or two before a race-specific session. This means using recovery methods such as easy jogging and light stretching to reduce muscle soreness and tightness. It also means eating high-carbohydrate meals to ensure adequate glycogen levels. Immediately before the race-specific session, runners should perform a warm-up complete with jogging, flexibility exercises, and technique strides. It's also good practice to warm up in training shoes and then put on racing flats or spikes for the session, especially for anaerobic intervals, race-specific intervals, and time trials. Lightweight racing shoes can make a big difference in running mechanics and economy, but they obviously don't offer the support and shock absorption of training shoes. By wearing racing shoes in race-specific training sessions, runners condition the muscles and connective tissue in their feet and lower legs to withstand the greater impact.

The sample race-specific interval sessions in table 7.5 are for the beginning of the preparation period for a competitive season. The total session volume is less than that of the event specialty. For example, a 3,000-meter runner might do an

Table 7.5 Sample Sessions: Race-Specific Interval Training

Duration of repetitions: 1/3-1/2 of event specialty
Intensity: Race pace
Frequency: 2-4 repetitions
Recovery: 20-60 seconds
Total volume per session: 60-100% of event specialty

	Sample Sessions for the Early Preparation Period		
Event specialty	Beginner CA[a] = 12-14 TA[b] = 0-2	Intermediate CA = 14-16 TA = 2-4	Advanced CA = 16-18 TA = 4-6
800 m	2 × 300 m with 60 s recovery	2 × 300 m with 45 s recovery	2 × 300 m with 30 s recovery
1,500 m to 1 mi	2 × 500 m with 60 s recovery	2 × 500 m with 45 s recovery	2 × 500 m with 45 s recovery
3,000-5,000 m and cross country	2 × 1,000 m with 60 s recovery[c] 2 × 1,500 m with 60 s recovery[d]	2 × 1,000 m with 60 s recovery[c] 2 × 1,500 m with 60 s recovery[d]	2 × 1,000 m with 60 s recovery[c] 2 × 2,000 m with 60 s recovery[d]

[a]CA = chronological age in years

[b]TA = training age in years

[c]Session for 3,000- to 3,200-meter specialist

[d]Session for 5,000-meter specialist

Paul Baur

Pine Crest School
Fort Lauderdale, Florida

Paul Baur serves as the program director and head coach of cross country and track at Pine Crest School in Fort Lauderdale, Florida. In his first three years at Pine Crest (2012-2014), the boys' and girls' high school cross country teams captured five district titles and two regional titles, and the girls' team finished second in two consecutive state championships. In track, Baur's Pine Crest teams won five district titles, and the girls' team finished third in two state championships. Before taking the position at Pine Crest, Baur coached at Westminster Academy (Fort Lauderdale, Florida) for seven years. Over this period, he coached 73 district champions, 22 regional champions, 9 state runners-up, 5 state champions, and 96 All-State athletes. Baur also earned the Broward County Coach of the Year honor six times.

What are some of your favorite race-specific workouts for high school runners?—We design our favorite workouts to simulate the challenges our runners will face in championship meets. As an example, our state cross country meet is held in North Florida, in Tallahassee, on a hilly course. The "wall" is a steep 100-meter hill that the runners have to go up and over twice. We don't have hills in South Florida, so we do our hill training on bridges. Our favorite is a bridge in Fort Lauderdale that's 400 meters from bottom to top—so, it's 800 meters from one end, up and over, to the other end. This is how we prepare our athletes for throwing in surges throughout a cross country race, even on the hills. One of our favorite hill workouts involves continuous running with surges over varying distances as we run up the bridge. Most important, we have our runners surge all the way to the top of the hill and through the flat part before the downhill starts. Most young runners give the effort to reach the top of a hill, but then they immediately relax on the flat part. Our approach is to grind out the hill and then surge hard when it flattens out. Having trained for this surging tactic, our runners break away from competitors before the downhill.

To prepare for championship races in track season, we like to do varying distance interval training. For a midseason workout, we might do three sets of 700, 500, 300, and 150 meters. We run the 700- and 500-meter repetitions at mile race pace and the 300- and 150-meter repetitions at 800-meter race pace. We do a continuous roll-on recovery, which means gradually slowing after each repetition and then building up the speed leading into the next one. The roll-on distance might be 300 meters after the 700- and 500-meter repetitions and 200 meters after the 300- and 150-meter repetitions. This method really forces our athletes to continue to give a hard effort throughout the workout. At the end of the set, they have to dig deep and give close to maximal effort when they are already tired—it's just like throwing in a surge at the end of a race. Between sets, we take three to five minutes of walking, some jogging, and a break for water before the next set.

How do you incorporate mental training into race-specific workouts?—I really believe in a variety of methods for mental training. In cross country, we spend a lot of time talking with our athletes about strategies for running different courses. Our kids are smart, but we still have to teach them the best ways to run a course. This planning makes our runners confident going into a cross country race—they feel like they have an advantage over their competitors. We also do a lot of pace work through interval training and tempo runs. These workouts help our runners feel comfortable at their goal pace for races.

In track, we prepare our athletes to be mentally and physically ready for multiple events in a single meet. Our state meet in Florida takes place on one day, so our kids might run the 4 × 800-meter relay, the 1,600, and the 3,200 all in a span of eight hours. To be mentally prepared for the biggest stage at the state meet, they must accomplish this challenge before they get there. So, in meets leading up to state, we have our athletes compete in multiple races—for example, the 400 and 800, the 800 and 3,200, or the 3,200 and 4 × 400 relay—with relatively little time between them.

We also like to simulate the demands of different parts of races. To mentally and physically prepare our runners for fast starts, we might begin a workout with some 50-meter accelerations or a fast 300-meter run. Also, to simulate racing tactics, in interval sessions we might start a repetition in lanes and have our runners cut in at the break line to practice proper breaking in the first 200 meters of a race. Or to prepare athletes for fast finishes, we'll have them start behind teammates and run them down over the course of a repetition.

In interval training sessions, how do you determine the duration of the recovery period between repetitions?—Years ago, a coach told me that younger athletes, especially girls, can't handle jogging between reps and should walk instead. But the more I read and hear from leading coaches and sport scientists, the more I believe that even the youngest, least experienced, and least fit runners should use the active roll-on recovery method. Still, I do consider training age, fitness levels, the point in the season, and racing goals in everything we do. If I think an athlete would benefit most from continuous effort, I shorten the total distance of a workout and the distance of repetitions, and we incorporate some jogging and walking for the recovery. That's usually how we start the season. As the season progresses, the distances get longer. At the end of track season, when we're preparing for championship meets, we run shorter repetitions close to race pace, and we take more recovery time between reps. Our athletes hit their goal times for the reps, and they feel comfortable jogging between them because we've taken that approach to recovery in early-season training.

How do you individualize race-specific training?—One of our approaches to individualizing training is to have our girls cover shorter total distances than our boys even though they race the same distances. With our girls, we're more cautious with volume because they can be at greater risk for injury, especially stress fractures. Also, over the years I've found that some girls don't respond well to short, high-intensity interval training. These athletes race faster with more tempo training. I really listen to my athletes

Paul Baur *(continued)*

when they talk about which training methods make them feel strongest. We also split our runners into training groups based on their natural inclinations for distance running and their event specialties. For cross country, we might have kids come out who, in the upcoming track season, will specialize in the 300-meter intermediate hurdles, the 400, or the 800. We limit their overall volume and have them do shorter repetitions in interval workouts, and we find that they still perform their best in cross country.

---

initial session of 2 × 1,000 meters. Over the course of the preparation period, the total volume might increase from 60 to 100 percent of the target racing distance. In this progression, distance is added to a base speed, building the race from pieces to cover longer and longer distances at goal pace.

Time Trials (Practice Races)

As the competitive season approaches, there's no better way for runners to both develop and test their competitive fitness than to do time trials, or practice races. Several weeks before the competitive season, for example, a 3,000-meter runner might do a 1,500-meter or 2,000-meter time trial. Or, the runner could do a series of time trials at distances both shorter and longer than 3,000 meters.

In addition to conditioning the body for racing, time trials are a great way to develop mental fitness through practicing pacing strategies and race tactics. No matter what the outcome, time trials can boost confidence and motivation. If athletes hit their goal times, they confirm that they're on target in preparing for the upcoming competitive season. On the other hand, the disappointment of falling short of goals for time trials can boost motivation to train harder and perform better next time. In addition, easing up on training before time trials and simulating a race warm-up is great practice. The simulated preparation will make runners more comfortable and less nervous in early-season competitions.

Early-season competitions can be designated as practice races for honing pacing skills and tactical strategies. This approach fits nicely into the schedules of high school runners in the United States, who typically have two track meets a week at the season's start. The first meet, often a dual meet in the middle of the week, might be designated as practice for the skill of even-paced racing or the tactic of midrace surges or fast finishing sprints. Then, the second meet, usually a big multiteam competition on the weekend, is for real racing. This approach gives distance runners the opportunity to experiment with various distances and strategies without excessive pressure.

Developing Race-Specific Mental Fitness

We all know that competitive success in distance running heavily depends on peak *mental fitness*, or qualities including self-confidence, motivation, willpower, and pacing and tactical skills. Race-specific training sessions offer perfect opportunities for developing these qualities. Key methods, described in the following sections, are mindfulness training, pace work, and tactical practice.

Mindfulness Training

In chapter 4 we introduced mindfulness training as directing awareness and attention to internal (body) and external cues. We gave an example of a 25-minute training run in which runners are instructed to be mindful of different cues in successive five-minute segments. As you may recall, these were the sounds of breathing; feelings of any tension in the shoulders, neck, and face; the mechanics of arm and upper body movements; the position of the feet on landing and the action of the lower legs on propulsion and takeoff; and awareness of the running form and breathing sounds of teammates. The objectives of mindfulness training are to deepen awareness of what's going on in the present moment, and to make appropriate adjustments in form, pacing, and tactics.

We strongly recommend that coaches regularly integrate mindfulness training into race-specific sessions. During an aerobic interval session on the track, for example, the coach can direct runners to take inventory of body cues: *How's your breathing? Relaxed or too hard? Are you extending at your ankle joint when you push off the ground? Do you feel any tension in your shoulders?* Then, when trouble spots are identified, runners should make the necessary adjustments. For example, if they hear and feel themselves taking heavy, plodding steps, they can try to adjust the stiffness of their leg muscles for a springier stride. Or, if their shoulders are riding up to their ears, they can lower and relax them. Through regular mindfulness training, runners develop the ability to naturally attend to relevant cues in competition.

Pace Work

More than any other aspect of mental fitness, skill in pacing separates elite runners from average runners. Runners with good pacing skill have a deep awareness of internal and external cues to gain a sense of how fast they're running. The cues include feelings of muscular effort, breathing intensity, and visual input from objects they are passing. They must then mentally compare all of this sensory information with their memories of what their goal pace should feel and look like. By no means is pacing a simple skill! On top of this complexity, the best runners can perform mental arithmetic to calculate split times and compare them with targets they're shooting for.

Coaches should design race-specific training sessions to support young runners in developing pacing skills such as the ability to calculate split times and make necessary adjustments. Let's say that George's goal for 5,000 meters is 16:15, which calls for 400-meter splits of 78 seconds each. For today, the coach has planned an aerobic interval session on the track: 3 × 1,600 meters at race pace. George's goal pace for each 1,600 is 5:12. As George completes each 400-meter lap, his coach calls out the cumulative time. During the first 1,600 repetition, for example, the coach calls out "78 seconds" for 400 meters and "2:38" for 800 meters. Having studied his pacing chart, George knows that his goal times for the first two laps are 78 and 2:36. So, as he passes 800 meters and hears his split, George mentally calculates how long the last 400 took, and he figures out that he slowed down by two seconds. For an extra challenge, the coach asks George to call out his last 400-meter time as well as the next 400 split he'll need to get back on pace. This exercise actually trains the brain, which ultimately regulates running pace.

In another training method for developing pacing skill, the coach gives feedback by blowing a whistle to indicate target pace at designated distances. For example, suppose a group of runners is doing an anaerobic interval session of 5 × 400 meters with a goal of 68 seconds each. For each 100-meter split, their goal time is 17 seconds. Each 100 is marked by a cone. During the session, the coach blows the whistle every 17 seconds in a 400-meter repetition. The runners have to judge whether to speed up or slow down based on where they are in relation to the cone. This exercise trains runners to associate their efforts with specific paces and to make adjustments when they're off pace.

Tactical Practice

In chapter 4 we described tactical approaches to racing, including even-paced and negative-split running, front running, surging, and kicking. The best way to develop and sharpen these tactics is to practice them in race-specific training sessions. These sessions should focus on specific areas for tactical improvement in each athlete. Take the example of Erica, a 17-year-old whose best events are 800 and 1,600 meters. During last year's track season, Erica was usually among the top runners, in contention for winning most races, until the last 200 meters. She had a pattern of fading over the last 200 and giving up several seconds to her competitors. For the upcoming track season, the coach is planning race-specific workouts with the objective of improving Erica's finishing kick. In aerobic interval sessions, for instance, the coach will adjust Erica's split times so that she must sprint

Active Rest as a Training Method

Earlier in the book we pointed out that physiological adaptations to distance training actually occur during rest and recovery periods, such as during sleep or the day after an intense workout. Of course, proper nutrition and adequate rest are keys to restoring energy and improving physiological capacities. However, positive adaptations to training can be accelerated with methods of active rest. Examples are 20- to 30-minute sessions of easy jogging, cycling, or swimming. Active rest might also involve stretching, massage, a cold treatment with ice packs or an ice whirlpool, or a hot treatment with heating pads. These methods increase the rate of blood flow to the muscles, restoring energy and providing nutrients for regeneration. Coaches should plan methods of active rest following every high-intensity training session. For methods such as massage and cold or heat therapy, coaches should seek guidelines from the school or club athletic trainer.

all-out over the final 200 meters to achieve her goal times for each repetition. In other interval workouts, the coach will instruct Erica to deliberately run three to five seconds behind her teammates until the last 200 meters, where she will be challenged to sprint and catch up. Creative approaches to practicing racing tactics can be tailored for runners who need to improve their front-running, surging, and negative-split tactical skills.

Striding Ahead

To help you remember the details of race-specific training, we've summarized the methods in table 7.6. Race-specific methods spark major improvements in performance when applied correctly. Remember, however, that because they can maximally stress the runner's body, coaches must apply these methods with caution. Successful implementation depends on having a strong foundation of general fitness and progressively increasing training loads over time. Now that you've learned about the general and race-specific training methods, you're ready for the first steps of designing training programs: assessing the runner's readiness and setting racing and training goals.

Table 7.6   Methods for Developing Race-Specific Fitness

Method	Intensity	Duration	Frequency (number of repetitions)	Recovery	Total volume
Interval tempo running	80-85% of HRmax	3-10 min per repetition	2-10	30-90 s	2-6 miles (3,200-10,000 m)
Continuous tempo running	80-85% of HRmax	12-40 min	1	None	2-6 miles (3,200-10,000 m)
Aerobic intervals	85-95% of HRmax; 3,000 to 5,000 m race pace	600 m to 1 mile per repetition	2-10	Run-to-recovery ratios of 1:0.5, 1:1, or 1:1.5	0.75-5 miles (1,200-8,000 m)
Anaerobic intervals	5-15% faster than 1-mile race pace	200-800 m per repetition	2-8	Run-to-recovery ratios of 1:2 to 1:4	0.3-2 miles (600-3,200 m)
Race-specific intervals	Race pace	1/3-1/2 of event specialty per repetition	2-4	20-60 s	60-100% of event specialty
Time trials	Race pace	50-200% of event specialty	1	None	50-200% of event specialty

8

Program Building

Training for young distance runners is like a long journey. Of course, instead of cars, buses, or planes, the vehicles are the training methods described in chapters 6 and 7. Just like planning a trip, designing a training program requires figuring out how to get from here to there. In our case, the landmarks are an athlete's current level of fitness and ultimate performance goals for an upcoming season. Our approach to planning training programs involves the five-step process illustrated in figure 8.1. This chapter covers the first two steps: (1) assessing starting fitness level and training, racing, and health history for each athlete and (2) setting racing and training goals. Coaches who take these steps can confidently determine the best training methods and loads for their runners.

Step 1: Assess Starting Fitness and Review History

Before beginning any journey, it's best to take stock of your starting point. For coaches, this means evaluating each runner's initial fitness level and training, racing, and health history. This information is essential for setting appropriate goals, choosing the best training methods, and determining how to progressively increase training loads. The following sections outline a comprehensive approach to this first step in designing a training program. The process requires a good record-keeping system. We provide an athlete assessment form that coaches can use as is, perhaps by reproducing it in a computer spreadsheet, or adapt to their needs and purposes. Note that the form includes the term *macrocycle*, which refers to one complete season of cross country or track.

The best time to assess the starting points for runners is at least a few weeks before training begins. The sooner coaches complete the assessments, the more time they will have for planning the details of their training programs.

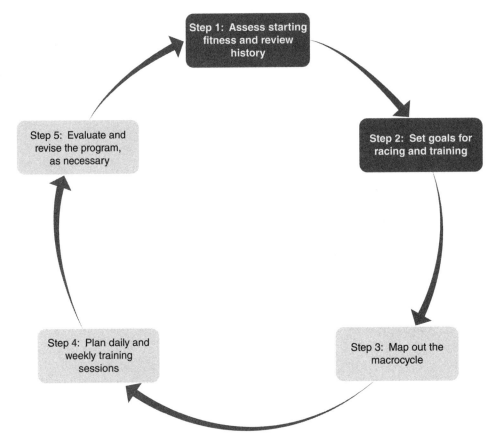

Figure 8.1 Five-step process for designing training programs. This chapter addresses the first two steps.

Developmental Status

Section I of the athlete assessment form provided in this chapter is for recording a runner's developmental status. One of the key items is training age, which we defined in chapter 1 as the number of years an athlete has trained regularly for distance running. An awareness of training age helps coaches make their programs progressive, ensuring that their runners improve from season to season. They can use training age to set limits on distances to cover in workouts and races. Training age also helps coaches decide which methods to use now and which to delay until later for certain athletes. For example, to develop strength endurance, we recommend that runners whose training age is less than two years do circuit training before progressing to more strenuous weight training.

Other developmental factors are height, weight, and body composition. Changes in these measures since the previous assessment must be noted. For instance, if a boy has grown several inches over a single summer, his training program should be adapted accordingly. He'll need to do extra technique and strength-endurance training to better control his longer limbs. To avoid injuries associated with rapid

Athlete Assessment Form

Name: _____

Date: _____ Date of last assessment: _____

I. Developmental Status

Chronological age: _____ years _____ months

Training age: _____ years _____ months

Height: _____ Weight: _____ Body fat %: _____

Change since last assessment:

Height: _____ Weight: _____ Body fat %: _____

II. Current Fitness Assessment

Flexibility

	Poor 1	2	3	4	Excellent 5	Comments
Hip flexors						
Hamstrings						
Calves						

Strength Endurance

Exercise	Score (number of repetitions)
Push-up	
Curl-up	
Chin-up (unassisted)	
Dip (unassisted)	

Technique

	Poor 1	2	3	4	Excellent 5	Comments
Upper-body posture						
Arm action						
Foot strike						
Action of the leg joints on landing						
Knee lift						

Aerobic Power

$\dot{V}O_2$max (if lab testing is available): _____

Longest continuous aerobic run from previous macrocycle (season): _____

3,000-meter time trial: _____

From L. Greene and R. Pate, 2015, *Training Young Distance Runners*, 3rd ed. (Champaign, IL: Human Kinetics).

Anaerobic Fitness and Speed

Time trial distance	Time
60 meters	
100 meters	
400 meters	

Race-Specific Physical Fitness

Time trial distance	Time

Race-Specific Mental Fitness

	Poor 1	2	3	4	Excellent 5	Comments
Motivation						
Confidence						
Concentration						
Ability to relax						
Pacing skill						
Tactical skill						

III. Training History: Summary of the Previous Macrocycle

Dates of the previous macrocycle: _____ to _____

	General preparation	Specific preparation	Pre-competition	Main competition
Training units Average number of units per week				
Strength endurance Average duration of circuit training sessions per week				
Average load lifted in weight training sessions per week				
Hill running: average volume per week				
Cardiorespiratory fitness Continuous aerobic running: average volume per week				
Continuous aerobic running: average pace per mile or kilometer				
Aerobic fitness Tempo running: average volume per week				
Tempo running: average pace per mile or kilometer				
Aerobic intervals: average volume per week				

(continued)

Training History *(continued)*

	General preparation	Specific preparation	Pre-competition	Main competition
Aerobic intervals: average pace per mile or kilometer				
Anaerobic fitness Anaerobic intervals: average volume per week				
Anaerobic intervals: average pace per mile or kilometer				
Race-specific physical fitness Time trials and practice races: average volume per week				
Time trials and practice races: average pace per mile or kilometer				
Highest volume of running in a week				
Average volume of running per week				

IV. Racing History

Personal Records

Event	Time	Date	Meet	Comments
800 meters				
1,500 meters				
1,600 meters				
1 mile				
3,000 meters				
3,200 meters				
2 miles				
5,000 meters				

Performances From Previous Macrocycle

Date	Meet	Event	Time	Place	Comments

V. Health History

Type of injury, illness, or medical concern	Period of injury, illness, or medical concern	Comments

From L. Greene and R. Pate, 2015, *Training Young Distance Runners*, 3rd ed. (Champaign, IL: Human Kinetics).

growth, he should maintain or even reduce his volume of continuous aerobic running and race-specific training until his growth stabilizes.

Our athlete assessment form includes places for recording weight and body fat composition. These measures can guide decisions about whether to alter a runner's diet for better health and performance. However, the measurement of body fat composition requires special instruments and expertise. In addition, any ensuing dietary advice should come from a qualified health professional, such as a physician or a licensed sport nutrition expert. Under no circumstances should a coach without such qualifications advise runners to change their diets for weight loss or gain. A coach who has strong concerns that a runner's weight is negatively affecting her health should talk with the runner's parents. If they have similar concerns, the coach should recommend that they seek advice from a qualified health professional.

We have not included biological maturation on the athlete assessment form. Like body fat composition, an accurate assessment of maturation, or biological age, requires expertise beyond the scope of this book. The best measurement of maturation, skeletal age, involves X-raying the bones to determine how much they have ossified, or hardened. However, coaches can get a sense of each athlete's maturation by observing some of the hallmarks of pubertal change (see table 1.1 in chapter 1). Obvious changes in secondary sex characteristics, such as lowering of the voice in males and breast development in females, indicate that puberty is underway.

Starting Fitness Levels

Chapters 6 and 7 describe training methods for developing 10 fitness capacities: flexibility, mobility, strength endurance, neuromuscular fitness, technical skill, cardiorespiratory fitness, aerobic power, anaerobic fitness, race-specific physical fitness, and race-specific mental fitness. By assessing each runner's entry level of fitness in these areas, coaches can identify which training methods to emphasize in each runner's program (see section II of the athlete assessment form). For some fitness capacities, the most objective tests are administered by exercise physiologists in the laboratory. The best measure of aerobic power, for example, is a $\dot{V}O_2$max test on a treadmill. Because most coaches don't have access to this type of testing, we suggest more practical fitness tests in the following sections.

Flexibility

The muscle groups that tend to be tight in distance runners are the hip flexors, hamstrings, and calves. The hip flexors, which cross the hip joints in front of the body, are responsible for swinging the legs forward and lifting the knees in the running stride. The hamstrings, which cross the hip and knee joints on the backs of the legs, flex the knees during the swing phase and extend the hips at the end of the swing phase and during the stance and takeoff phases. The calf muscles are stretched upon foot strike, creating elastic energy, and they generate propulsive force during takeoff. Excessive tightness in these three muscle groups can negatively affect stride mechanics and cause injuries. Tests of flexibility in these and other muscle groups for runners should be administered by a qualified athletic trainer or physical therapist. The results can then be used to develop an effective and safe stretching routine.

Strength Endurance

Coaches should evaluate runners' strength endurance when designing circuit and weight training sessions. This involves determining the maximum number of repetitions of circuit and weight training exercises that runners can do before fatiguing and losing form (see the instructions for determining repetition maximum values, or RM, in chapter 6).

Coaches can use strength-endurance tests to identify areas for improvement and to determine whether athletes are developing strength endurance progressively. For example, an athlete who can do only 15 abdominal curl-ups in the assessment before a cross country season will benefit from extra circuit training to develop the abdominal muscles. If the athlete improves to 35 curl-ups in next year's assessment, she and her coach will be confident that the extra training paid off.

Technical Skill

The assessment form includes five features of running biomechanics, which coaches can evaluate to plan technique training. Refer to the technique tips in chapter 5 for details on how to identify strengths and weaknesses in these aspects of form.

Aerobic Power

The best assessment of aerobic power, a $\dot{V}O_2$max test conducted in an exercise physiology lab, isn't an option for most youth programs. A 3,000-meter time trial is a field test that correlates with lab measures of $\dot{V}O_2$max, because running at race pace for 3,000 meters maximally stresses the aerobic system. However, one concern about using a time trial to assess changes in aerobic power is that external factors, such as the weather, can influence performance. If the current assessment is based on a time trial in poor conditions—say, it's hotter and windier than the day of the previous time trial—a false sense of the athlete's aerobic power could result. Therefore, coaches should be cautious when interpreting time trial results.

Anaerobic Fitness and Speed

Assessment of anaerobic fitness and speed is useful for determining whether runners would benefit from more anaerobic training and speed development. In addition, this evaluation guides decisions about which events runners should specialize in during track season. We recommend a 400-meter time trial because it requires a substantial amount of energy from the anaerobic pathway. For runners with relatively slow 400-meter times, coaches should design progressive training to develop anaerobic fitness and speed. Such training helps slower runners even if they specialize in the longer events, such as 3,000 and 5,000 meters. Training for faster runners might need to emphasize building more endurance to maintain their speed. Distance runners with fast 400-meter times have the potential to excel at 800- and 1,500-meter races.

Coaches might also want to test strictly for speed, especially for 800-meter specialists. For this purpose, time trials for 60 and 100 meters are useful.

Race-Specific Physical Fitness

A great way to assess race-specific fitness is a time trial held a few weeks before the new training program begins. This test is especially useful for assessing the starting point for beginners who have limited training and racing experience. Coaches can use the results for both planning training sessions and setting racing goals for the upcoming season. Preseason time trials may not be as necessary or useful for intermediate and advanced runners; coaches of these athletes can gain a good sense of their race-specific fitness from their performances in races at the end of the previous season.

Race-Specific Mental Fitness

There are no objective tests for mental fitness in young distance runners. Even so, coaches who have worked with runners for at least a season should have a good sense of their levels of confidence, motivation, concentration, ability to relax, pacing skill, and tactical skill. They can score these capacities on a scale of 1 to 5. Again, scores on the low end indicate areas for improvement through well-targeted training.

Training History

Section III of the athlete assessment form is for summarizing the volume and intensity of training from the previous cross country or track season. Recall that a complete season is called a *macrocycle*. This term comes from a systematic approach to planning training called *periodization*, which is detailed in chapter 9. For now, note that periodization involves dividing up a macrocycle into phases. Our approach divides a macrocycle into four phases of preparation and competition:

- General preparation
- Specific preparation
- Precompetition
- Main competition

Coaches can use records from the previous macrocycle to decide how much to increase training loads in the upcoming macrocycle. Let's say that Bryce averaged 12 miles (19 km) a week of continuous aerobic running during the general preparation phase of the last cross country season. For the upcoming season, the coach might increase Bryce's average weekly volume to 15 or 16 miles (24 or 26 km) during this phase.

Here are some guidelines for recording training history in section III.

- **Average number of training units per week.** A training unit simply refers to the use of a given method in a daily workout. For example, if a runner stretched and performed technique drills on a Tuesday, she completed two units—one for flexibility and one for technique. To record this item in the assessment form, add up the number of units an athlete completed in each training phase, and divide by the number of weeks in the phase.

- **Average duration of circuit training sessions per week.** For each training phase, add up the time taken to complete each circuit training session and divide by the number of weeks.

- **Average load lifted in weight training sessions per week.** First, calculate the load lifted in a single weight training session by multiplying the number of repetitions of an exercise by the load lifted. For example, if the athlete performed 12 bench press repetitions with a 50-pound (22.7 kg) load, the total for that exercise would be 600 pounds (12 × 50 = 600). After figuring the load lifted for each exercise, add them up. To reduce this sum to a more manageable number, divide it by 2,000 pounds (1 ton), which gives you a measure of the weight lifted. Then, average the loads for all sessions by dividing by the number of weeks in the training phase.

- **Average running volume and intensity per week.** For each of the running methods (continuous aerobic running, tempo running, aerobic intervals, anaerobic intervals, and so on), add up the miles, kilometers, or minutes covered in each phase and divide this total by the number of weeks. Then, for runs timed on marked courses or on tracks, calculate the average pace per mile or kilometer.

As you can see, assessing training history requires keeping detailed daily records. On the following pages, we present sample logs that coaches can use to quickly summarize daily and weekly training sessions. The sample log for recording daily sessions shows the volume and intensity of a continuous tempo run for a runner named Kelsey. The workout for the day was a 20-minute continuous tempo run at 80 percent of Kelsey's maximal heart rate (206 bpm), or 165 bpm. Kelsey covered 2.7 miles at an average pace of 7:20 per mile. The coach's comments at the bottom of the form show that the session went well. Kelsey's tempo run is recorded in a weekly summary. The coach can calculate weekly totals for each training method at the bottom of this form. Then, use these weekly totals to determine the average training loads to record on the athlete assessment form.

The record keeping involved in the assessments we've covered takes a lot time and detailed work. We have a few suggestions for making the process organized and efficient. Coaches can record daily training results for their runners using a standard spreadsheet program on a computer. Another option is for runners to record their own training and deliver their logs to the coach every week or two. Runners who keep their own training logs draw motivation from reflecting

---

Sample Log for Recording Daily Training

Name: *Kelsey*

Date: *Monday, March 21*

Method: *Continuous tempo running*

Planned session: *1 x 20 minutes at 80% HRmax (165 bpm)*

Total volume:

Distance: *2.7 miles*

Duration: *20 minutes*

Intensity:

Average pace per mile: *7:20*

Comments: *Handled the session easily and in good form. Pretty even pace the whole way. Heart rate was 168 at the end of the run.*

---

on the written records of their hard work and improvement. It's inspiring and fun for runners to look back at challenging workouts in which they performed well. For more inspiration and guidance, runners can fill their training logs with motivational sayings and tips from running magazines and books. In addition, by regularly reviewing their training and racing histories, runners gain insight into training methods that lead to their best competitive results.

Racing History

Section IV of the athlete assessment form is for recording information about personal records and race results from the previous season. There are two main reasons for keeping racing history records. First, the coach and athlete can use this information to set performance goals for the upcoming season. Second, the records can reveal performance patterns and reasons for both good and disappointing outcomes. For example, by examining a runner's times from the previous track season, the coach can determine strengths and weaknesses in the training program. Take the example of a runner whose 1,500-meter times dropped consistently over the season (4:48, 4:42, 4:37, and 4:34). Looking back on these race results, the coach should feel confident that last season's training resulted in steady improvement, leading to the athlete's best performances at the end of the season, in championship meets. In contrast, if the runner's times had slowed as the season progressed (4:38, 4:45, 4:46, and 4:50), the coach would wonder why. Did the runner burn out because the training was too intense at the start of last season? Or did the program lack sufficient race-specific training for improvement? This sort of questioning helps coaches make adjustments in their runners' programs for upcoming seasons.

Weekly Training Summary

Name: *Kelsey*

Week of: *March 21-27*

Day	Circuit training	Weight training	Hill running	Continuous aerobic running	Tempo running	Aerobic intervals	Fartlek	Anaerobic intervals	Race-specific intervals or time trials
Monday					20 min at 7:20 pace (2.7 miles)				
Tuesday									
Wednesday									
Thursday									
Friday									
Saturday									
Sunday									
Week totals									

Record training results using the following measures:

Circuit training: duration of session in minutes

Weight training: weight lifted and duration of session in minutes

Hill running: distance covered

Continuous aerobic running: distance covered or duration and pace per mile or kilometer

Tempo running: distance covered or duration and pace per mile or kilometer

Aerobic intervals: distance covered and pace per mile or kilometer

Fartlek: distance covered or duration

Anaerobic intervals: distance covered and pace per mile or kilometer

Race-specific intervals and time trials: distance covered and pace per mile or kilometer

Health History

Section V of the athlete assessment form provides space in which to record information about injuries, illnesses, and other health concerns. Coaches can use this information to adapt programs for injury and illness prevention. Let's say that David's assessment form showed that he strained his calf muscles in both legs during the first few cross country races of the season over the last two years. David's coach hypothesized that the injury might have been caused when David switched running shoes. All summer long he ran in training flats with a high, supportive heel, which didn't stretch the calf muscles. Then, at the start of the racing season, David began wearing his low-heeled spikes in race-specific training sessions and competitions. The sudden change to spikes put extra tension on his calves and might very well have caused his muscle strains. To prevent the injury in the upcoming season, David's coach included more calf-stretching exercises in the program.

Pat Tyson

Gonzaga University
Spokane, Washington

Pat Tyson has the unique distinction of having coached successfully at all levels. Before taking the position of head cross country and track coach at Gonzaga University in 2008, he coached college runners at the University of Oregon and the University of Kentucky. Previously, over a 20-year period, he developed a national-class program at Mead High School in the state of Washington. His cross country teams at Mead qualified for the state championships 18 consecutive years. They won 12 state titles and never placed worse than third. In Tyson's last three years at Mead, his teams placed third, fourth, and fifth at the Nike Cross National Championships. In the 1970s, Tyson ran cross country and track at the University of Oregon, where he competed in three NCAA Cross Country Championships. Tyson is the author of *Coaching Cross Country Successfully*.

What advice do you offer coaches for supporting year-to-year improvement in young runners who excel at an early age?—It's important for coaches to plant the seeds for ensuring progressive improvement. Goals are an important component. In my program, we establish a culture of expectation for all runners on the team to achieve their yearly goals. Take the example of a sensational high school freshman boy who runs 4:30 for the mile. For his sophomore year, we might set a goal of 4:19, and then we'll aim to break 4:10 in his junior year. And we'll see how close we can get to 4:00 in the senior year. We're going to plan specific workouts to achieve these goals. These workouts will plant the seeds of self-trust, confidence, and belief in the coach. I like to simplify workouts to achieve challenging performance goals. I do this by giving my athletes manageable training goals. For example, we break down a 4:30 mile into four 400-meter runs at 67.5 seconds. If the athlete can run this pace as a freshman, in his sophomore year it shouldn't be so difficult to run four 400s in a row at 64.9 seconds, which is sub-4:20 pace. By the athlete's senior year, we would expect to be close to 4:00. So, in interval workouts he would be running 400s in under 60 seconds and repeat 800s in 2:00 with short recovery. With this approach, when kids line up to race, they'll be physically capable of achieving their goals, and they'll have the confidence, too.

What qualities in high school runners best predict success at the college level?—To reach the college level and be successful, high school runners need to have a tremendous amount of desire. My old college coach, the legendary Bill Dellinger, used to say that runners who have talent without desire won't make it to the next level. If they have a little talent and strong desire, they will reach their potential. But when high school runners have both talent and desire, it's scary how much they can achieve. Another key is being a self-starter. In making the transition from high school to college, it's very important for young runners to find a coach they trust and believe in. The runner's success also depends on being able to communicate well with the coach.

To excel at the college level, you don't necessarily need to be a superstar in high school. Great coaches can develop good high school runners into top college runners. On the women's side, for example, a 5:10 or 5:12 high school miler can be developed into a sub-4:50 miler or a 16:00 5,000-meter runner in college. But they need that high level of desire. When you're not as talented as the very best runners, you need to have the mentality of a giant killer.

How do you organize training sessions to meet the needs of elite young runners as well as teammates at lower levels of development, fitness, and talent?—It's not fair to hold the elite runner back to the level of other runners on the team. I've worked hard to build programs with lots of athletes at different levels who can train with others. But if you have one standout who is better than everyone else by far, you can still arrange the workouts so that everyone benefits. You might, for example, have athletes of lesser ability run every other interval with the elite athlete. Or, let's say that the A-level runner is doing repeat 800s. You might have your B group run the first 400 of each repetition with the superstar. The key is to make all the runners feel that they are part of the team and to make sure that each individual gets the necessary training. In interval sessions, that means emphasizing that all runners should train at their own goal race paces. In the best situation, younger kids in the B group will shadow excellence by seeing what the older, more experienced kids in the A group are achieving. When kids in the B group have the desire to train with kids in the A group over time, that's how you get major breakthroughs.

What advice do you offer parents of high school runners who have the potential to earn a scholarship and compete at the college level?—The most important advice for parents is to be careful of the recruiting process. It's easy to get caught up in the hype of collegiate sports, where everybody seems like a superstar. Parents need to understand that there aren't that many scholarships for cross country and track. The first concern for high school runners and their parents should be a good education. Also, you have to do your homework to find a college with a good fit for both academics and athletics. And it's very important to find out what the college coach is really like. How does the coach deal with injured runners? What about class conflicts? Does the coach pressure runners to make athletics more important than academics? Another key point is that parents need to understand their roles, which are to provide love and support, but also to give their children some space to ultimately make the decision about where to go to college.

Pointers for Parents

This chapter covers many factors that determine success in distance running. However, young runners differ in their potential for development in each area. It's important for parents to be aware of differences in key predictors of performance success. They include genetic and psychological factors, coaching effectiveness, and family support.

- **Genetic factors.**

  As described in chapter 2, the physiological determinants of distance-running performance include aerobic power, muscle fiber type, and enzyme activity in the energy pathways. Whereas most physiological factors can be significantly improved through training, their ultimate potential is limited by genetics. Understand, then, that the genes you passed on will play a major role in determining the heights your child reaches in distance running.

- **Motivation and determination to succeed.**

  No matter how gifted runners are genetically, they will not reach their performance potential without superior motivation and determination. Whereas these qualities can be improved through training, they largely come from within the athletes themselves based on their interests, values, and goals. By talking with your daughter or son about these psychological qualities, you can provide the best support.

- **Coaching effectiveness.**

  Throughout this book we've emphasized that distance running success depends on progressive, well-rounded training programs based on sound principles that account for individual differences. The quality of any training program depends on the knowledge, skill, and commitment of the coach. Fortunately, most distance running coaches are knowledgeable and committed to ensuring the best outcomes for their athletes. What should parents do, however, when they have concerns about the ability and credibility of their child's coach? We refer you to the excellent advice of sport psychologist Dr. Greg Dale in chapter 4. He recommends that parents act as consultants for their children, encouraging them to talk directly with the coach about concerns with the training program. If your child asks for advice, Dr. Dale recommends that you "role-play," which means taking the perspective of the coach in responding to how your daughter or son is planning to discuss the situation. This will give your child helpful practice for talking with the coach.

- **Support of family.**

  Never underestimate your influence in shaping your young runner's path to success. When it comes to emotional support, you have the strongest impact through offering encouragement and praise, and helping your child stay grounded in responding to success or dealing with disappointment.

In addition, he worked out a plan for David to start wearing his racing shoes in training sessions earlier in the season, so he could break them in gradually.

Step 2: Set Goals for Racing and Training

In previous chapters we discussed goals as powerful tools for building runners' motivation and confidence. Goals are also essential for guiding coaches as they design training programs. Let's talk now about the goal-setting process and how its products—goals for racing and training—help coaches make sound decisions about training methods and loads.

Racing Goals

Carla is a talented and highly motivated 14-year-old high school freshman. Her training age is two years. Carla's best 1,600-meter time as a 13-year-old was 5:47—excellent for her age. Considering her progressive training to date, Carla's coach sees the potential for her to break 5:00 for 1,600 meters by age 17, during her senior year of high school. It's a goal that Carla is excited about and willing to work hard for. She knows that a sub-5:00 1,600 will earn her a college scholarship, and she wants to keep running after high school. A month before the track season starts, Carla and her coach meet to discuss long-term and short-term racing goals. They begin by setting the long-term goal of 4:55 in four years, a 52-second improvement over Carla's current PR.

Two points are worth noting about Carla's scenario. First, the goal-setting process ideally begins with long-term goals. The stuff of fantastic dreams, long-term goals are powerful motivators. But they also inspire a realistic attitude, helping runners focus on the steps they need to take now to reach their destinations. Second, coaches should involve runners in goal setting. When runners are part of the process, the goals are more personal and motivating.

For Carla, the stepping-stones to running 4:55 for 1,600 meters will be yearly short-term goals. What strategy should Carla and her coach use to set these goals? They could simply divide the total improvement desired by the number of years: 52 seconds ÷ 4 years = 13 seconds per year. Thus, Carla would shoot for 5:34 at age 14, 5:21 at age 15, and so forth. Although this strategy seems sensible, it might not be the best approach considering that most young runners don't improve at a constant rate over the years. That's because improvement is influenced by factors other than training, especially developmental factors such as growth and maturation, which don't necessarily occur in a linear way.

Carla has already experienced many of the maturational changes of puberty. As a result, her coach figures that growth and maturation won't be major factors. Because Carla has been training for only two years, her coach predicts the potential for relatively big chunks of improvement early in her high school career. Considering these factors, Carla and her coach set goals to lower her 1,600 meter time by 18 seconds at age 14 and then by progressively smaller amounts each year thereafter (15, 12, and 7 seconds). They agree on the following goal times:

Age	Goal	Improvement
14	5:29	18 seconds
15	5:14	15 seconds
16	5:02	12 seconds
17	4:55	7 seconds

In all likelihood, Carla won't improve by exactly 18 seconds and run 5:29 in her freshman track season at age 14. She might run a little, or even a lot, faster. Suppose that she runs 5:20 and finds herself 9 seconds ahead of schedule. Fast-forwarding to Carla's sophomore year, would you change her 1,600-meter goal? We recommend keeping the age-15 goal at 5:14 instead of lowering it. Considering the easier challenge for Carla's sophomore year, we would advise the coach to alter her training program slightly, emphasizing improvement in general fitness capacities such as strength endurance and technique. If Carla can run 5:14 at age 15 without putting a lot of extra stress on her body from high-intensity running, she'll leave more room for improvement in her junior and senior years. This approach is based on the principle that young runners should never overtrain to reach their goals. Indeed, for long-term improvement as well as injury prevention, young runners should actually do the *least* stressful training necessary to achieve yearly goals.

In a different scenario, suppose that Carla doesn't reach her goal of 5:29 at age 14. Perhaps she is healthy and has a good year, but runs only 5:36. Carla and her coach must now decide whether 5:14 is within reach when setting goals and planning training for the next year. If reaching her goal means increasing training loads to levels that might cause injury, then it's best to make the goal a bit slower, perhaps 5:20. If Carla can run 5:20 at age 15, she'll still be in reach of her long-term goal and, most important, she'll have taken steps to avoid injury.

The same principles can be used to set place goals. A 14-year-old who placed 64th in the district cross country championships might have dreams of placing in the top 5 by age 18. Before each season, the coach and athlete should work out the progression for reaching this goal. As in setting time goals, they should consider how developmental factors will influence the runner's potential for improving his place finish in various meets.

Training Goals

If long-term racing goals mark the final destination of a runner's journey, training goals are the intermediate checkpoints along the way. Well-planned training goals guide the selection of daily training methods and loads. When setting these goals for individual runners, coaches should consider three main factors: developmental objectives, training history, and racing goals.

Table 8.1 shows training objectives that are based on the developmental principles from chapter 1. These objectives will help coaches select methods that

Table 8.1 Developmentally Based Training Objectives

Training age	Objectives
0 to 2 years	Gain experience using all methods of training, each to a small degree.
	Acquire good technique.
	Build a base of strength endurance and cardiorespiratory fitness.
	Develop the ability to race at an even pace.
2 to 4 years	Refine technique.
	Reinforce strength endurance and cardiorespiratory fitness base.
	Begin to develop race-specific physical fitness by introducing the advanced training methods: tempo running, aerobic intervals, anaerobic intervals, race-specific intervals, and time trials.
	Improve even-pacing skill and begin to sharpen varied-pacing skill.
	Develop the ability to use various racing strategies.
4 to 6 years	Continue using the general methods to develop the fitness base.
	Develop race-specific physical fitness by increasing the volume of advanced training methods.
	Refine racing strategies that work best for the individual.

account for the athlete's maturation, fitness, and experience. Developmentally appropriate training goals for runners up to two years in training age include improving fitness capacities such as strength endurance, cardiorespiratory fitness, and technique. They don't, however, include developing high levels of anaerobic fitness, which is more appropriate for runners over four years in training age.

Each runner's training history, as recorded in step 1 of the program-building process, provides key information for setting training goals for the phases of a macrocycle. For example, the coach might set goals for the following aspects of training:

- Total number of miles or kilometers per week
- Average weekly miles or kilometers for each of the running methods (continuous aerobic running, tempo running, aerobic intervals, and so on)
- Paces (minutes per mile or kilometer) for the various running methods
- Longest continuous aerobic run and tempo run to be attempted
- Average weekly loads of general training methods such as circuit, weight, and technique training

Concrete scientific guidelines don't exist for how much to increase training loads from one macrocycle to the next. However, common sense and a long-range view can guide the way to sound decisions. Take the case of an athlete whose longest continuous aerobic run from the previous macrocycle was 7 miles (11.3 km). A sensible increase in volume for the upcoming macrocycle, one that would support progressive improvement, might be 2 miles (3.2 km). Or, consider a runner who averaged 2:42 in his best aerobic interval session of 4 × 800 meters. In the upcoming macrocycle, this runner might shoot for a goal of averaging 2:36 to 2:38 for 5 × 800 meters.

Of course, the runner's racing goals should influence decisions about optimal training methods and loads. Let's follow up on Carla, the 14-year-old who ran 5:47 for 1,600 meters as a 13-year-old and who is shooting for 5:29 in the upcoming track season. When Carla does race-specific interval training, her goal time for 1,600 meters will be a guide for pacing her repetitions. Carla's race-specific interval training might include the following sessions, all of which are based on the pace required to run 5:29 for 1,600 meters:

- 3 × 500 meters in 1:42 to 1:43 with 45 seconds of recovery
- 2 × 800 meters in 2:44 to 2:45 with 60 seconds of recovery
- 1 × 1,000 meters in 3:24 to 3:26 and 1 × 500 meters in 1:42 to 1:43 with 60 seconds of recovery

We close this section with a very important point about training goals: although they are powerful motivators, they work only when runners understand what it takes to achieve them. Therefore, coaches must clearly communicate the objectives for every training session. This means conveying details about training intensity and target paces.

Striding Ahead

This chapter covered the first two steps to planning an effective training program. The products are a formal assessment of each runner's starting point and a set of goals for racing and training. Together, these form a road map for the runner's training journey. With the starting point, final destination, and intermediate checkpoints clearly defined, coaches and athletes can begin to bridge the gap between these points by refining their travel plans, so to speak. The next steps in the planning process involve detailed mapping and choosing the best vehicles, or training methods, for getting from point to point. That's our focus in chapter 9, in which we explain how to assign appropriate methods for various phases of training and competition.

9

Planning Training

In chapter 8 we took the first two steps in the process of building training programs: (1) assessing runners' starting fitness levels and reviewing their histories and (2) setting goals for training and racing. This chapter focuses on the third and fourth steps in our process: (3) mapping out the macrocycle (season) and (4) planning daily and weekly training sessions (see figure 9.1). Using our travel analogy, these two steps are like making an itinerary for a long journey. Once you've established your starting point and set your sights on your final destination, you're ready to chart your course with details. This includes identifying when you'll begin certain stages of the journey, when you plan to reach important landmarks along the way, and what means of transportation, or training methods, you'll use to go from point to point.

Steps 3 and 4 answer questions such as these:

- When, during a season, should you emphasize certain training methods?
- How much should each method contribute to the total training load as the season progresses?
- How should you alternate and combine training methods from day to day?
- How can you organize training to ensure peak performance in the most important competitions?

In this chapter we help you answer these questions by applying a highly organized approach to planning training, called *periodization*. It's an advanced system that leading coaches use to build complete and progressive programs.

Step 3: Map Out the Macrocycle

Periodization involves dividing an entire training program into shorter periods. Then, for each period, methods and loads are assigned to meet a runner's training

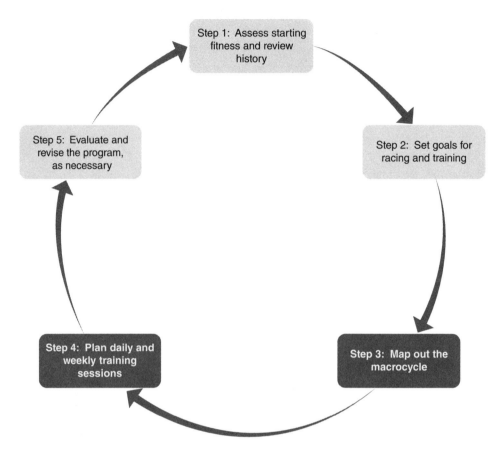

Figure 9.1 Five-step process for designing training programs. This chapter addresses the third and fourth steps.

and racing goals. Figure 9.2, for example, divides a four-year high school career into smaller and smaller periods that are repeated in cycles. As defined in chapter 8, a macrocycle comprises one complete cross country or track season. Our sample macrocycle is divided into three major periods:

- *Preparation,* which emphasizes training
- *Competition,* which focuses on racing
- *Transition,* which provides recovery after the season's final race and before a new season begins

The preparation and competition periods are divided into shorter phases, which consist of three- or four-week cycles of training called *mesocycles.* The next smallest cycle, called a *microcycle,* lasts one to two weeks. Microcycles are made up of *sessions,* or single workouts. Finally, a single session consists of *units,* which are simply training methods such as flexibility exercises, continuous aerobic runs, and weight training. If you're new to learning about periodization, this terminol-

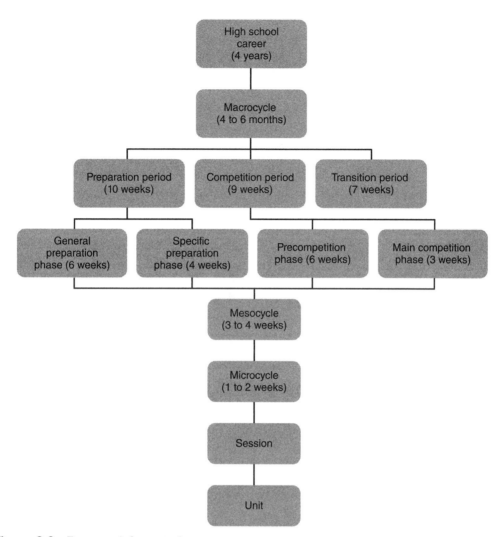

Figure 9.2 Framework for periodization.

ogy can be a bit confusing. Along the way in this chapter, we explain the terms in more detail and give lots of examples for clarification.

A helpful way to map out a macrocycle is to create a periodization chart, which we've done in figure 9.3. This chart is a sample macrocycle for a typical cross country season in the United States. The season spans four months from the first day of training on July 1 through the competitive period ending on November 4. The chart also includes the transition period from the end of the cross country season (the week of November 11) to the beginning of training for outdoor track (the week of December 30). Note that the main competition phase is longer for elite runners, who compete in postseason regional and national championships after the state meet.

For many young runners in the United States, the calendar year includes two macrocycles, one for cross country and one for outdoor track. This is called a

Athlete: _____

Season		Cross country						Track
	July	August	September	October	November	December	January
Periods	Preparation		Competition			Transition	Preparation
Phases	General preparation	Specific preparation	Precompetition	Main competition		Transition	General preparation
Mesocycles	1	2	3	4	5	6		1
Microcycles	7/1 7/8 7/15	7/22 7/29 8/5	8/12 8/19 8/26 9/2	9/9 Lower Richland:Dual / 9/16 Sumter: Dual / 9/23 Francis Marion Invtl. / 9/30 Coaches' Classic Invtl.	10/7 Rock Hill Invtl. / 10/14 / 10/21 District / 10/28 Regional / 11/4 State	11/11 11/18 11/25 12/2 12/9	12/16 12/23 12/30	

Figure 9.3 Periodization chart for cross country.

double-periodized year. Including a third macrocycle for indoor track results in a triple-periodized year.

The periodization chart in figure 9.3 provides a framework for designing the training program. Filling in this framework for each phase of training involves first doing the following:

1. Focusing on the main training objectives
2. Identifying the methods for accomplishing these objectives

Determining how much each method should contribute to the entire training load Although our example for carrying out these steps involves a cross country season, the principles and practices apply to planning for a track season as well.

General Preparation Phase

In the periodization chart in figure 9.3, the preparation period is divided into two phases: general preparation and specific preparation. The general preparation phase is primarily for building a base of fitness, emphasizing capacities such as technical skill, strength endurance, and cardiorespiratory fitness. In the specific preparation phase, loads of general methods gradually decrease as race-specific methods become more prominent. In our example, the general preparation phase covers 6 weeks, or about one-third of the preparation and competition periods, which total 19 weeks. Devoting about one-third of the macrocycle to general preparation enables runners to build a strong base. Remember, the stronger the base is, the greater the potential for developing high levels of race-specific fitness will be. For beginners, coaches might even choose to lengthen the general preparation phase to one-half of the macrocycle.

The next step after dividing up a macrocycle is to identify the training objectives and methods for the shorter periods. For example, table 9.1 shows key objectives and methods for the general and specific phases of preparation. The table also includes recommendations for approximately how much each method should contribute to the total training load during a microcycle (one or two weeks). The percentages are based on the amount of time runners devote to training per week. Let's say that during the general preparation phase for cross country, a runner trains for 6 hours (360 minutes) a week. For each microcycle in this phase, we recommend devoting approximately 30 percent of the training load to developing cardiorespiratory fitness. So, during a typical week, the runner would spend approximately 108 minutes training for cardiorespiratory fitness ($360 \times 0.30 = 108$). As shown in the last column of table 9.1, the training might be spread across two to four units in the weekly microcycle. For example, to log 108 minutes of cardiorespiratory training, the runner might do a 54-minute run on Monday and Thursday. Or, for variety, she might do a 40-minute run on Monday and a 68-minute bike ride on Thursday.

We want to provide coaches with a solid framework for deciding how much training to assign. However, each runner's unique characteristics ultimately determine the correct load. Take the case of physically mature track runners who

Table 9.1 Training Objectives, Methods, and Loads for the General and Specific Phases of the Preparation Period

Main objectives	Key methods	Relative training load (%)	Units per microcycle
GENERAL PREPARATION PHASE			
Flexibility	Stretching exercises	10	3-6
Mobility	Games (ultimate Frisbee, keep-away, flag football)	10	2-4
Strength endurance	Circuit training, weight training	20	2-4
Technical skill	Technique drills, strides	10	2-4
Cardiorespiratory fitness	Continuous aerobic running, cycling, swimming	30	2-4
Aerobic power	Interval tempo running, fartlek	7.5	1 or 2
Anaerobic fitness	Anaerobic intervals	2.5	1 or 2
Recovery between training sessions	Easy jogging, cycling, swimming	10	2-4
SPECIFIC PREPARATION PHASE			
Flexibility	Stretching exercises	15	3-6
Mobility	Games	5	1 or 2
Strength endurance	Circuit training, weight training, hills	15	2-4
Technical skill	Technique drills, strides	10	2-4
Cardiorespiratory fitness	Continuous aerobic running	20	1-3
Aerobic power	Continuous tempo running, interval tempo running, aerobic intervals	15	2-4
Anaerobic fitness	Anaerobic intervals	5	1 or 2
Race-specific fitness	Race-specific intervals, time trials	5	1 or 2
Recovery between training sessions	Easy jogging, cycling, swimming	10	3-6

specialize in the middle distances, 800 and 1,500 to 1,600 meters. Because success in these events depends heavily on high levels of aerobic power and anaerobic fitness, advanced middle-distance runners might need less training for general cardiorespiratory fitness than we recommend in table 9.1. For the general preparation phase leading up to track season, coaches might assign only 15 to 20 percent of the total load to cardiorespiratory training methods for these runners. In turn, they would increase the percentage of training devoted to developing aerobic power and anaerobic fitness. Here's the take-home message: although the guidelines in this chapter are based on scientific and developmental principles of training, coaches need to adapt them according to the event specialties and needs of their individual athletes.

Table 9.1 shows that half of the training load during the general preparation phase is devoted to developing cardiorespiratory fitness (30 percent) and strength endurance (20 percent). The key methods for developing strength endurance are circuit training, weight training, and hill running. For at least the first mesocycle of this phase (three or four weeks), it's best to use circuit training to build a base for weight training and hill running. We recommend devoting another 30 percent of training to developing flexibility (10 percent), mobility (10 percent), and technical skill (10 percent). In the case of a runner who trains 6 hours (360 minutes) in a one-week microcycle, about 36 minutes of that time would be spent stretching; 36 minutes, playing mobility games; and 36 minutes, doing technique work.

In chapter 6 we pointed out that high-intensity training, including speed development, should be a regular, year-round feature of a young runner's program. So, even though general training methods dominate the general preparation phase, race-specific methods should still be included. We recommend devoting 10 percent of training to developing aerobic power (7.5 percent) and anaerobic fitness (2.5 percent). During this phase the main methods for developing aerobic power are tempo running and fartlek. Anaerobic fitness will come from the short bursts of fast running in mobility games such as ultimate Frisbee and flag football. Finally, the general preparation phase also features recovery methods, such as easy jogging and swimming, to speed regeneration after demanding workouts. Because the training intensity is fairly low during this phase, recovery methods account for only about 10 percent of the training load.

Specific Preparation Phase

In the periodization chart in figure 9.3, the specific preparation phase lasts four weeks, or one mesocycle. This may not seem like a long time, but it doesn't take as long to build race-specific fitness as it does to build general fitness. In addition, the types of training that runners do during the specific preparation phase carry over into the competition period.

As you can see in table 9.1, the major difference between the two preparation phases is that the specific phase involves less general training and more race-specific training. For example, the recommendation for the percentage of training time devoted to developing aerobic power doubles from 7.5 percent to 15 percent of the program. In a one-week microcycle, this increase could come from adding an extra tempo run, fartlek session, or aerobic interval session. We've also increased anaerobic fitness and race-specific training. Cardiorespiratory fitness and strength endurance, which accounted for 50 percent of the training load in the general preparation phase, now make up only 35 percent of training in the specific preparation phase. The shift from general to specific training methods builds a bridge from the preparation phase to the competition phase to prepare runners for the challenges of racing.

Precompetition Phase

In the macrocycle for cross country outlined in figure 9.3, the competition period is divided into two phases: precompetition (six weeks) and main competition (three weeks). These phases correspond to the regular season (precompetition) and the playoffs and championships (main competition) in other sports. Training during the precompetition phase emphasizes methods that progressively build race-specific fitness by simulating the physical and mental demands of competition. In this phase runners also gain high levels of fitness and tactical skill through racing.

Table 9.2 presents recommendations for the percentage of contributions of training methods in the two competition phases. Take a few minutes to compare the relative training loads for given methods in tables 9.1 and 9.2. You'll see, for example, an increased contribution of race-specific training, including race-specific intervals and time trials or practice races, in the precompetition phase. Other high-intensity methods, such as aerobic intervals and anaerobic intervals,

Table 9.2 Training Objectives, Methods, and Loads for the Precompetition and Main Competition Phases of the Competition Period

Main objectives	Key methods	Relative training load (%)	Units per microcycle
PRECOMPETITION PHASE			
Flexibility	Stretching exercises	15	3-6
Mobility	Games (ultimate Frisbee, keep-away, flag football)	0	0
Strength endurance	Circuit training, weight training, hills	15	1-3
Technical skill	Technique drills, strides	5	1 or 2
Cardiorespiratory fitness	Continuous aerobic running	15	1 or 2
Aerobic power	Continuous tempo running, interval tempo running, aerobic intervals	10	2-4
Anaerobic fitness	Anaerobic intervals	5	1-3
Race-specific fitness	Race-specific intervals, time trials	15	2-4
Recovery between training sessions	Easy jogging, cycling, swimming	20	3-6
MAIN COMPETITION PHASE			
Flexibility	Stretching exercises	20	3-6
Mobility	Games	0	0
Strength endurance	Circuit training, weight training, hills	10	1-3
Technical skill	Technique drills, strides	10	1-3
Cardiorespiratory fitness	Continuous aerobic running	0	0
Aerobic power	Interval tempo running, continuous tempo running, aerobic intervals	15	2-4
Anaerobic fitness	Anaerobic intervals	5	1-3
Race-specific fitness	Race-specific intervals, time trials	15	1-3
Recovery between training sessions	Easy jogging, cycling, swimming	25	3-6

continue to make up a relatively large portion of the training load. As a result of increases in high-intensity training in the precompetition phase, runners need to spend more time recovering, using methods such as easy jogging and swimming,

Early-season races in the precompetition phase are like stepping-stones, especially to the championship races in the main competition phase. A major objective during the precompetition phase is to gain experience, skill, and comfort in races. In low-key races, coaches should encourage their athletes to purposefully experiment with a variety of tactics, such as even pacing, negative-split pacing, and front running. Such practice prepares runners for the many tactical scenarios that could arise in more important competitions, and it helps them find racing strategies that work best for them.

Some runners, especially beginners, might set new PRs every time they race during the precompetition phase, but that shouldn't be the objective of early-season competitions. Runners should focus on tactics, technique, and time goals that gradually lead to new PRs. The risk of setting PRs in early-season races is that runners might not continue to improve as the competition period progresses. As a result, they may fall short of their goals in championship meets.

One of the major questions about racing in the precompetition phase is whether runners should *train through*, which means competing without taking recovery days before and after a race. Some coaches believe that runners who reduce their training load before and after early-season races lose fitness and valuable training time. These coaches thus have their athletes train through these races. We discourage training through because it leaves runners fatigued from hard training in the days before a race. In this condition, they risk injury, poor performance, and related losses of confidence and motivation. Even when runners aren't out to set PRs in early-season races, they should still be physically rested and mentally sharp. By tapering, or reducing the training load in the days leading up to races, runners gain valuable practice in preparing for competition for the best outcomes.

Main Competition Phase

The main competition phase consists of important races at the end of the season. For beginners who haven't yet reached the performance level to qualify for championship meets, these races might be the last few dual meets and invitationals of the season. For intermediate and advanced runners, the major races are city, regional, state, and national championships. Regardless of the runner's developmental stage, coaches should reinforce the goal to perform at the highest level in the final races of the season. Beginners who develop a pattern of peaking in the last few dual meets of a season will be preparing to excel in championship meets later in their careers.

The overall objective of training during the main competition phase is maintaining race-specific fitness and form. This requires training at speeds close to race pace. We recommend devoting about 35 percent of training time to advanced methods for sharpening aerobic power (15 percent), anaerobic fitness (5 percent), and race-specific fitness (15 percent). Although fast running is a staple of training during this phase, sessions shouldn't be exhausting. In interval training, for example, the repetitions should be relatively short, and runners should take ample time for recovery between them. Runners should finish interval sessions feeling light and energized, as if they could do several more repetitions without fatiguing. In addition to maintaining race-specific fitness, this approach to running fast without draining energy is great for sharpening mental fitness. When race-week training consists only of easy, slow running, runners often feel sluggish and tired, which can lead to doubts and worries about upcoming races.

Another important method for maintaining race-specific fitness and form during the main competition phase is technique strides (repetitions of 100 to 150 meters at race pace). Runners can perform these in several sessions during the week of a race.

In the main competition phase, many training sessions involve fast running, so a significant amount of time—approximately 20 percent of the load—should be devoted to warming up and stretching. Recovery is vital during this phase, particularly in the last few days before the race and a day or two afterward, so we recommend that recovery methods make up about 25 percent of training.

Transition: Recovering, Regenerating, and Reflecting

Our discussion of periodization has focused on the preparation and competition periods. We can't forget the transition period, though, because it is a critical part of the young runner's program and development. The transition is the period between the last race of a season and the first day of training for the next season. The objectives during the transition period are to recover from the stress of training and racing and to regenerate physical and mental energy for the upcoming macrocycle. In our sample macrocycle, the transition period lasts seven weeks, from early November to the end of December (see figure 9.3).

Transition is a time to take a break from serious training. However, it doesn't necessarily mean complete rest and inactivity. Some runners might use the time for low-intensity running or participating in other sports and activities just for fun. For coaches, the transition period is a time to reflect on each runner's training and racing over the previous months and to plan the upcoming macrocycle. During the transition, coaches can begin planning by completing the assessment process described in chapter 8.

Step 4: Plan Daily and Weekly Training Sessions

To summarize our approach to periodization so far, we mapped out a macrocycle by dividing it into phases. Then we identified the training objectives for each phase and assigned how much each training method contributes to the total training load. Now we're ready to take the next step, planning daily and weekly training sessions, which are organized by microcycles (one- or two-week periods) and

Pointers For Parents

This chapter addresses some highly technical and advanced approaches to planning training programs. Given our focus on the principles and practices of periodization, the chapter is intended mostly for coaches. However, parents can also benefit from learning about this systematic method of planning. Here we offer some advice for how parents can be involved in the process:

- **Reinforce lessons about the importance of planning.**

  Like so many other aspects of training for distance running, periodization can teach valuable lessons that go beyond athletics. When young runners appreciate the importance of taking an organized and detailed approach to planning for training and competition, they may relate the lessons learned to their education and even to personal matters. You can reinforce the importance of planning through your everyday words and actions. Let your child know that for challenging and complex endeavors in life, successful outcomes usually depend on careful forethought rather than haphazard decisions.

- **Be prepared for plans that go awry.**

  A key ingredient for bringing plans to fruition is an unwavering positive attitude. But as the saying goes, "The best laid plans of mice and men often go awry." When minor setbacks and detours derail your young runner's plans, you can help him get back on track. In the event of a small bump in the road, offer your moral support and strong encouragement to overcome the challenge. For more serious matters, such as injury or illness, you obviously have the responsibility for ensuring that your child gets the best health care. This requires learning about the medical resources in your community and seeking the best health professionals, especially those with expertise in sports medicine.

- **Acknowledge your child's training process and progress.**

  It's truly amazing to watch young runners develop higher and higher levels of fitness, skill, and confidence, leading to improved performances over time. Seeing all the hard work pay off is a great reward of coaching. As the parent of a young runner, you also need to be aware of, as well as to regularly acknowledge, areas of improvement as the products of well-designed training programs. Suppose, for example, that your child has been working extra hard on developing a strong finishing kick or better hill-running technique. Your recognition and praise of improvement in these areas will help boost her confidence and motivation to keep working hard and improving.

mesocycles (three- or four-week periods). At this point, the following questions are most important:

- What are the best ways to arrange training methods over the period of a microcycle or mesocycle?
- In a single workout with multiple units of training, what is the optimal order?
- On which days of the week should runners do the most demanding high-intensity sessions?
- How many days of relatively low-intensity training should separate demanding workouts?
- How can a good progression of training loads be ensured over the microcycles and mesocycles of a season?

We'll answer these questions by presenting guidelines for planning daily and weekly training sessions. To illustrate how to apply the guidelines, we've designed four sample microcycles, one for each phase of the preparation and competition periods (see tables 9.3-9.6). The sample microcycles are intended for intermediate cross country runners (training age: two to four years) who race 3,000 to 5,000 meters. The training loads in the sample microcycles correspond to the recommendations in tables 9.1 and 9.2.

Organizing Units in a Single Training Session

Most daily training sessions consist of more than one unit. For example, on a day when runners stretch and do technique drills, they complete two units of training. In such a session, the coach could even add a unit of circuit training without overdoing it. The session's effectiveness greatly depends on how the individual units are ordered. The following principles and guidelines, although not hard-and-fast rules, will guide coaches in making decisions about the best way to order training units in a single session.

- **Low-intensity units should precede high-intensity units.** Monday's session in the first set of sample training sessions (see table 9.3) consists of two units of training. The first unit, a continuous aerobic run at 70 to 80 percent of maximal heart rate, is performed at a relatively low intensity compared with the second unit, which is a game of ultimate Frisbee. The first unit shouldn't cause severe muscular fatigue. Instead, it should warm up the muscles and prime the cardiovascular system for the bursts of anaerobic sprinting and jumping that the runner will do in the second unit.

  A unit of high-intensity, race-specific training should not precede a unit of low-intensity, general training on the same day (except for doing stretching exercises after a tempo run or an interval session). Runners who do intense anaerobic interval sessions before continuous aerobic runs risk overtraining and injury.

- **Runners should not do technique units when overly fatigued.** In all of the sample microcycles, units of technique training occur early in the session, following a warm-up with stretching exercises. Technique training should not follow a unit that causes deep muscle fatigue, such as circuit training or anaerobic intervals. The reason is that the fatigue might prevent runners from executing and learning good form.

- **Units of continuous aerobic running should precede units of strength-endurance training.** In a session that includes running and strength-endurance training, it's usually best to run first. For example, a continuous aerobic run should precede circuit or weight training, as illustrated in the session on the first Monday of the sample sessions for the precompetition phase. The muscle fatigue caused by the strength-endurance unit could lead to injury if it is followed by a run.

Organizing Training Sessions in a Microcycle

Let's say that a coach is planning an upcoming microcycle and has decided to combine a continuous aerobic run with mobility games on one day and stretching with an interval tempo session on another day. On what days of the microcycle should the coach place these two sessions? What methods should be scheduled for the other days of the microcycle?

This section helps coaches figure out how to arrange sessions within microcycles. The sample microcycles in tables 9.3-9.6 are either 7 or 10 days long. To illustrate the pattern of training during the general preparation phase in table 9.3, for example, we chose a seven-day microcycle for simplicity: it's convenient to think about training on a weekly basis. Nevertheless, coaches may need to lengthen the seven-day microcycle if it doesn't allow runners to recover sufficiently. Beginners may need an extra day or two of recovery after high-intensity sessions, such as the interval tempo workout on Wednesday in the seven-day microcycle. If so, coaches should add these recovery days, lengthening the microcycle, perhaps to 9 or 10 days.

On the other hand, some intermediate and advanced runners may be able to handle more units of training than we've included in our sample microcycles. One way to increase their training load is to schedule additional units on two or three mornings per week. Coaches can plan morning sessions for recovery methods, continuous aerobic running, or even strength-endurance training. These extra units help young runners who have the desire and potential to continue beyond high school prepare for the two-a-day sessions that many college and world-class runners regularly do.

The following principles and guidelines will help coaches organize training sessions in a microcycle:

- **Repeat key training methods for a given phase regularly in the microcycle.** To reach higher and higher levels of fitness, runners must consistently repeat key training methods while progressively increasing their loads. For example, a primary objective of the specific preparation phase is to develop a high level of aerobic power using methods such as tempo running and aerobic interval training. During this phase, runners should repeat these methods several times in a microcycle. A general rule is to repeat key methods at least once in a 7- to 10-day period. In the 10-day microcycle for the specific preparation phase (see table 9.4), we've included two units for developing aerobic power: an interval tempo run on the first Tuesday and aerobic intervals on Saturday. If these two training sessions were spread out over a longer period, such as once every three weeks, they wouldn't stress the aerobic system enough for positive adaptations. Including the tempo run that we've scheduled on Wednesdays of our sample microcycle for the general preparation phase, our program includes 10 tempo runs, one per week, over the 10 weeks of the entire preparation period.

  Although repetition of methods is essential for improvement, coaches should vary elements of their training programs to avoid monotony. For example, if a weekly plan includes two continuous aerobic runs, the coach can change up the courses—maybe a flat dirt road on one day and a hilly golf course on the other. Or, if runners are doing two or three circuit training sessions in the microcycle, the coach can vary the exercises and change the venue of the workout.

- **Avoid using the same training method two days in a row.** Although key training methods in a microcycle should be repeated, developing fitness isn't simply a matter of training, training, and more training. Instead, repeated cycles of training with sufficient recovery do the trick. As a general rule, at least one day should separate the repetition of a demanding training method. If a runner does circuit training on a Monday, she should wait at least until Wednesday before repeating the method, to allow the stressed muscles to restore energy and to undergo the physiological adaptations that improve strength endurance. This doesn't necessarily mean that Tuesday should be devoted to recovery methods or complete rest. If, for example, the circuit session on Monday primarily stressed the muscles of the upper body, the runner's legs might be fresh enough for a continuous aerobic run on Tuesday.

  Low-intensity or recovery days should both precede and follow high-intensity days. When coaches plan high-intensity sessions such as race-specific intervals or anaerobic intervals, they should also plan enough recovery so that runners are physically regenerated and mentally fresh for the next challenging workout. One day of recovery exercise (e.g., easy jogging, cycling, or swimming) is usually sufficient. Be aware, however, of individual differences in recovery rates. Some runners, particularly beginners, may need more recovery or complete rest before they are ready to train hard again. On the day before a demanding session, runners should use either recovery methods or low-intensity methods such as continuous aerobic running or technique strides.

Consider two exceptions to the rule that runners shouldn't repeat the same training method on successive days. First, recovery methods can be used two days in a row, particularly in the days leading up to a race. Second, elite runners who compete in track meets with semifinals the day before the finals should do back-to-back days of race-specific training to simulate these racing demands.

- **Assign race-specific training methods on the days of the week that competitions are usually held.** In the sample microcycle for the specific preparation phase in table 9.4, we've scheduled a session of aerobic intervals for Saturday. During the precompetition phase, this session might be a 5,000-meter time trial. Both of these workouts closely simulate the physical and mental demands of competition. We've scheduled the sessions for Saturday because that's the day of the most important races during cross country season. It's also a good idea to schedule race-specific training sessions at the time of day that the most important races will be held. If cross country races are scheduled for 8:00 a.m., the coach should plan several race-specific training sessions for that time. These sessions could be held on successive Saturdays during the specific preparation and precompetition phases. This approach instills a pattern in which the runner is prepared to take on the greatest physical and mental challenges when it counts the most.

- **Race weeks should include sessions with low volumes of fast running and sessions of recovery.** The sample microcycle for the main competition phase in table 9.6 illustrates this guideline. During the race week, Monday, Tuesday, Wednesday, and Friday include units of fast running. One objective of these sessions is to activate the neuromuscular pathways that will be used in the race. Another objective is to boost the runner's comfort and confidence in her ability to maintain race pace. The most important thing to remember about these sessions is that they should not be so intense that they drain energy. For example, the interval session scheduled for Monday and the 150-meter technique strides on Tuesday and Friday are for practicing pacing and good form rather than for stressing the physiological systems to reach a higher level of fitness. The key to avoiding fatigue during these sessions is to shorten the repetition distance and lengthen the rest interval.

Table 9.3 Sample Sessions: General Preparation Phase

(Intermediate-Level, 7-Day Microcycle for Cross Country)

Monday	**Unit 1: Cardiorespiratory fitness (continuous aerobic running)** 35-40 min at 70-80% of HRmax
	Unit 2: Mobility and anaerobic fitness 20-min game of ultimate Frisbee
Tuesday	**Unit 1: Warm-up and flexibility** Stretching exercises[a]
	Unit 2: Technical skill (drills[b]) High-knee marching: 3 × 30 m Skipping: 3 × 60 m Butt kick: 3 × 30 m High-knee running: 3 × 40 m
	Unit 3: Strength endurance (circuit training[c]) 1 × 4-station circuit
Wednesday	**Unit 1: Warm-up and flexibility** Stretching exercises[a]
	Unit 2: Aerobic power (interval tempo running) 4 × 4 min at 80-85% of HRmax with 60 s recovery, or 30 min fartlek
Thursday	**Unit 1: Recovery** 20-30 min of easy jogging or swimming
Friday	**Unit 1: Cardiorespiratory fitness** 70 min of cycling, or 35-40 min of running at 70-80% of HRmax
	Unit 2: Mobility and anaerobic fitness 20-min game of flag football
Saturday	**Unit 1: Warm-up and flexibility** Stretching exercises[a]
	Unit 2: Technical skill (strides) 12 × 150 m
	Unit 3: Strength endurance (circuit training[c]) 1 × 4-station circuit
Sunday	Rest

[a]See guidelines for stretching and illustrations of exercises in chapter 6.

[b]See illustrations and instructions for technique drills in chapter 6.

[c]See illustrations and instructions for circuit training in chapter 6.

Table 9.4　Sample Sessions: Specific Preparation Phase

(Intermediate-Level, 10-Day Microcycle for Cross Country)

Monday	**Unit 1: Cardiorespiratory fitness (continuous aerobic running)** 45-50 min at 70-80% of HRmax
	Unit 2: Mobility and anaerobic fitness 20-min game of ultimate Frisbee
Tuesday	**Unit 1: Warm-up and flexibility** Stretching exercises[a]
	Unit 2: Aerobic power (interval tempo running) 4 × 6 min with 60 s recovery at 80-85% of HRmax
Wednesday	**Unit 1: Warm-up and flexibility** Stretching exercises[a]
	Unit 2: Technical skill (drills[b]) High-knee marching: 3 × 40 m Skipping: 3 × 70 m Butt kick: 3 × 40 m High-knee running: 3 × 50 m
	Unit 3: Strength endurance (weight training[c]) 2 sets of lower- and upper-body exercises
Thursday	**Unit 1: Warm-up and flexibility** Stretching exercises[a]
	Unit 2: Anaerobic fitness (anaerobic intervals) 4 × 400 m at 5-15% faster than race pace for 1,500-1,600 m with 3-4 min recovery
Friday	**Unit 1: Recovery** 20-30 min of easy jogging or swimming, or rest by taking the day off completely
Saturday	**Unit 1: Warm-up and flexibility** Stretching exercises[a]
	Unit 2: Aerobic power (aerobic intervals) 4 or 5 × 800 m at 5,000-meter race pace with a 1:1 recovery[d]
Sunday	**Unit 1: Recovery** 20-30 min of easy jogging or swimming, or rest by taking the day off completely
Monday	**Unit 1: Warm-up and flexibility** Stretching exercises[a]
	Unit 2: Strength endurance (hill training) 6 × 300 m uphill with easy jog recovery (downhill)
Tuesday	**Unit 1: Warm-up and flexibility** Stretching exercises[a]
	Unit 2: Technical skill (drills) See the previous Wednesday's session
Wednesday	**Unit 1: Warm-up and flexibility** Stretching exercises[a]
	Unit 2: Race-specific fitness (race-specific intervals) 2 × 1,000 m at race pace with 90 s recovery

[a]See guidelines for stretching and illustrations of exercises in chapter 6.

[b]See illustrations and instructions for technique drills in chapter 6.

[c]See illustrations and instructions for weight training in chapter 6.

[d]1:1 recovery means that the interval between repetitions lasts as long as the repetition itself.

Table 9.5 Sample Sessions: Precompetition Phase

(Intermediate-Level, 7-Day Microcycle for Cross Country)

Monday	**Unit 1: Cardiorespiratory fitness (continuous aerobic running)** 40 min at 75% of HRmax
	Unit 2: Strength endurance (circuit training[a]) 2 × 4-station circuit
Tuesday	**Unit 1: Warm-up and flexibility** Stretching exercises[b]
	Unit 2: Race-specific fitness (race-specific intervals) 3 × 1,000 m at race pace with 90 s recovery
	Unit 3: Anaerobic fitness (anaerobic intervals) 3 × 300 m at 5-15% faster than race pace for 1,500-1,600 m with 3-4 min recovery Or, replace units 2 and 3 with a 5,000-meter race (dual meet)
Wednesday	**Unit 1: Recovery** 20-30 min of easy jogging or swimming
Thursday	**Unit 1: Warm-up and flexibility** Stretching exercises[b]
	Unit 2: Aerobic fitness (continuous tempo running) 15-20 min at 80-85% of HRmax
Friday	**Unit 1: Recovery** 20-30 min of easy jogging or swimming
Saturday	**Unit 1: Warm-up and flexibility** Stretching exercises[b]
	Unit 2: Race-specific fitness 5,000-meter time trial or invitational cross country race
Sunday	**Unit 1: Recovery** 20-30 min of easy jogging or swimming

[a]See illustrations and instructions for circuit training in chapter 6..

[b]See guidelines for stretching and illustrations of exercises in chapter 6..

Table 9.6 Sample Sessions: Main Competition Phase

(Intermediate-Level, 7-Day Microcycle for Cross Country)

Monday	**Unit 1: Warm-up and flexibility** Stretching exercises[a]
	Unit 2: Aerobic power and anaerobic fitness (aerobic and anaerobic intervals) 3 × (1 × 600 m and 1 × 200 m with 30 seconds jog recovery between the 600 and 200), running the 600 at 5,000-meter race pace and the 200 at a controlled sprint, with complete recovery between sets
Tuesday	**Unit 1: Warm-up and flexibility** Stretching exercises[a]
	Unit 2: Technical skill (strides) 8 × 150 m at race pace
	Unit 3: Strength endurance (circuit training[b]) 1 × 4-station circuit
Wednesday	**Unit 1: Warm-up and flexibility** Stretching exercises[a]
	Unit 2: Aerobic power (interval tempo running) 4 × 3 min at 80-85% HRmax with 90 s recovery
Thursday	**Unit 1: Recovery** 20-30 min of easy jogging
Friday	**Unit 1: Recovery** 20-30 min of easy jogging
	Unit 2: Technical skill (strides) 8 × 150 m at race pace
Saturday	5,000-meter cross country race
Sunday	**Unit 1: Recovery** 20-30 min of easy jogging or swimming, or complete rest

[a]See illustrations and instructions for stretching exercises in chapter 6..

[b]See illustrations and instructions for circuit training in chapter 6. .

Vern Gambetta

Gambetta Sports Training Systems
Sarasota, Florida

Vern Gambetta is an internationally renowned expert in sport training. He has served as a conditioning coach for numerous professional sports teams. A cofounder of USA Track & Field's Coaching Education program, Gambetta is a consultant for national initiatives aimed at developing young distance runners, including the Nike Oregon Project. He has authored many books, including *Following the Functional Path: Building and Rebuilding the Athlete* and *Athletic Development: The Art and Science of Functional Sports Conditioning*.

Courtesy of Vern Gambetta.

Why should young distance runners train to be "complete athletes," developing all-around fitness?—Although the obvious answer is to improve performance, the most important reasons are to "bulletproof" young runners and to enable them to train and race at higher intensities. By developing a complete foundation of fitness, young runners are less likely to be injured. It's given that they will gain cardiorespiratory endurance through training. But if they don't work on coordination, flexibility, core and overall body strength, and speed, these components will be limiting factors to increasing training intensity and improving racing performance. Also, overall athleticism will enable young runners to compete successfully over a greater range of events—they won't get locked into being only a 1,500-meter runner or a 3,000-meter runner. For young endurance athletes, the ability to run a range of events is very important.

An especially important point for coaches is that we're not talking about huge investments in time for methods devoted to developing overall athleticism. However, these methods must be consistent, integral parts of the program throughout the phases of a season.

During early phases of preparation, what are some examples of training sessions for developing speed?—I'll begin with a philosophical statement. I've always believed that for middle-distance and long-distance runners, speed development is part of an essential process throughout all phases of a season. If coaches don't regularly include speed work in their programs, they are setting their runners up to be beat when it counts the most. I define speed work as running at least a little faster than goal race pace. It's not always necessarily all-out sprinting.

We lay the foundation for speed development with technique drills and exercises for developing specific strength, good posture, and the ability to strike the ground with neuromuscular control and power. After training runs, my young runners do eight to twelve 60-meter strides in which they work on good mechanics, posture, and arm action. In these sessions, they learn how to run fast through fatigue. As a coach, I'm there reminding them to do things such as quicken their stride rather than lengthen it to the point of overstriding. We make it a gamelike situation. For example, in a pack of six runners, one will accelerate for 30 or 40 meters, and the group has to go with him. So all runners learn how to control their mechanics. This session addresses a major problem that I see with many young runners: they lack the ability to change gears in the middle of a race. That's a very important quality to develop when you're young.

What are the main goals for training during the championship season?— Especially during the latter part of the championship season, the number one training objective is to sharpen, hone, and fine-tune fitness. Coaches sometimes forget that, and they make the mistake of increasing training intensity to very high levels. Instead, we want to reduce training volume and *maintain* intensity, not raise it. Many coaches during the championship season have a tendency to do one more repetition and to push runners to their limits. My rule of thumb is to do one fewer repetition. I want my athletes to be physically and mentally fresh.

Another main goal is race simulation, in which we're preparing for different scenarios in championship races. So, let's say we're doing a session of 6 × 400. To simulate a fast start, we'll run the first two repetitions a little faster than average race pace. The next two 400s might be progressive: they start slower than race pace for the first 200 meters and then pick it up a little to simulate tempo changes. The last two 400s might be progressively faster to prepare for fast finishes.

During the championship season, we also want to keep up the elements of strength training, postural and core work, and stretching. Of course, we'll spend a little more time on recovery and easy running—maybe running in the pool in cold water. The key element, as the old cowboy said, is "dancing with the one who brung you." That means not using training methods that are different from the ones that got you to the championship season in the first place.

What general advice do you offer coaches for helping their athletes improve progressively from season to season?—Coaches sometimes focus too heavily on increasing their athletes' running mileage as a goal for progression. Instead, I think we should focus on progressively increasing the number of training days and sessions per week over time. Take the example of 14-year-old boys or girls in their first year of high school. I would have them train five or six days a week, once a day. The next year, we might go to seven sessions a week. Depending on the athlete's maturation, by age 16 we might do eight sessions a week, which means doing two-a-day workouts twice. During the last year of high school, we might increase to 10 or 11 sessions a week (two-a-day workouts three or four days a week) in some phases of the year. From year to year, we should focus on increasing the number of sessions for strength training and core work each week. It's also important to progressively increase the duration of the longest run and tempo runs, as well as various types of interval work. Finally, we have to think about the number of competitions, which should also increase progressively over time. To me, progression is about exploring and expanding a young runner's possibilities and capabilities.

Organizing Microcycles in a Mesocycle

After arranging units within sessions and sessions within microcycles, the next step is to organize the microcycles within a mesocycle, tying together individual weeks of training into a block of three or four weeks. Coaches should use these guidelines to organize the microcycles within a mesocycle:

- **Repeat key methods throughout the mesocycle, gradually increasing the training load.** Let's say that, for the specific preparation period, the coach has set up a mesocycle that's made up of three 1-week microcycles. A continuous tempo run is planned for the first Monday of the first microcycle. A good plan is to repeat tempo running several times throughout the mesocycle, perhaps assigning it for the next two Mondays. As we've discussed, this cyclical pattern ensures that runners stress key elements of fitness, adapting for improvement on a regular basis. Of course, for improvement to occur, the training load for each method has to increase systematically. For example, over three successive Mondays in a mesocycle, the coach might increase the duration of the continuous tempo run from 14, to 16, to 18 minutes. Gradual progression should always be the aim.

- **Schedule an unloading microcycle at the end of each mesocycle.** A common practice in periodization is to set up mesocycles in a pattern that increases the training load over the first two or three weeks and decreases it in the last week. This pattern is illustrated in figure 9.4, which shows an increase in running volume over the first two weeks of two successive mesocycles, each lasting three weeks. In the first mesocycle, we've scheduled 25 and 32 miles (40 and 51 km) of running in successive seven-day microcycles. Then, after a week of reduced volume, the runner starts the second mesocycle at 32 miles (51 km) and increases to 37 miles (60 km) across the two weeks. In addition to increasing the distance, the pace should get progressively faster over these "building" weeks.

In figure 9.4, notice how the volume drops in the third week of each mesocycle. These weeks are called *unloading microcycles* because the training load decreases. As a general guideline, coaches should reduce the training volume by 25 to 50 percent of the highest volume in the mesocycle. We've lowered the mileage by 40 percent from the second (32 miles, or 51 km) to the third (19 miles, or 31 km) week of the first mesocycle. The unloading microcycle gives runners extra recovery from training and fuels motivation for taking on higher levels of training.

During the precompetition and main competition phases of the season, unloading microcycles lead up to races. The reduction in training load results in a timely regeneration to prepare for the physical and mental demands of competition.

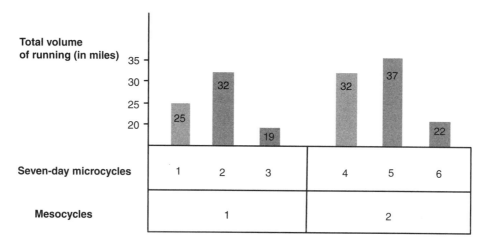

Figure 9.4 Building and unloading microcycles in two successive mesocycles.

Striding Ahead

This chapter's guidelines for using periodization provide a solid framework for designing training programs. For the best outcomes, however, coaches must consider which patterns of training work best for individual athletes. Let's say that, for a given runner, a coach has planned one recovery day after high-intensity anaerobic interval sessions. If the runner is not fully recovering after one recovery day, the coach needs to adjust the schedule by adding an extra recovery day after this method. This sort of flexibility and revision in planning training is the theme of chapter 10.

Before moving on, we want to make one more point about planning daily and weekly training: it's vital that the coach discuss training plans with runners. An open line of communication is crucial to finding out which training methods work best for each runner. A great way to start the conversation is to hand out a weekly workout schedule a few days before it begins. The runners and coach can discuss the plan and make suitable changes. In addition, runners can use the plans to prepare physically and mentally for upcoming challenges. For example, athletes who know that they will be running a time trial on Saturday can prepare by eating a high-carbohydrate meal and getting a good night's sleep on Friday. During the week, runners can also plan their strategies for the time trial and perform mental imagery to fine-tune mental fitness.

10

Dealing With Setbacks

Coaches who plan training following the steps in chapter 9 gain a world of confidence in their programs. They know where their athletes are going as well as how to help them get there safely. The detailed planning that characterizes periodization lessens the chances of major obstacles blocking a runner's journey to performance goals. Nevertheless, no matter how much forethought goes into planning training programs, minor setbacks and detours are inevitable. At some point, every runner experiences gaps in training as a result of injury, illness, loss of motivation, personal challenges, stretches of bad weather, or other reasons. In this chapter we discuss how to evaluate programs and help runners get back on course after unexpected detours. Here we take the final step in our five-step process for designing training programs (see figure 10.1).

Evaluating Training and Racing Outcomes

The sure signs of a successful program are healthy and motivated runners who, over time, are training and racing at higher and higher levels. In chapter 8 we talked about assessing factors such as improvement, health, and motivation after each season— that's the first step to planning training for the following season. To make necessary adjustments in a program *during* the season, which is the focus of this chapter, coaches must evaluate their runners' training and racing on a day-to-day basis.

Evaluating Training Performance

Sometimes it's easy to take a wrong turn in training without realizing it. Therefore, coaches need to watch closely and make sure their runners stay on track. One way to do this is to regularly confirm whether the runners are doing what is actually planned in their training. Let's say that a runner has been allotted around 25 percent of the general preparation phase to developing strength endurance

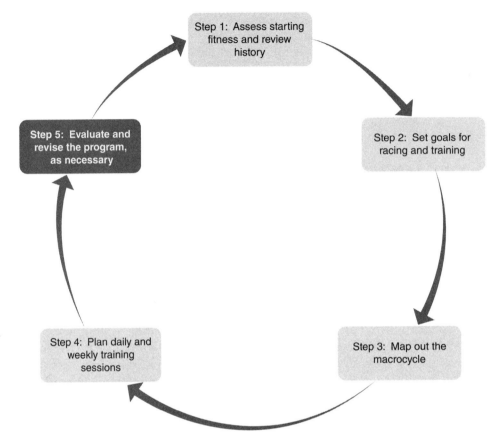

Figure 10.1 Five-step process for designing training programs. This chapter addresses the last step.

with circuit and weight training. During a given week, suppose the runner's training time for these methods totaled less than 10 percent—maybe he had to miss practice on the day of a planned circuit training session. Usually it's no problem to miss one workout. If, however, the runner repeatedly skips sessions devoted to a particular training method, he won't develop the targeted fitness capacity, which limits his potential for achieving his racing goals. Strategies for getting back on course when the actual training load deviates from the planned program are addressed later in this chapter.

Another way to evaluate training on a daily basis is to use indicators such as heart rate and running time. Say, for example, that the objective of a session is to develop cardiorespiratory fitness with continuous aerobic running. If the runner's pace is too fast, as indicated by a heart rate above the recommended range of 70 to 80 percent of maximum, she may not be able to maintain it long enough to adequately stress the cardiovascular system for positive training outcomes. Sometimes it's tempting to let the runner keep going because she's feeling good and working hard. The workout may even lead to a breakthrough in confidence.

However, straying off-course from training plans usually leads to negative results, including suboptimal fitness and injuries.

Finally, coaches can evaluate the training program by regularly asking runners for feedback with questions such as these:

- How do you think your training is going?
- How are your legs feeling after yesterday's interval workout? Are they sore?
- How is your breathing? Are you working harder than we planned?
- How did your technique feel on that last stride? Can you tell whether your arms are crossing the front of your body?
- Do you think you had enough recovery time yesterday to work hard today?
- Are you psyched to run these 200s in under 35?
- Did you like that workout? How would you change it to make it better?

By asking questions such as these, coaches open lines of communication for feedback that is so important for making changes to the program, when necessary.

Evaluating Racing Performance

The ultimate test of a training program is whether runners are performing up to their capabilities and improving in races. If runners are meeting their racing goals, there's no need to change the program other than to progressively increase training loads. As the saying goes, "If it ain't broke, don't fix it!" If, however, runners' performances aren't up to par, the coach must search for reasons and revise the program accordingly.

Runners might fall short of their racing potential for several reasons. Some shine in training sessions but flicker out in races. For these runners, psychological factors such as nervousness, lack of confidence, poor concentration, or ineffective tactics are at the root of poor competitive performance. To identify the specific causes, coaches must become detectives by asking themselves the following questions:

- Is the runner tight and anxious before the race starts? Maybe he's too nervous.
- Does the runner have doubts about whether she can achieve her goal? Maybe she lacks confidence.
- Does the runner fall behind on uphill sections of cross country courses? Maybe he's not concentrating on the right cues for good uphill running technique.
- Does the runner finish the race with too much energy left? Maybe she isn't pacing herself properly.

The answers to these questions will help the coach adapt the training program to focus on the aspects of mental fitness that need improvement.

In another scenario, a runner has a high level of mental fitness but simply lacks the physical fitness to achieve his goals. This is evident in competitions in which the runner starts out on goal pace and in good position but fades as the

Pointers for Parents

Preventing injuries and illness tops the list of parents' roles in sound training programs for young runners. In support of these roles, the following pointers recall important lessons from earlier in the book:

- **Remember the critical roles of sleep and nutrition.**

  As discussed in chapters 2 and 3, adequate sleep and good nutrition are keys to ensuring optimal health and performance in distance running. You can help by preparing balanced and nutritious meals with sufficient calories to replace the energy burned in training. In addition, you might remind your child that experts in sports medicine recommend getting at least eight hours of sleep every night.

- **For parents of girls, be aware of the female athlete triad.**

  In chapter 3 we described the female athlete triad, which is an unhealthy condition of deficient energy levels, abnormal menstrual function, and low bone mass. If you are the parent of a female runner, you and your daughter should know the signs of this condition. If your daughter has not had a menstrual period by age 15, or if she has infrequent periods after menarche, she should be evaluated by a physician who is familiar with the female athlete triad. The most important factor for prevention is to ensure that adequate energy is available through the diet.

- **Help your child keep running fun.**

  Appreciate the fact that your child's participation in youth running can build a foundation for a lifetime of good physical and mental health. However, this invaluable outcome depends on cultivating a positive attitude about running for performance and exercise during youth. As we've stressed throughout the book, a key is to ensure that young athletes view running as fun. You can help by watching for signs of overtraining or burnout, such as excessive fatigue or loss of motivation. In response, you might suggest that your child talk with the coach about cutting back on training. Most important, offer unconditional love and convey the attitude that what truly matters is giving your best effort and enjoying training and competition.

- **Seek the best health care professionals for your child.**

  If your young runner suffers an injury or illness that requires professional care, seek a sports medicine physician who is familiar with running and has experience in providing health care for competitive runners. The ideal health professional is a physician who understands how training, diet, sleep, and other factors influence risks of injury and illness. A hallmark of a good sports doctor is a commitment to addressing the underlying causes of injury or illness rather than simply treating the symptoms.

race progresses. If a lack of mental fitness is not the problem, it's likely that the runner is simply not physically prepared. Take the case of Vijay, whose goal is to break 2:10 for 800 meters. This season he has struggled to break 2:16. A careful review of Vijay's recent training shows that he has been far from hitting goal times in race-specific sessions. The fastest 400-meter repetition he ran in training was only 67 seconds, a 2:14 pace for an 800-meter race. He has also done only a few 200-meter repetitions that were faster than race pace. The reason for Vijay's disappointing racing performance is clear: he simply hasn't prepared his body for running under 2:10. Remember, it's vital to keep records of daily training to make this type of assessment.

Revising the Training Program

Part of the challenge of coaching distance runners is adjusting the program to account for individual differences and to meet individual needs. This is the art of coaching. It requires creativity and flexibility to steer runners toward their goals. These coaching skills are essential because, as we've said, the road to the runner's goals can have potholes and detours. This section addresses strategies for avoiding setbacks and for getting back on course should setbacks occur.

Getting Back on Course After Detours in Training

Table 10.1 summarizes strategies for getting back on course after detours in training. For example, a common setback is no longer improving performances in training and competition. In this situation, coaches should look for signs of overtraining and undertraining. *Overtraining* refers to excessive amounts of stressful work that break the body down so that it can't recover within a few days. Some signs of overtraining are long-lasting fatigue and muscle soreness, injury, illness, difficulty falling asleep at night and waking in the morning, changes in mood, and loss of motivation. Some signs of undertraining are a lack of progress in workouts that should be easy for the runner to complete and failure to improve in races. A runner who is undertraining is simply not challenged physically and mentally by workouts.

In cases of overtraining or undertraining, coaches need to identify the core problem and make adjustments accordingly. Consider a runner who has been training for less than a year and who complains of muscle soreness for several days after doing anaerobic interval sessions. To avoid serious injury, the coach must cut back on the load for this method. If the anaerobic interval training accounts for 5 percent of the total load in a given phase, an option is to cut it back 1 or 2 percent. Over time, this form of high-intensity work can be increased as the runner matures and develops the conditioning to handle it.

How should coaches make adjustments when athletes have to miss workouts? Let's go back to the runner who missed a circuit training session. At the end of the week, the coach evaluates this runner's program and finds that the contribution of strength endurance falls short of the planned load. In the case of missing just

Table 10.1 Detours and Setbacks in Training:
Strategies for Revising the Program

Potential detours and setbacks	Ways to get back on course
Lack of improvement in fitness over time	Look for signs of overtraining and undertraining.
	Identify and remove developmentally inappropriate training methods.
	Cut back on excessive training loads if overtrained.
	Add to training loads if undertrained.
Failure to meet training objectives for a given session	Stop the session if the runner is extremely fatigued and losing form.
	Adjust target heart rates and paces to set the right intensity.
Common cold, upset stomach, or other short-term illnesses	Take time off from training until health completely returns.
	See a family physician for treatment.
Injuries	Take time off from training until the injury completely heals.
	See the school's athletic trainer or family physician for treatment.
	Use supplemental training methods if possible (swimming, cycling, water running, circuit and weight training).
Unexplained off days	Be positive and upbeat: "It's only a bad day; we'll make up for it."
	Seek the source of the problem and eliminate it in the future.

one workout, the coach might not make any adjustments. If, however, the runner misses several sessions, especially if the cause is injury or illness, the coach is faced with a dilemma. Should the runner skip over the lost training and advance to where his teammates are? Should he go back and complete the workout and then catch up with teammates over time? Or should he go back to the start of the training journey and rebuild a fitness base?

The best answer depends on how much training the runner has missed and how much fitness he has lost. No firm guidelines exist for getting back on course after missing training. Generally speaking, however, the more fitness the runner lost, the farther back the runner must go in the training journey, using general methods such as continuous aerobic running and circuit and weight training to rebuild fitness. The danger of advancing a runner to where he would have been had he not missed training is that he likely won't be able to handle the greater loads and might suffer an injury or illness.

Another bump in the road is failing to meet training objectives in daily sessions. Usually, this is the result of running too fast or too slow, thus missing the target on the intended training effect. Consider a runner whose 3,200-meter goal is to break 11:30. Very early in the precompetition phase, the coach has planned a race-specific interval session of 3 × 1,000 meters at 3:33 to 3:38, a range that includes this runner's race pace of 3:35. On the first repetition, she struggles to hit 3:38. If the coach senses that she isn't fit enough yet to do the last two repetitions in 3:33 to 3:38, the coach should not hesitate to change the workout on the spot.

Dealing With Side Stitches

One of the most common setbacks in training and racing is the side stitch, or a sharp pain just under the ribs, typically on the right side of the body. Side stitches have several causes. First, they tend to occur in runners who are just starting to train and are relatively unfit. These runners may get stitches because their respiratory muscles—the diaphragm and muscles attached to the ribs—fatigue and cramp as a result of insufficient blood flow and oxygen delivery. Like the leg muscles, the respiratory muscles work very hard during high-intensity running, and stitches seem to occur when runners breathe vigorously. Because highly fit runners tend to experience fewer stitches, it's possible that they have conditioned their breathing muscles to receive and use more oxygenated blood. Thus, one key to getting rid of stitches is to improve fitness through progressive increases in training.

Second, stitches tend to occur in runners who train soon after drinking a lot of water or eating. Food and water in the stomach can cause pressure that triggers pain by pulling on muscle and connective tissue. A solution is to allow several hours for food to digest before running. However, runners should not avoid drinking water just to prevent a stitch—doing so could risk dehydration. Instead, they should drink several small cups of water rather than one or two large cups in the hours before training and racing.

When a side stitch occurs while running, experts suggest stopping, bending over at the waist, and massaging the painful area. Another method is to tighten the abdominal muscles and breathe deeply. At first this might worsen the pain, but within a minute or so the stitch should go away.

Shortening the distance of the last two repetitions from 1,000 to, say, 800 meters, will enable the athlete to stay on goal pace.

To keep runners on course, coaches inevitably have to alter their training programs. However, they shouldn't make changes hastily and without careful thought. Sometimes, runners veer off-course from training plans simply because they have bad days. Many circumstances may cause disappointing results in a training session: a sleepless night, an upset stomach, a side stitch, bad weather, a demanding test in school, or even an argument with a friend. When runners are having really bad days, the coach might need to stop the session and, in an upbeat way, suggest that they try again the next day. It's important to give them the option to try again so they can regain confidence. It doesn't make sense to let young runners fail to achieve training objectives and risk losing confidence if there's a good reason for a temporary setback. When things aren't going very well, the coach should seek the source of the problem, let the runner know that it's only a bad day, and try to eliminate that problem in the future.

Getting Back on Course After Detours in Racing

Bad races occur for a variety of reasons, including those summarized in table 10.2. As discussed, some runners who are in great shape physically and have impressive training sessions fall short of their racing goals because they lack mental fitness. In this situation, coaches are challenged to identify weaknesses in mental fitness and then design training and racing experiences to improve them. Consider Julia, who was especially nervous before races and had many disappointing results. Her coach noticed that before training sessions, which were going very well, Julia was relaxed, talkative, and playful. On race days, however, she isolated herself from teammates and took on a serious attitude. Sensing that Julia might be putting too much pressure on herself before races, her coach suggested that she hang out, warm up, and joke around with her teammates to help her relax. They tried this plan and it worked. Being around her teammates helped Julia relax and avoid getting nervous. Her subsequent performances were better than ever.

If a lack of confidence is the problem, the coach should adapt training sessions to ensure success. As discussed in chapter 4, success in training breeds confidence for racing. One strategy is to make goal times in training sessions a bit easier to reach until the athlete gains the physical fitness and confidence to achieve more demanding goals. Or, the coach might schedule workouts that the runner enjoys and always seems to master. Other training changes are extra attention to relaxation techniques, more work on pacing control, and time set aside for visualization of successful racing outcomes. To elevate confidence levels, coaches should also remind athletes about recent workouts and races that went especially well.

Table 10.2 Detours and Setbacks in Racing: Strategies for Revising the Program

Potential detours and setbacks	Ways to get back on course
Shortcomings in mental fitness	Evaluate elements of mental fitness: confidence, concentration, pacing and tactical skill, relaxation, anxiety, fear, and motivation.
	Design training and racing experiences to improve mental fitness in weak areas.
Shortcomings in physical fitness	Evaluate elements of physical fitness (e.g., technique, strength endurance, cardiorespiratory fitness, aerobic fitness).
	Evaluate recent training sessions to determine whether they simulate racing demands.
	Design training to improve weak areas and stress the body to meet racing demands.
Injuries or illnesses	Hold off on racing until completely recovered and healthy.
	Stay on treatment and therapy schedules; use supplemental training methods if possible.
Unexplained off days	Seek the source of the problem and eliminate it in the future.
	Use poor performance as a source of motivation to do better next time.
	Put running in its proper perspective.
	Race again as soon as possible.

Pinpointing weaknesses and making changes in training to eliminate them are also the keys to getting a runner back on course when he lacks the physical fitness to attain his racing goals. In this case, the coach must analyze racing performances to detect physical weaknesses. Perhaps the runner's form falls apart in the last half of the race. This indicates that he needs to work on strength endurance and technique. Maybe the runner can't respond to midrace surges and finishing sprints. He probably needs more varied-pace training that stresses the fast-twitch muscle fibers and anaerobic energy pathways.

Probably the most common reason for disappointing performances in distance running is simply having an off day. As with off days in training, the key to preventing them in races is to seek the source of the problem. If a runner has an upset stomach and a side stitch, perhaps she ate too soon before competing. A painful blister that makes a runner slow down could be the result of wearing a new pair of spikes without first breaking them in. A runner may feel tired before the race starts because she didn't sleep well the night before because of nervousness. Identifying the cause of an off day permits the runner and coach to devise a plan for eliminating the problem in the future. To avoid the side stitch, the athlete can try eating an hour earlier. Wearing new shoes a few times in training before racing in them can prevent blisters. To be fresh and well rested on race day, a runner can take her mind off racing the night before by watching television, reading a favorite book, or listening to relaxing music before going to sleep.

Often, there's no obvious reason for what went wrong in a race. Take the runner who is healthy and fit and whose recent training has been perfect. She feels great before the race starts. But during the race, it all falls apart, and there's no clear explanation for the disappointing result. Even the world's best distance runners have had this experience many times in their careers. Successful runners and coaches take advantage of these disappointments to get back on course for future races. Using poor performance as a source of commitment to do one's best in the next race can raise the level of motivation and determination to succeed. Coaches must repair the emotional wounds of bad races as quickly as possible and direct the runner's focus to the next race. It's important to race again as soon as possible after unexplained off days to keep doubts about fitness and ability from building when there's likely no reason for them.

Sometimes, runners have a few unexplained bad races in a row. From our own experiences, we know well the disappointment that comes from this sort of setback, but we also see an opportunity for coaches and parents to help young runners put athletics into perspective. When young runners realize that the sun will come up tomorrow and that the coach, family, and friends will be there with encouragement, they learn a wonderful lesson about sport and about life. Young runners who love to train and race have many workouts and competitions to look forward to down the road. Bad races are just temporary detours along the way.

One last bit of advice about setbacks in racing: runners should try to finish every race they start unless they suffer an injury or experience pain during the event. Some runners get in the habit of dropping out of races because they're

Adam Tenforde, MD

Redwood City, California

Dr. Adam Tenforde was a five-time National Collegiate Athletic Association All-American and part of three national championship team titles while competing for Stanford University. After college, his career highlights include finishing ninth at the 2004 Olympic Trials in the 10,000 meters and a runner-up finish at the 10,000-meter road national championships. His personal bests on the track include 4:10 for the mile, 13:39 for 5,000 meters, and 28:23 for 10,000 meters. As a physician specializing in physical medicine and rehabilitation, Dr. Tenforde continues to enjoy running. He qualified to run the Boston Marathon in 2014 and has a career best marathon of 2:43. His research focuses on preventing overuse injuries and optimizing bone health in runners.

SG Photographic, Inc.

To help prevent injuries, what are some key elements that coaches should include in training programs?—Overuse running injuries are common in young runners. In one research study we conducted at Stanford, a majority of male and female high school runners reported a history of one or more prior overuse injuries (see the Risk Factors for Running Injuries sidebar later in this chapter). The knowledge we gained about factors that were associated with these injuries can guide coaches to incorporate injury prevention into a running program. Training programs should incorporate gradual increases in volume and intensity, because higher training volume is a risk factor for injury. In general, I recommend not increasing total mileage or the distance of the longest run by greater than 10 percent per week. Running on soft and level surfaces, such as grass, and replacing running shoes every 350 to 500 miles (563 to 804 km) may also reduce the risk for injury. Although we don't have good current research evidence, generalized strength and conditioning may improve biomechanics (running form) and help prevent injuries. A common issue I see in runners of all ages is poor core and hip strength. When the muscles supporting the pelvis are weak, this can result in altered biomechanics, which can cause injury. Performing exercises that use body weight resistance, instead of machines, is usually enough to develop muscle strength and improve coordination. I recommend body weight exercises that simulate running, such as single-leg squats. The goal should be to develop muscle endurance and not muscle bulk.

My research has focused on the prevention of stress fracture injuries. Exercises that incorporate jumping and multidirectional loading may be helpful, given that early sports participation in basketball and soccer has been observed to reduce the risk for stress fractures in runners. Health benefits from participation in sports outside of running highlight a key concept: young runners should be encouraged to participate in a variety of sports during childhood and adolescence.

In addition to developing new skills from participating in other sports that may improve running performance, variety in activities may reduce the risk for burnout and overuse injuries. My wife, Kate Tenforde (O'Neill), made the 2004 Olympic team in the 10,000-

meter track event. Through middle school, she competed in swimming. She didn't start to focus on running until high school and college, but the earlier cardiorespiratory training in the pool likely helped her become a better runner. I enjoyed participating in soccer and basketball when I was younger, and I didn't start training throughout the year for distance running until I was a high school junior.

Stretching is an area with conflicting data on its role in injury prevention. Performing active or dynamic stretching prior to exercise may be more helpful than static stretching, because active forms of stretching increase blood flow to muscles and prepare the body for more strenuous activities. Running drills are commonly performed to improve running mechanics. Static stretching typically should be reserved for after a run.

During workouts, to reduce risks of injury, what should coaches pay special attention to, and what actions should they take?—The most valuable advice I ever received was "Listen to your body." The goal of a workout is to stress the body and result in adaptive changes, including increased cardiorespiratory fitness and strength. A hard workout may result in fatigue, but a runner should not push through pain or injury during a workout. Related to this concept, it's valuable for coaches to educate their runners on the purpose of each workout and help each runner become a student of the sport. By understanding the purpose of a workout and the importance of recovery between hard efforts, a young runner is likely to perform better during each training effort and reduce the risk for cumulative fatigue or pushing through pain that may result in injury.

Coaches should monitor for changes in running mechanics and encourage each runner to maintain good form; deterioration in running form may indicate that an athlete is overexerting. Monitoring heart rates during workouts and recovery can be helpful to target the desired running efforts intended for each workout.

What advice do you offer coaches of young runners whose injury risks are related to flaws in technique?—Coaches should encourage each athlete to address deficits in biomechanics and strength. Core strengthening and lower-body exercises to improve strength and endurance and running drills to improve biomechanics may be valuable to start at a younger age. When I started running in high school, I had an asymmetrical arm swing. My coaches helped me correct this issue by having me hold a small stick in my hand to emphasize keeping my thumb pointing up and fingers gently curled. I corrected this issue within a few months, which resulted in improvements in my form.

After an injury or illness, what factors should coaches and runners consider when deciding when and how to resume training?—The most important aspect of recovery from an injury or illness is for the athlete to have open and honest communication with his or her physician, coach, and parents. Running should resume gradually depending on the type of injury sustained, and an athlete should ask his or her sports physician to provide guidelines for return to activity and symptoms to monitor. I have found that providing a handout is useful to runners to guide the gradual increase in mileage and duration of runs. For example, a runner recovering from a bone stress injury might alternate running days with recovery days. We often recommend that a recovering runner start with five minutes of running one day, rest the next day, and then on the next day run five minutes twice with a one-minute break in between. It's important for the runner to monitor for the return of the pain or symptoms from the initial injury and then to communicate this information to the coach and sports physician.

fatigued or they've fallen off pace for a PR. These runners may never fully challenge themselves because the thought of quitting is always present. Even if it requires slowing down to a jog on off days, runners should try to finish the race. However, under no circumstances should coaches or parents encourage runners to finish races when they are experiencing pain and extreme discomfort from an injury, cramp, or health-threatening response to very hot or cold weather.

Dealing With Injuries

Given the physical demands of distance running, a fine line separates peak performance and injury risk. Over a long career, despite following a sound training program, few runners will completely avoid getting hurt, so it's important for coaches, parents, and runners to know the causes, symptoms, and approaches to treating and rehabilitating running injuries. Common causes of injuries include the following:

- **Training errors:** Sudden, sharp increases in training volume and intensity; overuse (running more miles or kilometers than the body can handle); failure to take sufficient recovery time between demanding workouts; running too much on very hard or very soft surfaces

- **Anatomical abnormalities:** Flat feet, high arches, excessive pronation or supination, knock knees, bowed legs, inwardly rotated thigh bones, unequal leg lengths

- **Muscle imbalances:** Differences in the strength of opposing muscle groups (hamstrings and quadriceps, calf and tibialis anterior, hip flexors and hip extensors), differences in the flexibility of opposing muscle groups, excessively tight or loose muscles

- **Poor technique:** Excessive turning and twisting motions, overstriding, striking too hard on the heel or forefoot

- **Inappropriate footwear:** Insufficient cushioning, inadequate control for excessive pronation or supination, insufficient arch support, overly worn shoes

- **Suboptimal nutrition:** Insufficient intake of calories, fluids, calcium, electrolytes, or other nutrients

By considering the causes of running injuries, coaches might find that some aspect of their training programs increases injury risk. By eliminating the risk factor or adding training methods that counteract it, they can prevent injuries. For example, impact-related injuries, such as shinsplints and stress fractures, are often caused by running long distances on hard surfaces such as asphalt roads. Runners can reduce their risk for these injuries by training on dirt roads and trails.

To effectively deal with injuries, both athletes and coaches must heed their symptoms and understand the best approaches to treatment and rehabilitation

Common Running Injuries

To prevent and treat running injuries, coaches and runners benefit from knowing their causes, symptoms, and rehabilitation methods. Following are descriptions of some common running injuries; an extensive discussion of running injuries is beyond the scope of this book.

Stress fractures are tiny breaks that occur in the bones of the feet, shins, thighs, and hips. The symptoms include localized pain and tenderness on the surface of the affected bone. This injury is commonly caused by overuse, or the excessive loading of the bones from the repetitive stress of running on hard surfaces. Stress fractures tend to occur in girls who, as a result of inadequate caloric intake and excessive training, experience athletic amenorrhea, or cessation of normal menstruation. Cyclical increases in estrogen levels, which occur with regular menstruation, are necessary for maintaining bone density. Diagnosing a stress fracture is typically complicated because the fracture may not show up on X-rays for several weeks after the onset of symptoms. To avoid serious bone damage and to promote healing, athletes who experience the symptoms of stress fractures should stop running and see a sports doctor. If a stress fracture is diagnosed, rehabilitation involves alterations in training and diet, a change in footwear or the use of orthotics, and cardiorespiratory training methods such as swimming, pool running, and cycling that don't stress the affected bone.

Plantar fasciitis is an inflammation of the band of connective tissue that runs along the insole of the foot from the heel to the arch. This injury is characterized by gripping pain and tenderness in the arch, close to the fleshy part of the heel. The pain is especially intense in the morning and during running. Plantar fasciitis is common in runners who have flat feet and who overpronate. Recovery time from this injury can often require several weeks or months of reduced or no running. Doctors may prescribe exercises for strengthening muscles in the feet, orthotics, anti-inflammatory medication, and steroid injections.

Achilles tendinitis is the degeneration and inflammation of the Achilles tendon, which connects the calf muscles to the heel bone. The main symptoms of this overuse injury are pain, tenderness, and swelling along the tendon. The pain is especially severe when athletes run on their toes, up hills, and in low-heeled racing flats or spikes. Runners with tight calf muscles are at particular risk, so they should regularly stretch these muscles. In some cases, rehabilitation time can be lengthy because the Achilles tendon receives limited blood flow and is stressed in daily activities such as walking. The main treatments—icing, anti-inflammatory medication, and ultrasound—increase blood flow to the tendon to reduce inflammation and promote healing. Swimming and deep-water running are good training methods for maintaining fitness while the tendon heals.

Patellofemoral pain syndrome results from cartilage degeneration behind the kneecap. Runners with this syndrome experience stiffness and grinding pain in the knee, especially after sitting for long periods and bending the knee in activities such as squatting and stair climbing. Patellofemoral pain syndrome occurs most often in runners with

(continued)

Common Running Injuries *(continued)*

knock knees, bowed legs, and flat feet. Another cause is strength imbalances between the hamstrings and quadriceps. Doctors recommend anti-inflammatory medicine and exercises that strengthen the quadriceps and stretch the hamstrings.

Osgood-Schlatter syndrome refers to inflammation, tenderness, and pain where the patellar tendon (in front of the knee) attaches to the tibia, or shin bone. This syndrome, which is unique to young athletes, develops as a result of a combination of rapid bone growth and repetitive stress. During the adolescent growth spurt, the bones grow faster than the muscles and connective tissue. When the growth of the tibia outstrips that of the patellar tendon, the tendon pulls hard on its attachment site at the top of the shin. The excessive tugging causes irritation and pain. In addition, the force can lead to small bony formations and fractures. In most cases, the swelling and pain go away with reduced running and skeletal maturation.

Iliotibial band syndrome refers to inflammation and pain caused by the rubbing of the iliotibial band tendon against the lateral side (outside) of the knee. The iliotibial band runs along the lateral side of the thigh from the hip to the knee. In adult runners the syndrome is typically caused by a combination of repetitive stress from running and tightness of the iliotibial band and the muscles around it. In young runners an additional cause is rapid growth of the femur. Runners should cease running, ice the injured area, and stretch the iliotibial band (see chapter 6) and hamstring muscles (see chapter 6).

Shinsplints is a term referring to pain and tenderness along the shin bone. When the pain runs along the inner side of the shin from a few inches (around 5 or 6 cm) below the knee to the ankle, doctors refer to the injury as **medial tibial pain syndrome**. The pain associated with this syndrome is caused by inflammation of the tissue that lines the bone. When the pain is on the outer side of the shin, the cause may be **compartment syndrome**—swelling of the muscles in the lower leg, which overstretches the elastic sheath that covers the muscles and creates pressure on nerve endings in the muscles. Runners with shin pain should consult a sports doctor because appropriate treatment depends on the cause, which is difficult to self-diagnose, and because continuing to run without appropriate treatment can result in stress fractures.

(see the Common Running Injuries sidebar later in this chapter). Although some injuries require immediate medical treatment, others, especially those caused by chronic overuse, may not pose an immediate danger. In some cases runners can self-treat these injuries, ideally under the supervision of a sports doctor or certified athletic trainer. Self-treatment of many running injuries involves RICE, which stands for rest, ice, compression, and elevation. Rest can mean a complete cessation of all training for at least a few days, but for many injuries it's possible to keep training with supplemental methods to maintain fitness. For example, runners with knee pain will make their injuries worse if they continue to run, but they can maintain a high level of cardiorespiratory and muscle fitness by swimming and doing upper-body circuit training.

Some leg and foot injuries that keep athletes from running are not affected by activities such as cycling and deep-water running. In deep-water running, the athlete mimics the running action while suspended in a pool by a flotation vest. Because cycling and deep-water running can elevate the heart rate for prolonged periods, they're great for maintaining cardiorespiratory fitness. The duration of supplemental training depends on the injured runner's familiarity with the exercise. For example, injured runners who have never done deep-water running might start out with only 10 or 15 minutes a day and gradually build up to a duration that approaches their longest continuous aerobic run. Runners who are accustomed to riding bicycles can start cycling at 45 minutes or more.

The second component of RICE, applying ice to the injured area, is often very effective for reducing swelling and pain as well as for promoting healing. Injuries that involve chronic inflammation, such as plantar fasciitis and Achilles tendinitis,

Risk Factors for Running Injuries

To prevent injuries, coaches and runners benefit from knowing factors that increase their risk. This was the aim of a study conducted by Dr. Adam Tenforde and colleagues at Stanford University (Tenforde et al., 2011). The researchers surveyed 748 high school distance runners (442 girls and 306 boys) between 13 and 18 years old, asking them to report previous injuries, training mileage, and performance bests in the mile and 5K. Most of these young runners, 68 percent of the girls and 59 percent of the boys, reported at least one injury from a list that included Achilles tendinitis, ankle sprains, iliotibial band syndrome, knee pain, plantar fasciitis, and shinsplints. The proportion of these injuries was greater for girls. For example, 41 percent of the girls and 34 percent of the boys had experienced shinsplints. Around 6 percent of the girls and 3 percent of the boys had had at least one stress fracture. Compared with noninjured runners, those who reported injuries were older and covered more miles in their weekly training. For girls, significant risk factors for injury included greater amounts of running on pavement and faster performance times in the mile and 5K.

Based on their findings and other related research, Tenforde and coauthors concluded that high school runners can reduce injury risks by limiting running on hard surfaces and by performing injury-specific strength training and balancing exercises. The researchers' recommendations are summarized in table 10.3.

Table 10.3 Exercises for Preventing Common Running Injuries

Type of injury	Recommended exercises for injury prevention
Shinsplints	Walking on the heels (3 × 30 steps for each foot)
Patellofemoral pain syndrome	Double-leg squat (see chapter 6)
Iliotibial band syndrome	Hip abduction exercises (lying on side and raising straightened leg to a 45-degree angle)
Achilles tendinitis	Heel raiser (see chapter 6)

Adapted from Tenforde et al. (2011).

respond especially well to ice treatment. The protocol is to simply apply a plastic bag filled with crushed ice to the injured area. To avoid freezing the skin, the runner should place a thin cloth between the bag and the injured area. Freezing water in a paper cup and using it to perform an ice massage is another option. A general guideline is to apply ice two or three times a day for 10 to 20 minutes each time. We strongly recommend that runners consult a sports doctor or athletic trainer for an injury-specific icing protocol.

Compression of the affected area is also often an effective treatment for injuries that cause swelling. The most common method of compression is applying an elastic bandage. The placement of the bandage depends on the injury and the person. Athletic trainers know the proper techniques for wrapping injuries.

The fourth component of RICE, elevation, involves raising the injured area to reduce blood flow to it, thereby reducing swelling. A runner who has a knee injury, for example, should lie on a bed or couch and elevate the affected leg with a pillow or two. The leg should be raised slightly above the heart.

Going Off-Course for Variety and Fun

When you're on a long journey, sometimes the most effective and fun way to reach your destination is to venture off on side roads and unpaved paths. It's the same with training for distance running—it can be worthwhile to experiment with training methods and doses that deviate from the planned program. Occasional training detours that add variety and fun are essential because they keep young runners motivated, interested, and engaged. When they are limited to completing the assigned workouts day after day, week after week, and month after month, they can become bored with running.

The key to cultivating interest in training is to make the program as varied as possible. Coaches can use a variety of training methods, exercises, and drills from day to day. We also recommend changing the training venue and environment regularly. Every so often, coaches should surprise their athletes with a change that spices up the day's training. For example, instead of announcing ahead of time that the team will do its continuous aerobic run on the beach, a 10-mile (16 km) drive from school, the coach might just show up at practice that day with a van and pile everyone in. Or, on a day scheduled for an interval tempo session, the coach might change the workout to a controlled fartlek just for variety. On recovery days every now and again, the coach might even surprise the team by canceling practice altogether and taking everyone to the movies.

Training methods that are inherently fun should be a regular part of the program. Especially in the general preparation phase, coaches should include games such as basketball, soccer, ultimate Frisbee, and keep-away several times each week. They can also spice up training methods that aren't inherently fun, such as recovery sessions, by adding variety and making them playful. For example, on a recovery day during the spring, runners can go swimming in a local pond or river, or they can go mountain biking. In winter, a recovery session might be 20 minutes of cross-country skiing. If the recovery session is an easy 20-minute run, the whole team can run together, talking and joking along the way. If the course goes through a park, the runners can play a game in which they earn points for being the first one to spot a chipmunk, sparrow, deer, or other animal. If the course goes through an urban neighborhood, they can spot cars of different makes and colors rather than animals.

Sometimes, experienced coaches and runners unexpectedly change training and racing plans on a hunch that a detour might lead to a breakthrough. A coach might postpone an important race-specific interval session until the next day if the wind is blowing hard on the day that the session is scheduled. A 1,500-meter runner might abandon a racing plan to start her finishing kick over the last 300 meters if she feels strong and has the energy to surge and break up the field with 800 meters to go. Coaches and athletes should act on these hunches every so often because they might be shortcuts on the road to reaching goals. Then again, they might take runners way off course, but they can learn important lessons from such detours if they keep track of how they veered off-course so they can avoid those roads in the future.

Above all, the most important feature of a training program is an atmosphere of fun because, without it, young runners will not be motivated to improve themselves through hard work and dedication. Coaches and parents foster this atmosphere when they adopt the philosophy that youth sport is about doing one's best and enjoying the journey on the road to self-improvement. When they're not pressured to win, young athletes are truly motivated by the challenge of this journey. However, they want to have fun along the way. Good coaches and engaged parents realize this and use their creativity to make sure that training and competitive experiences are challenging and fun.

Coaches who follow sound, scientific guidelines for designing and adapting training will surely challenge their young runners with sessions that develop physical and mental fitness. However, as complex as designing training can be, it can sometimes be easy compared to creating an atmosphere of fun and enjoyment, which requires thought and ingenuity on a daily basis. Our advice to coaches who want to add more fun to daily training is to listen carefully to their athletes to find out what they enjoy most about running and about their lives as teenagers. Maybe they'd like music playing over the speaker system at the track every once in a while. They might enjoy dressing up in running costumes on special holidays such as Halloween and St. Patrick's Day (and seeing their coach in costume, too!). Most enjoy team parties and awards banquets at which everyone is recognized. Runners rely on their coaches to build team morale and camaraderie with special experiences and events that add excitement to their training.

Striding Ahead

We congratulate you on your efforts to learn about training for young distance runners and applying the science of distance running to the artistry of coaching, parenting, and running itself. We leave you with one last bit of advice for ensuring successful and safe training journeys in the future: Keep asking for directions! You can always learn more about training. As sport science and training theory evolve, you will encounter new ideas and training methods to consider applying to your own program to make it even better.

You will be rewarded in many ways by learning more about running. Reading books and running magazines, attending clinics, and discussing ideas and strategies with others who share your interest are all ways to keep learning. If you're a coach, you'll experience the incredible satisfaction of improving your ability to help young athletes achieve their goals. In addition, your own experience will be enriched because you'll be engaged in an exciting discourse with other coaches and sport scientists about the best methods for developing young runners. Perhaps you'd like to learn more about exercise physiology, or maybe you want to set up a computer system for keeping training records and tracking your athletes' progress. To advance your coaching skills, you'll need to keep seeking knowledge about training for young runners.

If you're a parent, you'll do a great service to your child by learning more about nutrition, the effects of training on maturation and growth, and other areas that influence your young runner's health. Positive distance-running experiences have tremendous potential for establishing behaviors and values that contribute to a lifetime of good health. It's your responsibility, along with the coach and your family physician, to ensure that your child has good experiences in training and competition. To meet this responsibility, you'll need to continue learning about youth distance running.

If you're a young runner, you should realize that learning more about distance running is vital to progressing and developing in future years. The coach takes the wheel at the beginning of the training journey, but as you gain experience over the years, you gain more control over your own training program. After all, who knows better than you what training is working and what is not? As an advanced runner, you can learn about your body and how it responds to training and racing, and you can share some of the responsibility of directing the journey with your coach. When you and your coach work together in this way, you increase your potential for success. Most important, if you commit to learn more about running, you'll gain knowledge and experience that will be the source of a lifetime of good health.

We wish you success in your journey in youth distance running. Perhaps our paths will cross along the way!

References

Bar-Or, O., and Rowland, T. 2004. *Pediatric exercise medicine: From physiologic principles to health care application.* Champaign, IL: Human Kinetics.

Barrack, M.T., Rauh, M.J., and Nichols, J.F. 2010. Cross-sectional evidence of suppressed bone mineral accrual among female adolescent runners. *Journal of Bone Mineral Research* 25: 1850-1857.

Born, D.P., Sperlich, B., and Holmberg, H.C. 2013. Bringing light into the dark: Effects of compression clothing on performance and recovery. *International Journal of Sports Physiology and Performance* 8: 4-18.

Cermak, N.M., Gibala, M.J., and van Loon, L.J. 2012. Nitrate supplementation's improvement of 10-km time-trial performance in trained cyclists. *International Journal of Sport Nutrition & Exercise Metabolism* 22: 64-71.

Eisenmann, J.C., and Wickel, E.E. 2007. Estimated energy expenditure and physical activity patterns of adolescent distance runners. *International Journal of Sport Nutrition and Exercise Metabolism* 17: 178-188.

Gastin, P.B. 2001. Energy system interaction and relative contribution during maximal exercise. *Sports Medicine* 31: 725-741.

Halson, S.L. 2014. Sleep in elite athletes and nutritional interventions to enhance sleep. *Sports Medicine* 44 (Suppl. 1): S13-23.

Hasegawa, H., Yamauchi, T., and Kraemer, W.J. 2007. Foot strike patterns of runners at the 15-km point during an elite-level half marathon. *Journal of Strength and Conditioning Research* 21: 888-893.

Hoon, M.W., Johnson, N.A., Chapman, P.G., and Burke, L.M. 2013. The effect of nitrate supplementation on exercise performance in healthy individuals: A systematic review and meta-analysis. *International Journal of Sport Nutrition and Exercise Metabolism* 23: 522-532.

Larson, P., Higgins, E., Kaminski. J., Decker, T., Preble, J., Lyons, D., McIntyre, K., and Normile, A. 2011. Foot strike patterns of recreational and sub-elite runners in a long-distance road race. *Journal of Sports Science* 29: 1665-1673.

Lieberman, D.E. 2012. What we can learn about running from barefoot running: An evolutionary medical perspective. *Exercise and Sport Science Reviews* 40: 63-72.

Morris, C.J., Aeschbach, D., and Scheer, F.A. 2012. Circadian system, sleep and endocrinology. *Molecular and Cellular Endocrinology* 349: 91-104.

Murphy, M., Eliot, K., Heuertz, R.M., and Weiss, E. 2012. Whole beetroot consumption acutely improves running performance. *Journal of the Academy of Nutrition and Dietetics* 112: 548-552.

National Academy of Sciences. 2002/2005. Dietary reference intakes for energy, carbohydrate, fiber, fat, fatty acids, cholesterol, protein, and amino acids. www.nal.usda.gov/fnic/DRI//DRI_Energy/energy_full_report.pdf.

Nattiv, A., Loucks, A.B., Manore, M.M., Sanborn, C.F., Sundgot-Borgen, J., and Warren, M.P. 2007. American College of Sports Medicine position stand. The female athlete triad. *Medicine & Science in Sports & Exercise* 39: 1867-1882.

Nieves J.W., Melsop, K., Curtis, M., Kelsey, J.L., Bachrach, L.K., Greendale, G., Sowers, M.F., Sainani, K.L. 2010. Nutritional factors that influence change in bone density and stress fracture risk among young female cross-country runners. *PM&R: The Journal of Injury, Function and Rehabilitation* 2: 740-750.

Noakes, T. 2003. *Lore of running,* 4th ed. Champaign, IL: Human Kinetics.

Spencer, M.R., and Gastin, P.B. 2001. Energy system contribution during 200- to 1500-m running in highly trained athletes. *Medicine & Science in Sports & Exercise* 33: 157-162.

Tenforde, A.S., Sayres, L.C., McCurdy, M.L., Collado, H., Sainani, K.L., Fredericson, M. 2011. Overuse injuries in high school runners: Lifetime prevalence and prevention strategies. *PM&R: The Journal of Injury, Function and Rehabilitation* 3: 125-131.

Index

About the Authors

Larry Greene knows all about the challenges facing young distance runners. He won state championships in high school cross country and track, becoming a Florida state champion in cross country and the 2-mile run and finishing 10th in the national Junior Olympic Cross Country Meet as a senior. Greene's high school accomplishments earned him a scholarship to Florida State University, where he set the school record for the indoor 3,000-meter run and qualified for the NCAA championship meet three times. After college, Greene excelled as a distance runner. In 1984, he ran the fastest half marathon in the world (1:01:27) and finished 4th in the 10,000-meter run at the U.S. Track and Field Championships. In 1987, he finished 3rd in the half marathon at the U.S. Olympic Festival.

Greene is a scientific and medical writer in South Florida. He received an MS in movement science from Florida State University and a PhD in exercise science from the University of South Carolina. He has coached distance runners at the youth, university, and professional levels. He has also served as the director of the Carolina Marathon Youth Cross Country Run. His leisure interests include running, cycling, and cross-country skiing.

Russ Pate has been an exercise science instructor and researcher since 1972. He serves as a professor in the department of exercise science at the University of South Carolina, where his research is focused on the relationship between physical activity and health in children and adolescents. Pate is a lifelong distance runner. He has a personal best time of 2:15:20 in the marathon and competed in three U.S. Olympic Trials Marathons.

Pate has served as president of the American College of Sports Medicine (ACSM), the National Coalition for Promoting Physical Activity, and the National Physical Activity Plan Alliance. He has been recognized with awards by the American Alliance for Health, Physical Education, Recreation and Dance; the American College of Sports Medicine; the National Fitness Leaders Association; and the President's Council on Physical Fitness and Sports. He has also directed two U.S. Olympic Trials Women's Marathons.

Pate received a PhD in exercise physiology from the University of Oregon in 1974. In his free time, he enjoys running, reading, theater, traveling, and spending time with his family.